THE SOCIALIST PARTY
OF AMERICA

THE MACMILLAN COMPANY
NEW YORK · CHICAGO
DALLAS · ATLANTA · SAN FRANCISCO
LONDON · MANILA

THE MACMILLAN COMPANY
OF CANADA, LIMITED
TORONTO

THE SOCIALIST PARTY
OF AMERICA

A HISTORY

BY

David A. Shannon

New York
THE MACMILLAN COMPANY
1955

To

JANE

CONTENTS

PREFACE

IN the early years of the present century the Socialist Party of America was a young and virile organization that could not escape notice. Far stronger than any contemporary party on the left, the Socialist Party once excited the hopes of thousands and alarmed countless others. However one felt about the Socialists, they could not be ignored.

In recent years, of course, few political groups can be ignored more easily, but not until the past few years have professional historians shown much interest in investigating and writing the history of American Socialism. Since the end of World War II, long after the Socialist Party ceased to inspire or to disturb more than a handful of Americans, a small group of young historians has delved into the history of socialist movements. Their work has been fruitful, and today a reader interested in the field can learn much more from secondary accounts than he could eight or ten years ago. This volume, however, is the first attempt to write a book-length account of the history of the Socialist Party from its formation in 1901 until its disintegration in the late 1930's. I have attempted in this work to describe the Socialist rise and decline, to narrate the significant events in the party's history, and to analyze the reasons for its final failure.

This book is broad in scope as compared with many historical monographs, and undoubtedly further research would turn up interesting and significant details. It is not as comprehensive as a history of the Socialist Party could be. I should be gratified if my work should stimulate others to mine at the several places where further digging would be rewarding. I hope that this volume may be useful to them.

In the writing of a book an author inevitably puts himself into the debt of many people. I am happy to thank those who have aided me for their generous and valuable help. This volume's inadequacies, however, are entirely my own responsibility.

I want first to thank my colleagues, both those in the institutions where I have taught and others, who have offered me encouragement, advice, and stimulation. To Professor Merle Curti of the University of Wisconsin, a generous friend, an astute critic and teacher, and a distinguished scholar, I am especially indebted. To Robert J. Alexander, Daniel Bell, Ray Ginger, Robert Iversen, Arthur Link, Grady McWhiny, Henry May, Howard Quint, and Irvin Wyllie I owe special thanks.

The staffs of the following libraries deserve my gratitude: Carnegie Institute of Technology, Columbia University, Duke University, the Library of Congress, the University of Michigan, the Milwaukee County Historical Society, the National Archives, the New York Public Library, the Rand School of Social Science, Teachers College, the University of Wisconsin, and the Wisconsin State Historical Society.

Many sometime participants in the Socialist movement gladly tolerated my questions, answered my inquiries, and suggested ideas that proved to be useful. To the following people I am indebted: Freda Hogan Ameringer, the late Louis B. Boudin, the late August Claessens, the late Theodore Debs, Adolph Germer, the late Frederic Heath, Nina Hillquit, Harry W. Laidler, the late Algernon Lee, Theodore Muller, Frank O'Hare, James Oneal, Jacob Panken, Clarence Senior, the late A. M. Simons, J. G. Phelps Stokes, Norman Thomas, Anna Strunsky Walling, and Fred Warren.

Finally, I want to thank my wife, Jane Short Shannon, for her encouragement, for her cheerful acceptance of the history of the

Socialist Party as part of the household, and for helping out with the many dull and routine tasks connected with the making of a book.

DAVID A. SHANNON

Teachers College, Columbia University
December 18, 1954

THE SOCIALIST PARTY
OF AMERICA

I

THE EARLY SOCIALIST PARTY:
A REGIONAL SURVEY

THE more than one hundred men and women who stood in the
Masonic Hall at Indianapolis one summer day in 1901 singing the
"Marseillaise" had reason to celebrate. They had just finished founding the Socialist Party of America. They could look back with
satisfaction upon their work, for after many years of struggle and
growth the various socialistic organizations in the United States
were at last united within one party. Representatives of dissenting
groups that had fought one another for decades now sang together
the revolutionary air that for them symbolized leftist unity. All now
were within the fold of the new Socialist Party. Only the Socialist
Labor Party, led by that master of political invective Daniel De
Leon, and destined to remain a small and doctrinaire sect of Marxist
purists, remained outside the new organization. Also outside the new
party was a small group of well intentioned but ineffectual social
reformers who in their more daring moments called themselves
"Fabian Socialists." While these men and women accepted many of
the implications of Marxian socialism, they were repelled by its
class-struggle thesis and refused to join a party which made it an
article of faith.

The new party had behind it a long and strong tradition of
American economic heterodoxy. Almost from the time industrialism
first began in the United States, a few Americans had advocated some
kind of anticapitalistic scheme for society which, they hoped, would

eliminate industrial oppression and bring to those who toiled the full fruits of their labor. There had been Thomas Skidmore, who in the late 1820's had advocated a periodic redistribution of property. There had been followers of the Welshman Robert Owen and the Frenchman Charles Fourier who had tried to create semisocialistic communities as models for the reform of industrial capitalism. To trace the origins of the Socialist Party to these early nineteenth century social movements, however, would be a risky and not particularly fruitful endeavor. The party's real origins lay in the revolt against the social and economic conditions created by the mushrooming industrialism of America after the Civil War.

It is axiomatic that a society that produced a Carnegie, a Vanderbilt, and a Drew, that created a Pittsburgh, a Chicago, and a Lawrence, would also give birth to social discontent and to political protest movements. Of these movements there was an abundance. Grangers, Greenbackers, Populists, Single Taxers, trade unionists, anarchists, socialists—all had burning criticisms of the status quo. Most of these movements were not clearly anticapitalistic in their nature; most of them would not have abolished capitalism as such. They would only have removed those features of that economic arrangement which for the moment were causing them harm. But from the 1860's on there was some kind of organized socialist movement in the United States which looked forward to the establishment of some variety of socialism.

In the year that Ulysses S. Grant was reelected, Karl Marx moved the headquarters of the International Workingmen's Association, the First International, from London to New York. A few sections of the International had already been established among German immigrants. Upon this foundation was built in time the Socialist Labor Party, which in the 1890's blossomed under the leadership of De Leon and which today remains a very small but active independent organization. One group, most of them from the East but a few from the Midwest, at the founding convention of the Socialist Party in 1901 had come directly from De Leon's party, having split from the parent organization in the late 1890's.

Most of the delegates at this first Socialist Party convention, however, had no such direct relation to Marx, and, indeed, only a few had more than the haziest intellectual acquaintance with theoretical Marxism. Certainly the anticapitalism of many of the delegates derived more from Edward Bellamy's *Looking Backward* than from *Das Kapital*. In fact, many Socialists had formerly been members of Bellamy Nationalist clubs. Others came to Indianapolis from an experience in the Populist Party or Eugene V. Debs's American Railway Union or both. Debs himself had started his career as a Democrat and a craft unionist. When craft unionism proved itself inadequate to Debs, he built the industrially organized American Railway Union; and when a Democratic President, Grover Cleveland, broke the great ARU strike of 1894 and Debs went to jail, he became a socialist-oriented Populist.

In 1898, after flirting with the idea of establishing a socialist community in the Far West, Debs and his faithful followers organized the Social Democratic Party. Two years later this organization nominated Debs for President, and in the campaign he had the uneasy support of a large group of dissidents from the Socialist Labor Party, generally known as "Kangaroos." There were considerable rivalry and distrust between the Debsites and the former SLP members, and efforts to unite them and create a solid new party failed until several months after the election. Finally, in late July, 1901, the various socialist groups in the nation submerged their differences and formed the Socialist Party of America.[1]

More important than the feeling of satisfaction after the completion of a long and difficult job was a feeling of hope and promise. This new party, the singing delegates thought, was to lead suffering America out of the capitalistic wilderness and into the cooperative commonwealth. The new day was within sight. Had not Debs and his running mate Job Harriman polled nearly 100,000 votes the year before without even a unified political organization behind them, about three times the vote ever given a presidential candidate running on a socialist platform? Of the party's ultimate success there was no doubt. The question was when, not if, the American people

—the American working people—would see the logic of industrial history and vote the Socialist Party into office to socialize and democratize the American economy.

This faith in the party's success, the buoyant, optimistic view that Socialism was inevitable and probably fairly close, is one of the keys to understanding the Socialist Party before the 1920's. It helps to explain why factional disputes within the party were as intense as they were. If Socialism were indeed coming soon, the kind of Socialism it would be was important. Theoretical differences were of more than academic importance to those who thought the revolution was just around the corner. Such faith also helps to explain the dedication many people gave the movement, sacrificing what little comfort they might have been able to have to work anonymously and unceasingly for the Cause. The "Jimmie Higginses," the plain people of the movement who did the tedious, unrewarding tasks, those who stamped envelopes, passed out handbills, marched in parades, paced picket lines, and sold Socialist periodical subscriptions, had to have a faith that their work was for the benefit of mankind and that it would be successful. Their leaders assured them their faith was well founded. Morris Hillquit, leader of the New York City Socialists, an able, handsome young immigrant lawyer, told them at the Unity Convention in 1901 that Socialism was coming, although he did not know if it would come "today, tomorrow, or in ten years or half a century." They read Julius A. Wayland in his sensational weekly newspaper the *Appeal to Reason*. "Socialism is coming. It's coming like a prairie fire and nothing can stop it . . . . you can feel it in the air. You can see it in the papers. You can taste it in the price of beef . . . . the next few years will give this nation to the Socialist Party." [2]

Wayland's vision turned out to be something less than prophetic, but until World War I and the red scare following it the expectation of Socialist success sometime was not wholly without justification. For the party grew in every way, in membership, in vote, and in influence. Never before or since in the United States has a political organization with any kind of socialist orientation grown the way the

Socialist Party did for the first ten to fifteen years of its existence. The year the party was founded, Morris Hillquit estimated later, there were 10,000 members, but this figure is probably too high. When Debs ran for the Presidency the second time, in 1904, there were 20,763 paid-up Socialist Party members. Debs polled 402,283 votes in that election, over four times his vote of 1900. By 1908 party membership had more than doubled again, rising to 41,751, but the increase in Debs's vote that year was not so great. He received 420,713 votes. Between the elections of 1908 and 1912 the Socialists enjoyed their greatest growth. Their membership almost tripled, increasing to 117,984 in 1912,[3] and in the presidential election that year Debs polled 897,000 votes, about 6 per cent of the popular vote.

The influence and prestige of the party grew during these years also. In 1910 the Socialists of Milwaukee won the municipal elections and sent their leader, Victor Berger, to Congress. Four years later New York City Socialists elected Meyer London to Congress, and there was a Socialist or two in Congress for most of the years from then until the mid-1920's. Many towns had Socialist administrations. In 1911 there were thirty-three Socialist cities and towns, the more important, besides Milwaukee, being Berkeley, California; Butte, Montana; and Flint and Jackson, Michigan.[4]

But more important than the few elections won was the belief, among followers of the major parties as well as among Socialists, that the party was a political force to be reckoned with. To Theodore Roosevelt, for example, the Socialists were a growing threat, "far more ominous than any populist or similar movement in time past," that must be headed off by reforms of capitalism. He warned that if the major parties failed to reform American society the Socialists might well take more drastic steps, but he complained that his warning was not always well received. He wrote to William Allen White, "As you know, I have incurred the bitterest attacks, not merely from the socialist and anarchist crowd, but from those men of predatory wealth who prefer socialists and anarchists to my style of conservatism." [5] A majority of American voters, however, did endorse Roosevelt's style of conservatism, whether they voted

Republican or Democratic, during the period from the beginning of the century until World War I, and it was an era of unusually progressive politics. To say that Socialist breathing down the neck of major party reformers was the cause of the extraordinary spurt of social legislation is to oversimplify a complex situation, but it was undoubtedly one motivating factor of the whole progressive movement.

As Wayland had said, Socialism was "in the air." There was evidence of it everywhere. A prominent Roman Catholic clergyman, Father John A. Ryan, debated the merits of Socialism with Morris Hillquit, and the debate in published form had wide circulation.[6] A high-ranking cleric's debating Socialism publicly and fairly was unheard of until this period of social ferment, and is almost unthinkable today. Thousands of people read novels and articles by Socialist authors. Upton Sinclair's *The Jungle*, first published serially in the *Appeal to Reason*, was an unmistakable and bitter indictment of capitalism, and although Sinclair complained that the book's almost incidental portrayal of filth in the meat-packing industry hit the nation's stomach harder than its description of workers' hardships hit the nation's heart, the nation's heart was not missed altogether. Jack London's great popularity was primarily due to his adventure tales, but his class-struggle literature was also widely read. Prominent people in many walks of life—journalists, labor leaders, lawyers, educators, even millionaires—publicly cast their lot with the Socialist Party. It did appear that Socialism was destined to become a major force in American life.

The Socialist Party during these years of growth and promise was a broad political organization representing all shades of leftist conviction. Because of the nature of leftist political organizations since about 1920, Americans tend to regard all left-wing political organizations as political sects with rigid party lines, groups of doctrinaires jealous of their doctrinal purity. But this was certainly not the case with the Socialist Party during its early and vigorous years. The party then was a coalition of regional groups that had different, even conflicting, points of view. In this diversity lay the party's strength. By mid-twentieth century standards of left-wing organizations, such a conglomerate aggregation as this would be impossible, but the prewar Socialists enjoyed relative success precisely because they were so catholic in their organization.

In being all-inclusive, in being a fairly loose alliance of regional political groups, the Socialists unconsciously were following the pattern of the major political parties. As the party of Lincoln had within it Western agrarians and Pennsylvania manufacturers, so the party of Debs had within it Oklahoma sharecroppers and New York immigrant garment workers; as the champion political alliance of them all, the Democratic Party in the 1930's and 1940's, could accommodate such diverse leaders as John Rankin and Theodore Bilbo on the one hand and Jerry Voorhis and Herbert Lehman on the other, so the prewar Socialists embraced such contrasting figures as Victor Berger and William D. "Big Bill" Haywood. The leaders, arguments, programs, and policies that might appeal to the immigrant garment worker might not have attraction for an Oklahoma farmer or an Indiana railroader, but in a party organized on a regional basis the Oklahoma farmer and the Indiana railroader could have programs of their own and only the loosest sort of connections with the New York City organization. Had the Socialists during these years won congressional and presidential elections they would have had the same kind of political difficulties that confronted Harry S. Truman and that today plague Dwight D. Eisenhower. Political parties with such a wide base of popular support frequently have difficulty in governing, but they are a marvelous device for catching votes.

And the Socialist Party was firmly committed to the ballot box, to attempting to attain its objective, the cooperative commonwealth, through political and parliamentary action. The Socialists rejected first the syndicalists' antiparliamentary point of view and later the Communists' argument. But lacking the political adhesive of patronage and eventually even much hope of electoral success and patronage, they also gradually abandoned this coalition concept of party organization. The party's decline is the story of movement from an all-embracing political party in the direction of monolithic sect.

To describe the Socialist Party, then—or any national party, for that matter—it is necessary to survey its regional parts, to put the spotlight on each of its centers of strength. There were significant Socialist organizations in all areas of the country except the eastern and central South. Each of these had different emphases, and together they represented all shades of red in the political spectrum from anarchosyndicalist crimson to reformist pink.

The most articulate and one of the most important centers of Socialism was New York City, particularly lower Manhattan. Union Square and the garment district had bred socialism even before there was a Socialist Party. Here in earlier years had been the main strength of the Socialist Labor Party, and when De Leon's personality and policies had brought revolt within his party most of his former followers went into the Socialist Party. The rank and file of the New York movement were immigrants, largely Jewish needle trade workers from eastern Europe. To these hard-working people Socialism was more than just a political movement; it was a way of life. In some neighborhoods one grew up to be a Socialist, a reader of Abraham Cahan's *Jewish Daily Forward*, in Yiddish, or the *Call*, in English, and a member of one of the needle trade unions just as naturally as in some other parts of the country one grew up to be a Republican and a reader of the *Saturday Evening Post*.

These workers with the needle and scissors were the bulk of New York Socialism, but their leadership came from those whose tool was the pen. Lawyers, journalists, and teachers led; garment workers followed. There was an unusual number of intellectuals in the party in New York—perhaps because that city was and is the best labor market in the nation for those who have intellectual abilities for sale—and they were a group of not inconsiderable brilliance. Among the writers were William James Ghent, an able journalist and historian; Gustavus Myers, author of the deservedly famous *History of the Great American Fortunes;* Ernest Poole, author of

The Harbor, and his wife, Margaret; Howard Brubaker, Floyd Dell, Max Eastman, Robert Hunter, Charles Edward Russell, and William English Walling.[7] A comprehensive bibliography of the writers who were at one time or another members of the Socialist Party in New York would be an impressive document. Among the lawyers were Morris Hillquit, the leader of New York Socialism; Louis B. Boudin, labor lawyer and author of the interesting and controversial constitutional history of the United States, *Government by Judiciary;* and Meyer London, several times Socialist member of the House of Representatives. Among the teachers were Jessie Wallace Hughan, holder of a Ph.D. from Columbia University and a public-school teacher in the city, and Algernon Lee, Iowa-born and Minnesota-reared head of the Socialists' Rand School of Social Science.

The Rand School, one of the early institutions in the field of worker education, was a bridge between the intellectuals and the rank and file. Founded in 1906 with an endowment from Mrs. Carrie D. Rand, wealthy mother-in-law of the Iowa Christian Socialist George D. Herron, it offered courses in public speaking, English grammar and composition, socialist theory and history, stenography, and American history and government. Charles A. Beard, then a young professor at Columbia, was associated with it for several years. In 1911 he organized new courses in history and government and lectured in American history. From the catalogue description of his American history course, it appears that his students were fortunate in having a course more like *The Rise of American Civilization* that Beard and his wife published in 1927 than like the conventional political and military history of the day. Among others on the faculty in its first years were David Saville Muzzey, who taught a course in ethics, and Franklin H. Giddings, who gave an elementary course in sociology.[8]

At the Rand School students gained some familiarity with their intellectual comrades, and apparently considerable respect for them. At any rate, the New York rank and file was quick to give what honors it could bestow upon intellectuals and others who might give the party prestige. For example, Charles Edward Russell, the muckraking journalist, did not join the party until 1908, but in 1910 his new comrades nominated him for governor, in 1912 they pushed his candidacy against Debs for the presidential nomination, and in 1913 they nominated him for mayor.[9] A case even more curious is that of J. G. Phelps Stokes, whose prestige stemmed more from social position and money than from scholarship or literary reputation. He was elected a New York member of the National Executive Committee of the party just two years after he joined it.

It was natural that the leadership of the New York Socialists should go to a professional man who had risen from humble origins. Such a figure was the extraordinary Morris Hillquit. Born in 1869 at Riga, where his father was a teacher, he came to the United States when he was sixteen and joined the Socialist Labor Party soon thereafter. After his graduation from New York University Law School in 1893, he rose to a position of leadership in the party exceeded only by De Leon. He soon came into conflict with De Leon, who disliked anyone's attracting enough of a following possibly to threaten his position in what was becoming almost his own political sect. In the late 1890's this conflict came to a head when Hillquit and others formed the Rochester convention, or "Kangaroo" wing, bolted the SLP, and formed an alliance with the Western Social Democratic Party.

The bolt of the Kangaroos was, on the whole, a movement in the direction of a more conservative socialism. One of the main points of difference between the two groups, other than the clash of personalities, was trade union policy. De Leon had despaired of ever converting the American Federation of Labor to socialism and had founded the Socialist Trade and Labor Alliance, an organization of socialist union men that competed with the AFL unions for membership and contracts. Hillquit and the Kangaroos held that the sponsorship of such a dual union was a grievous error that had to be rectified. Socialism, they maintained, was dependent upon the support of the trade unions, and competition with the regularly constituted unions would militate against the AFL's ever embracing socialism.[10] Hillquit retained this opposition to dual unionism throughout his career, later opposing the Industrial Workers of the World not only on the grounds of its syndicalism but also because he considered it in competition with already established unions within the AFL.

In the conflict within the Socialist Party between those who held that Socialism would come gradually, through social evolution and by political means, and those who held that it would come only by revolution, Hillquit and most of the New York Socialists were clearly in the evolutionist camp. At the Unity Convention in 1901 he argued for the inclusion of "immediate demands" in the new party's platform, demands for immediate reforms to benefit workers and farmers without changing essentially the capitalist structure. The cooperative commonwealth someday, yes, but the improvement and reform of capitalism now. In mid-century terms, the "welfare state" was preferable to the uncontrolled industrial capitalism of the early part of the century and was worth working for. He rejected completely the revolutionist argument that any reform of capitalism, by ameliorating the condition of the working class, only postponed the revolution.

Consistent with its evolutionist approach, the New York organization put great emphasis on political action, on getting votes. Many Socialists in other parts of the country, and more than a few in New York itself, felt that in that city the party compromised its principles in the pursuit of electoral support. There was some foundation for this belief. Meyer London, for example, unabashedly chased votes, even if his actions violated the spirit of the party. Speaking before a mass meeting of unemployed in Union Square in 1915, London was severely heckled by a group of IWW's. One of these yelled out a question about what London was going to do in Congress—he had been elected for the first time the previous November—to bring the "Social Revolution." London's reply was frank. "I am elected for only two years, and that is too short a time in which to bring about the Social Revolution, so I am going to leave that job until later. I am going to do hardly anything to bring it about. You see, I have to be re-elected in 1916 and I have to retain some votes in my district." [11]

Although the New York leadership had revolted from the De Leonite ideology, it retained always some characteristics of that earlier socialist movement that derived as much from European as it did from American experience. The New York Socialists retained their rather slavish adherence to European socialist terminology and to interpreting the basic Marxian literature. Hillquit disputed De Leon's interpretation of Marx, but he was as much an exegete as his enemy. New York Socialists in general took pride in their knowledge of the theoretical works of Marxism, and they delighted in interlarding their speech with European Marxist jargon, a language that was all but meaningless to most of the nonsocialist and nonimmigrant public. Terms such as "dialectical materialism," "proletariat," and "bourgeoisie" usually left the uninitiated exactly that—uninitiated. The New Yorkers' knowledge of Marxist theory and their pride in that knowledge sometimes led them to adopt a condescending attitude toward their untutored comrades from the Western plains, who generally did not know surplus value from long division or *Capital* from *The Eighteenth Brumaire*, and did not care to know.[12]

But the nonintellectual rank and file of the New York movement had a much different attitude toward their radical brothers in the Mississippi Valley. The Jewish Socialist immigrants were immensely gratified when they went to party conventions in the American heartland and discovered "old stock" American Socialists and a truly indigenous Socialist movement. These immigrants were Socialist by upbringing; they wanted to be "Americanized"; but sometimes Socialism and being American seemed to them to be antithetical. The Western Socialists, however, were a living proof that it was possible to be as "American" as Kansas and still be Socialist. This feeling accounts for the unusual sentimentality the New York rank and file felt for Debs, the son of immigrant parents but American enough for the most prejudiced cultural nationalist, and red as flame. Debs, of course, was a figure who inspired love throughout the movement and even beyond it, but the demonstrations of affection he received in New York were more than usually sentimental and even pathetically maudlin.

In general, the New Yorkers exerted a conservative force in the Socialist Party. Their leadership was evolutionist, strongly opposed to class violence, prone to emphasize reform rather than Socialism in order to attract votes, and quite sensitive to the opinions of the AFL trade unionists. In time, under the impact of the Russian Revolution, part of the rank and file in New York was to revolt from its leadership, starting a split that was to leave the party weak and ineffectual; but until then most of the dissent within the New York organization came from a few radical intellectuals. It would be an error, however, to dismiss Hillquit as a reformer—as Charles Edward Russell called himself a "side-line reformer"—dabbling in Socialism and likely to desert before the first strong wave of adverse public opinion. Hillquit was a social democrat, albeit a cautious and usually conservative one.

Perhaps the most reformist group in the Socialist Party, if indeed it really was part of the Socialist movement, was the political organization of George R. Lunn of Schenectady. Lunn, originally from Iowa, was ordained a Presbyterian minister in 1901 and took a position as associate pastor of a Brooklyn church. Three years later he became the pastor of the First Dutch Reformed Church of Schenectady, where he remained for five years before moving to that city's United People's Church. While in that position Lunn became interested in municipal reform, then a popular activity of Protestant ministers with mildly disturbing social consciences, and joined the Socialist Party in the belief that organization was the best available instrument for reform of Schenectady. In 1911 he won the mayoralty election, running on the Socialist ticket with strong backing from non-Socialist progressives.[13]

Soon after taking office in January, 1912, Lunn had a major brawl with the Socialist local. Some of the less realistic of the Schenectady Socialists regarded Lunn's election as the dawn of the new Socialist day and expected Lunn immediately to introduce Socialism within Schenectady's city limits. Even had he had such power, Lunn certainly had no such intentions. Many in the Schenectady party feared—correctly, as it turned out—that Lunn had political ambitions for something more than the highest office that city had to offer and was using the Socialists as a steppingstone. The anti-Lunn men in the local, in order to prevent Lunn's building a political machine through his patronage powers, tried to make Lunn submit all municipal appointments, even to the police force, to the party local for approval. This Lunn refused to do, and thereafter he and his party were on uneasy terms, although Lunn kept up his party membership. There were sufficient grounds under the party's constitution to expel Lunn from the party as early as his first year in office—he had gone into Maine during the campaign of 1912 to urge Down East Socialists to vote for Wilson—but he was not expelled until the state committee took action against him in 1915 for conspiring with the party's Bureau of Information director, Carl D. Thompson, to turn the Schenectady Socialist newspaper over to the Municipal Ownership League. By this time he had already made a berth for himself with the Democrats, later serving them for two more terms as mayor, one term in Congress, one term as lieutenant governor, and several terms as state public service commissioner. After Lunn's expulsion Schenectady Socialism declined to insignificance. As one veteran Socialist put it years later, "There were many cranks in Schenectady who wanted Lunn to do the impossible, and he wasn't capable or desirous of doing even the possible." [14]

In the party's very earliest days Massachusetts seemed destined to become a center of Socialist strength, but the hope never materialized. The old Social Democratic Party had won elections at Haverhill, Massachusetts, in 1898 and 1899, sending one of its members to the state legislature and controlling the municipal administration. The success was only transitory; in 1900 the Socialist mayor John Chase was badly beaten in a bid for reelection. Carried into office in the wake of local labor disputes, the Socialists had been unable, because of constitutional inhibitions upon Massachusetts municipalities, to effect any significant changes. [15] This was the high-water mark of Bay State Socialism. The state's vote for Debs in 1900 was exceeded only by New York's, but thereafter the state ceased to play an important role in the party. Later Massachusetts was the home of some important units of the party's foreign-language federations, which will be described in the next chapter.

The Socialists of Pennsylvania were nearly as numerous as those of New York, but their forces were not concentrated as much into a small area and they were thus unable to enjoy as much electoral success. The nature of the Socialist organization in Pennsylvania made it almost a labor party. Only in Wisconsin was the alliance of the Socialists with the AFL as strong, and this connection with the trade unions was largely due to the efforts of the remarkable James Hudson Maurer.

Maurer was a "Pennsylvania Dutchman" from Reading with a long experience in the trade union and radical movements. He quite literally received his education in the labor movement. Forced by the death of his father to leave school before he learned to read, he received this elementary instruction from a Knights of Labor organizer while he was a machinist's apprentice. He joined the Knights on his sixteenth birthday, in 1880, and from then until the end of his life he was active in labor organizations. In 1893 he joined the Populists, with whom he remained until after their disastrous marriage with the silver Democrats in 1896. In 1899, quite on his own, Maurer discovered the Socialist Labor Party, joined it, and had some small success converting his German-speaking fellows to Marxism. Although he had not been involved in the scrap between De Leon and the Kangaroos, he left the Socialist Labor Party in 1901 and joined the new Socialist Party. Meanwhile, he had moved from the moribund Knights to the American Federation of Labor. Quite active in both the party and the AFL, he soon rose to a position of leadership in each. He represented Pennsylvania in the party's National Executive Committee for several terms, beginning in 1904; was its candidate for governor in 1906, and its successful candidate for the state legislature several times. In 1912 Maurer became president of the Pennsylvania State Federation of Labor, an office he held for several years, even during the war, when the presence of a Socialist in such a position caused Samuel Gompers no little concern.

The party's main strength in Pennsylvania was in the German region, especially in Reading. There were locals of respectable size in Pittsburgh and Philadelphia, but they were never so successful as their comrades at Reading. There was sufficient party strength at Reading to elect state assemblymen, and later, when the party was all but dead elsewhere, to elect a Socialist municipal administration. The Philadelphia local, before the war led by J. Mahlon Barnes, a cigar maker, was oriented more toward Hillquit's organization in New York than toward the rest of the party in Pennsylvania.

Maurer and the majority of Pennsylvania Socialists were in the conservative wing of the party. They believed in "step at a time" tactics, moving slowly, gaining political office, and working with the AFL unions. Except that their professed goal was the abolition of capitalism and the institution of a socialist democracy, the short-run programs and policies of Pennsylvania Socialism were little different from the non-Socialist labor movement or major party reformers. Maurer was a little apologetic for his reformism, but he maintained it was justified. Reform, he wrote, "is part of a necessary preparation for Socialism. So long as people think that politics is in its nature corrupt, they are not likely to understand what Socialism means. Only clean political action can usher in the new social order." [16]

Most of the Socialists of Ohio, Indiana, and Michigan considered such emphasis on political reform as "slowcialism." The general tone of the party in those states was considerably more radical than in either Pennsylvania or New York, but there were no Socialist political machines in any of these states comparable to those of Maurer and Hillquit. Seldom having a reasonable chance to win an election, these Midwestern Socialists were less likely than their Eastern comrades to shift their emphasis to a program designed to attract AFL unionists and non-Socialist reformers. Indeed, Socialists from these states sometimes looked a little ridiculous in their zeal to avoid what they called "truckling for votes." In Canton, Ohio, for example, the

Socialist candidate for mayor once came within a very few votes of election. He wanted to contest the election in court, but the Canton local refused to support him on the grounds that to do so would be an inexcusable surrender of the party's revolutionary principles to political opportunism. When the candidate insisted upon a contest, the local expelled him. Subsequently the courts held he had been elected, and he took office as an ex-Socialist. In Lima and Lorain, Ohio, also, the party locals repudiated mayors elected on their tickets, but in these cases there was evidence that the mayors were trying to build a personal political machine à la George R. Lunn.[17]

The majority of the Socialists in these states, however, were not syndicalists; they did not reject political action entirely. Their position was between the syndicalists on the left and the reformers on the right. It is true that Debs, the most important of these Midwestern Socialists, had helped to found the Industrial Workers of the World in 1905, but after De Leon "captured" the organization the following year Debs ceased his active support of it. He retained his IWW membership a while longer only because one of the Wobbly purposes was industrial unionism and organization of the unskilled worker, a cause for which Debs had worked ever since he had organized the American Railway Union. By 1908, when the syndicalists got firm control of the IWW, Debs had severed all connection with the organization.[18]

Debs believed firmly in industrial unionism in the economic field and militant Socialist agitation in the political field. Most of the differences between Debs and more conservative Socialists such as Hillquit, Maurer, and Victor Berger, leader of the Milwaukee organization, were differences of emphasis. They all believed in industrial unionism, but the conservatives, who made great efforts to win elections, were willing to speak only softly on this issue for fear of antagonizing some elements in the AFL; all of them believed in the immediate demands of the Socialist platforms, but the conservatives, in the hope of attracting non-Socialist reformist votes, often made these demands paramount and minimized the distinctively anticapitalist aspects of the Socialist program, much to the disgust of Debs.

Besides Debs, Socialist leaders in these states were Charles E. Ruthenberg, of Cleveland, and Marguerite Prevy, of Akron. Ruthenberg, a young white-collar worker, kept the fairly strong Cuyahoga County local firmly in the radical camp. After the war this local was one of the strongest in the communist movement. Mrs. Prevy, a handsome and forceful woman, was a close friend of Debs. She was an example of a phenomenon not at all uncommon among Socialists but one that always puzzled outsiders: a relatively well-to-do radical. Mrs. Prevy was a successful optometrist who invested her savings in local real estate. She did not have any illusions about capitalism, however, no matter how kind it had been to her, and she worked hard at recruiting for the party and at preaching her militant Socialism.[19] One can only guess what her tenants must have thought as they paid their rents to a landlady who gave them Socialist literature along with their receipts.

Chicago was a strong Socialist center in terms of membership and votes in presidential elections, but Chicago Socialists never enjoyed the success of their comrades in New York and Milwaukee. Chicago Socialists were not united. They represented all shades of opinion, and no one group of them was ever strong enough to dominate the others and build an effective political organization. Perhaps the presence in the city of the party's national headquarters, with its rather frequent shifts of personnel and its national rather than local interests, was a factor in Chicago Socialism's impotence.

Furthest to the left in the Chicago party was Charles H. Kerr and his associates in his publishing house, which issued Socialist classics and the monthly *International Socialist Review*. The *Review* in its early years was a magazine for intellectuals with a taste for abstract articles on Marxian theory. Its editor, Algie Martin Simons, who understandably used only his initials, printed translations of articles from *Archiv für Sozialwissenschaft* and other European periodicals. He once reprinted Frederick Jackson Turner's famous 1893 essay, "The Significance of the Frontier in American History," with the note that it was "without doubt the greatest contribution yet made in the application of the materialistic conception of history to American conditions." Interesting though the Turner essay may be, it hardly set up a clamor for Socialist Party membership, and in 1906 Kerr fired his brilliant but rather erratic Wisconsin Phi Beta Kappan with the remark that the magazine as Simons ran it was more likely to appeal to professors than to proletarians.

It appears, however, that Kerr's real reason for firing Simons was not that he was a highbrow, incapable of editing a mass-circulation magazine. A difference of opinion about the proper relationship of the Socialist Party to the IWW was probably the main reason for Simons's dismissal. The most important new direction of the *International Socialist Review* after Simons left its staff late in 1906 was not toward a simplification of its contents—at no time did it even approach the simplicity of the *Appeal to Reason*—but toward closer alliance with the Wobblies. And after the Western "Hallelujah, I'm a Bum" elements of the IWW won control of the organization at its 1908 convention, and the IWW became vaguely anarchosyndicalist, Kerr's *Review* was the warmest and almost the only supporter of the Wobblies among Socialist periodicals.

Simons had been one of the founders of the IWW in 1905 and had written in Kerr's magazine that if trouble should arise between the new organization and the party it would be "because of those who are so anxious to gain the favor of the A.F. of L. officials that they must heap their abuse on every one who does not kow-tow to their pure and simple god." But under Simons's editorship the magazine's enthusiasm for the IWW soon began to cool. Before the IWW's first birthday Max Hayes, who edited the *Review*'s labor department, became alarmed at the influence of De Leon in the new labor organization. De Leon, "that sorry old adventurer," and his followers were "running amuck and resorting to their old yell that whosoever refuses to join the I.W.W., instantly is a fakir, a traitor, and an all-around scoundrel." Simons dropped his support of the IWW during its second convention, in 1906, because De Leon "captured" the organization, and Kerr soon thereafter dropped him.[20]

After leaving the *Review* Simons became editor of the *Chicago Socialist*, which was soon to become the first Socialist daily news-

paper. (Soon thereafter there was a Socialist daily in New York and
Milwaukee.) On this newspaper Simons found a more conservative
group than that of his former comrades at Kerr's publishing house.
The *Chicago Socialist* was firm in its advocacy of industrial unionism, but it had never been more than lukewarm toward the IWW.
From the first it had feared that the "revolutionary" followers of
De Leon might wreck the attempt to organize labor industrially. "If
bona fide, experienced union men who have confidence in the rank
and file dominate the [1905 IWW] convention and are placed in
charge of the initiatory work of organization, the new movement has
a fair chance of becoming the most powerful, effective and benefi-
cial labor organization the world has ever known. But in case the De
Leon-Hagerty-Trautmann crowd succeed in dominating the convention . . . then the fate of the new movement is doomed to be a flat
failure from the beginning." The second convention of the IWW
realized the *Chicago Socialist*'s fears, and from then on that newspaper was a vigorous opponent of the IWW. William Trautmann,
general secretary of the IWW who within one year was expelled
from the AFL brewers' union for IWW activity and from the Socialist Party for allying himself with De Leon within the IWW, drew
the most fire. The "r-r-revolutionary Trautmann," according to the
Chicago Socialist editor, was a "big, hot air, rapid firing wind jammer
that can fire faker, faker, faker, faker, a hundred times a minute." [21]

Chicago was not, however, in the right wing of Socialism. The
majority of Chicago Socialists were not mere semisocialistic reformers. A group that could elect Barney Berlyn, a Dutch-Jewish cigar
maker and active trade unionist, to the party's National Executive
Committee for eight terms had to be more radical than that. Not that
Berlyn was by any means a flaming red, but Berlyn was of the labor
movement, not a middle-class reformer, and the difference is vast. It is
true that Seymour Stedman, a conservative Socialist lawyer, was prominent in the Cook County local, and for a brief period Chicago Socialists welcomed as a convert the millionaire Joseph Medill Patterson,
later the publisher of the anything but socialistic New York *Daily*

News, but most Chicago Socialists were strong trade unionists and middle-of-the-road social democrats.

It was in 1913, when Simons joined the staff of Victor Berger's *Milwaukee Leader*—Simons got around almost everywhere in his Socialist hegira—that he moved into the right wing of the Socialist Party. Milwaukee, city of beer, German brass bands, and bourgeois civic efficiency, was the strongest center of Socialist strength in the country. It was also one of the most conservative centers in the Socialist Party.

The history of Milwaukee Socialism is largely the story of Victor L. Berger, one of the giants of the American movement. Scholarly in appearance as only a Teutonic secondary schoolteacher can be, dignified to the point that his enemies considered him pompous, and with so little humor that the heavy-handed attempts at lightheartedness in his writing were pathetic, this Austrian immigrant was the most able machine politician and organizer in the party. His contributions to the party were not in his journalism, although he published German and English Socialist newspapers in Milwaukee throughout his career, nor in his role as a congressman, but in his welding together a strong political machine that to this day is a force in Milwaukee. More radical members of the party were disgusted with Milwaukee's caution, with its gradual "step at a time" policies, and with its general stuffiness—Trotsky's jibe that a convention of American Socialists looked like a meeting of dentists, while not a valid comment for the wild Westerners, certainly was an apt description of Milwaukee delegations—but the Milwaukee Socialists did build an organization that was successful politically.[22]

The secret of the success of the Milwaukee Socialists was their close alliance with the trade unions. Milwaukee AFL men were Socialists. Berger's newspaper, the *Social Democratic Herald,*[23] carried on its masthead the legend "Official paper of the Federated Trades Council of Milwaukee and of the Wisconsin State Federation of Labor." Popularity of the Socialist Party in the Milwaukee labor movement did not come of any "boring from within," of parliamentary trickery whereby the unions were put on record as supporters of Socialism, but by Socialists working hard in the trade union movement, getting the confidence and respect of the unionists, and converting them to their way of thought. Berger many times heatedly denounced efforts to "bore from within" in the sense of winning a vote or passing a pro-Socialist resolution. In writing of Max Hayes's unsuccessful attempt to get a pro-Socialist resolution through the 1902 AFL convention, Berger declared: "A resolution like this, even when [if] passed with a large majority, would mean little or nothing to the cause of Socialism in America. In fact experience in the past . . . has proven that resolutions of trades union congresses, even when going so far as to advise the members to vote the ticket of the Socialist party, amount to nothing in practice." Labor support of Socialism had to be freely given and genuine to have any value; anything else would be only a paper victory.

Labor support alone, however, was not enough to win elections. A strong party organization of the kind major parties use so successfully was another necessity. The Milwaukee Socialists had a party organization in every precinct to get their supporters registered, get them to the polls, and get their ballots counted. The party machinery could get literature into every house in Milwaukee within a few hours and in the proper language, English, German, or Polish. Victor Berger was the "boss" behind all these party activities and one of the bossiest "bosses" in a nation that had developed the art to a high degree. The Berger machine offered the Milwaukee electorate entertainment just as other political organizations realize the political possibilities of Roman circuses. In 1902, for example, Milwaukee Socialists offered the public a baseball game between the north-side and south-side Socialist organizations. The tickets were embellished with the red flag, and the *Herald* undoubtedly stimulated attendance when it announced that none other than Berger himself would be on the field as a substitute for the north siders. The box score of the game discloses that Berger did not get into the game even as a pinch hitter, but the sight of the Socialist "boss" in a baseball uniform, lager physique and all, must have been well worth the price of admission.[24]

Another factor in the Milwaukee Socialists' success was their appeal to that city's peculiar ethnic composition. There were and are three main ethnic groups in Milwaukee: the Yankees, the Germans, and the Poles. The Socialists had tremendous strength among the Germans, substantial influence among the Yankees, and their least power among the Poles. The Socialist membership was overwhelmingly German, so much so that there were many jokes among the Socialists in other parts of the country about their Teutonic Wisconsin comrades. One of these had to do with the Milwaukee Socialist who was explaining the failure of a Socialist candidate with a Polish name to win an election. "If we had had someone with a good American name like Schemmelpfennig we could have won." [25] Yet there were representatives of old Yankee stock prominent in the Milwaukee movement. Frederic Heath, whose forefathers on both sides of his family has crossed the Atlantic on the *Mayflower*, was editor of the *Herald*, and Carl D. Thompson, a former Congregational minister, held public office under Socialist auspices. The party's strongest Polish leader was Leo Krzycki of the Amalgamated Clothing Workers.

With its emphasis upon winning elections and its alliance with the local AFL unions, it is not surprising that Milwaukee Socialists were cautious evolutionary social democrats. If the Milwaukee Socialist leadership was to maintain its political strength and its trade union support, it could not get very far ahead of dominant social attitudes in the city. The Milwaukee organization was vigorously opposed to the IWW from its very beginning, and critical of those Socialists, including Debs, who supported the Wobblies. The *Herald* referred to the IWW's first convention as the "anti-A.F. of L. convention," and criticized what it considered the well meaning but misguided Socialists in attendance "who have allowed their feelings against Gomperism to be played upon to draw them out of the inside fight of [with] the A.F. of L.'s capitalistic misleaders—deserting the fight where it should be waged in order to impotently make faces at Gompers from the outside." This was the kernel of Milwaukee Socialism's labor principles: opposition to Gompers but dedication to the idea of winning the AFL to Socialism from the inside rather than fighting it from the outside. Frederic Heath expressed the sentiments of his comrades when he wrote to Gene Debs about the IWW: "I am loyal to the A.F. of L., but I am not loyal and do not care to be to Sam. Gompers. . . . I well, [*sic*] know, Gene, the insults you received from the Gompers crowd . . . but I cannot see why you are not able to keep your patience, especially when the conversion of the rank and file of the A.F. of L. was going so splendidly. The time is fast coming, even in spite of this miserable break of fighting the A.F. of L. from the outside, when it will be the Socialists who frame the policy and who guide the destinies of the federation."

Debs, the most important of the Socialist IWW supporters, thought the Milwaukeeans were sincere in their belief that they could, in his words, "turn the A.F. of L. inside out and make a clean industrial union out of it," but many on the left of the Socialist Party imputed dishonorable motives to Berger and his followers. These imputations of dishonesty were unfair. Berger was constant in his position; he did not compromise with Gompers. There were Socialists willing to accept Gompers and what he stood for, but the Milwaukee leadership was not among them. In 1912 Job Harriman, conservative Los Angeles Socialist leader, wrote to Berger criticizing his recent attacks on Gompers as "ill-timed" during a presidential election. When Berger read the letter he wrote notes for a reply at its bottom. "The time to fight him [Gompers] is all the time, because the American labor movement will remain reactionary as long as he has any influence." [26]

Pro-AFL in their trade union position, Berger and his followers were confirmed evolutionists, "step at a time" Socialists. Socialism, they believed, would come slowly, gradually evolving from capitalism as capitalism had evolved from feudalism, not from a cataclysm which would bring forth Socialism in a pure and finished form. One of Berger's favorite and oft-repeated mottoes was: "Socialism is coming all the time. It may be another century or two before it is fully established." But as for a revolution meanwhile, Berger wrote: "If there is to be a revolution some day, I and my crowd will surely be there. But that continuous threat of 'revolution' reminds me of a man who is continually brandishing a revolver which is not loaded." [27]

Berger's gradualist philosophy is evident in the measures he introduced in the House of Representatives. In the Sixty-second Congress, 1911–1913, besides a few private and local bills, he sponsored measures providing for old-age pensions, government ownership of the radio industry, abolition of child labor, self-government for the District of Columbia, and a system of public works for relief of the unemployed; resolutions looking toward the withdrawal of federal troops from the Mexican border, abolition of the Senate (a drastic approach to the problem of the "millionaires' club" before the seventeenth amendment to the constitution was ratified), woman suffrage, and federal ownership of the railroads. [28] With the possible exception of the measures calling for nationalization of the railroads and the radio industry, these bills and resolutions might well have been sponsored by some militant progressive of either of the two major parties. In fact, many measures like these have been sponsored—and passed— by non-Socialists since 1933. But when Berger introduced them he was criticized by many on the left of his own party because all these bills, even if passed, would not add up to Socialism. Even if Berger had agreed with his leftist critics and desired a more radical legislative program, the question might have been raised, What more could one lone congressman do? The answer, of course, would be, Nothing more. More, perhaps, could have been done if other segments of the party had adopted not only the idea of political action but political activity itself with the energy, determination, and organization of the Wisconsin group.

West of the Mississippi River, in Missouri, Kansas, Arkansas, Texas, and especially Oklahoma, was a kind of emotional and radical Socialism that caused Berger, Hillquit, and most moderate Eastern Social democrats to shudder. Berger and Hillquit, in their desire to be accepted by the socialists of Europe, were embarrassed by the presence in the American party of such wild-eyed Socialist evangelists as Kate Richards O'Hare. The dignified Berger wrote to the debonair

Hillquit, "As for your friend, Kate Richard[s] O'Hare, making the American Socialist Party ridiculous at the sessions of the International Bureau—why of course she will make it ridiculous." As it turned out, Berger's and Hillquit's fears were unfounded. Mrs. O'Hare's record of enrolling farmers from the Great Plains in the Socialist cause so impressed European socialists that Jean Jaurès invited her to come to France to advise the French leaders how to gain strength among the peasants.[29]

Mrs. O'Hare was unable to accept the invitation, but it is doubtful that she could have aided the cause of French socialism anyway, for the methods she knew were adapted only to the peculiar conditions of the southern Great Plains, with that region's heritage of religious evangelism and Populism. Socialist tent meetings, known as encampments, or newspapers such as the *Appeal to Reason* or the *National Rip-Saw* would have made no dent on the social viewpoints of French peasants, but they were conspicuously successful in the drought, wind, and grasshopper country.

Particularly colorful, and directly in the Great Plains tradition, was the Socialist encampment. An encampment, which was an extended outdoor Socialist meeting, usually lasted about a week and attracted an average crowd of five thousand people, who came from as far as seventy miles away, often by covered wagon. The Socialist organization furnished water, firewood, and toilet facilities; the farm families brought their own food and slept in their wagons or on the ground. The party raised what funds were necessary by passing the hat at meetings and by collecting contributions from merchants of the nearest town, who usually managed to overcome their antipathy toward Socialism when they thought of five thousand potential customers in the vicinity. On one occasion local merchants even displayed the red flag in their shop windows.

The program at these encampments, usually held in a grove of trees or a large tent, included music, classes in history and economics, and many speeches. The prairies rang with Socialist songs, some of them of Populist origin, which were based on familiar tunes. For example, there was the great favorite the "Red Flag" to the tune of

"Maryland, My Maryland" (with the chorus, "Then raise the scarlet standard high; Within its shade we'll live and die. Though cowards flinch and traitors sneer, We'll keep the red flag flying here"), and there was the maudlin "I Will Join the Party, Mother," based on the even more maudlin "Just Before the Battle" ("Yes, I'll join the party, mother, Join it body, mind and soul; With my comrades, like a brother, Fighting e'er to gain a goal"). When the versatile Oscar Ameringer, one of the best journalists and organizers in this area, and his three sons were present there was music by Beethoven, Mozart, Bach, and Schubert played by the Ameringer quartet, which brought "culture" to the encampments with, of all things, two trumpets, a French horn, and a tuba.

The classes at these encampments, no matter what their label, were concerned with Socialism. But besides such uniquely American Socialist books as Walter Thomas Mills's *The Struggle for Existence* and Ameringer's *Life and Deeds of Uncle Sam,* which has sold over a half-million copies and been translated into fourteen languages, the encampments used works by such academic authors of recognized merit as J. Allen Smith and Frederick Jackson Turner.

The music, the classes, and the camaraderie of kindred spirits after months on the lonely prairie were fine, but it was the spellbinding orators who drew the farmers into the encampments. The fiery Debs, for whom most Socialists had a personal admiration that was almost devotion, was the most popular of the encampment speakers. Despite Debs's elocution-school gestures, his burning sincerity was so great that when he pointed a bony forefinger at the crowd in his most characteristic mannerism each member of the audience thought he was speaking directly to him alone. Kansas-reared Kate Richards O'Hare, then of St. Louis, where she, her husband, and Phil Wagner published the *National Rip-Saw,* was nearly as popular as Debs. Caroline Low, a former Kansas City schoolteacher, had a considerable following, and there was the eccentric Walter Thomas Mills. Mills, a little man with a fancy beard who had the appearance of a Victorian college president or minister, was always influential among the Western farmers and occasionally a thorn in the side of the Socialist Party. Early in the party's history this Quaker, educated at Oberlin and Wooster, had led an attempt to capture the party in Nebraska, and he was later to leave the Socialists for A. C. Townley's Non-Partisan League. Socialism was a religion with these orators, with the possible exception of the enigmatic Mills; they were evangelists preaching the gospel of the cooperative commonwealth. It was the same with their embattled farmer-followers. Although born a Swabian peasant, Ameringer understood Great Plains Socialism better than most of his American-born comrades. Of these Socialist farmers he wrote:

. . . to these people radicalism was not an intellectual plaything. Pressure was upon them. Many of their homesteads were already under mortgage. Some had actually been lost by foreclosure. They were looking for delivery from the eastern monster whose lair they saw in Wall Street. They took their socialism like a new religion. And they fought and sacrificed for the spreading of the new faith like the martyrs of other faiths.[30]

Important as the encampments were in the Western movement, farmers could attend them perhaps only once a year. But every week they read and passed on to friends their copies of the *Appeal to Reason*, which preached, as an Eastern Socialist intellectual put it acidly but accurately, a "somewhat corybantic type of socialism." With its circulation of over a half-million, the Squeal of Treason, as it was known to many alarmed conservatives, was easily the most influential of all Socialist periodicals. Sold for only twenty-five cents a year, the *Appeal* could and did get into the poorest of homes with its emotional brand of Socialism.[31]

The *Appeal*'s purpose was to introduce people to Socialism, to make converts to the Socialist Party, rather than to provide news and deepen understandings for those already in the movement, although it did not altogether slight these functions. The publisher of the *Appeal*, Julius A. Wayland, asserted that "More people have had the subject [Socialism] thrust on their attention by the *Appeal* than all other influences combined. . . . It goes into new places or into new homes in old places and prepares the ground for the work of organizers and other literature." Its highly moral tone, its persistent and yet not blatant anti-Catholicism, and its vaguely Populistic approach to social problems made it a natural for converting disturbed Westerners to Socialism. The *Appeal*'s Puritanical moralism made it more than a little ridiculous to sophisticates, but readers avidly sought out headlines like "The Cause of Prostitution" (capitalism) or "Working Girls Seduced by Commercial Buccaneers." The hints of promiscuity in paragraphs like the following certainly did not hurt the circulation either: "In a letter from a member of an orchestra that plays for the delectation of the rich families that spend part of the summer at Newport, he writes me that the orgies that are nightly indulged in by the rich would shame the lowest brothels. . . . With wine and music and high feeding, he says they abandon all restraint, and the animal dominates the moral." The plight of the virgin in industrial capitalism was even celebrated in verse in "The Ballad of the Shop Girl."

> The wolf of poverty follows me on,
> Through the dingy streets of the town;
> So near to my side that his shaggy hide
> Can almost touch my gown;
> While after him the wolves of lust
> Are coming to drag me down.
> And many and fast the days whirl past
> While early I work and late;
> And along my path for the aftermath
> The basilisk watchers wait;
> And civilization bids me choose
> The grave or the harlot's fate.[32]

At one time eighty thousand salesmen-soldiers were selling subscriptions in the "*Appeal* Army." Probably the most famous of the soldiers was one Louis Klamroth, who rode a bicycle about the country selling *Appeal* credit cards, good for Socialist literature and a subscription when mailed to the *Appeal* office at Girard, Kansas. Despite being "Rotten-egged, knocked down and clubbed, drenched with fire hose and water bucket, arrested and deported," Klamroth sold over a hundred thousand subscriptions and thousands of Socialist pamphlets. Wayland knew no shame in his techniques to gain circulation. His subscription contests were the equal of anything William Randolph Hearst was ever able to devise. In 1904, for example, he offered a twenty-five-foot boat as the prize in a new circulation contest. It was Wayland's hope that the winner would use the craft to sell Socialist literature—presumably not neglecting the *Appeal*— along the Mississippi River and its tributaries and would call the vessel the "Flag Ship of the Socialist Propaganda Navy." [33]

All this sort of nonsense suggests that Wayland with his *Appeal* was a mere mountebank, or at least just a clown; nothing could be farther from the truth. He was a highly effective recruiter for radicalism. Although the *Appeal* was always vague as to just what it meant by Socialism, its indictments of capitalism were severe and its condemnations of injustice were vigorous. Besides sensational trash the *Appeal* carried articles of real merit. It was here that Upton Sinclair first published *The Jungle*. Here were published excerpts from the powerful *Modern Society* by E. A. Ross. Here Debs published his angry and revolutionary "Arouse, Ye Slaves," when Bill Haywood, Charles Moyer, and George Pettibone were arrested illegally in Colorado to stand trial on a "framed" murder charge. "They have driven us to the wall and now let us rally our forces and face them and fight," wrote Debs on this occasion. "If they attempt to murder Moyer, Haywood and their brothers, a million revolutionists, at least, will meet them with guns. . . . The worm turns at last, and so does the worker. Let them dare to execute this devilish plot and every state in the union will resound with the tramp of revolution." [34]

The vigor of the *Appeal* aroused action against it among conservatives, an indication of the paper's influence. President Roosevelt sent a copy of "Arouse, Ye Slaves," to his Attorney General along with a note: "This is an infamous article. Is it possible to proceed against Debs and the proprietor of this paper criminally? . . . please notify the Post-Office Department so that the paper may not be allowed in the mails, if we can legally keep it out."

Roosevelt could not legally keep the *Appeal* from the mails— Wilson could and did a few years later—but town postmasters illegally halted delivery of the *Appeal* frequently. On several occasions the *Appeal* complained that postmasters had notified the paper's office to cease mailing issues to certain subscribers because the subscriber had refused to accept the paper, only soon to receive inquiries from the reader as to why his paid-for subscription had stopped. The *Appeal* was involved in so many libel suits that Fred D. Warren, its managing editor, was recognized in the party as an expert whose advice was sought in such matters.[85] Warren's most important case grew out of the Haywood-Moyer-Pettibone affair.

Late in 1905 Frank Steunenberg, former governor of Idaho who had been elected with the support of the Western Federation of Miners but who had supported the mine operators while in office, was killed when he opened a booby-trapped gate at his home. The Pinkerton Detective Agency was put on the case and got a "confession" from a labor spy named Harry Orchard, who said he had been hired to kill Steunenberg by the officers of the WFM. Early in 1906 Denver police authorities cooperated with Idaho police in removing WFM officers Haywood, Moyer, and Pettibone from Denver and imprisoning them in Idaho. There was no legal extradition process. It was a clear case of flouting Anglo-American due process of law. The radical and labor press referred to their removal to Idaho as "kidnaping." This was when Debs wrote "Arouse, Ye Slaves." Subsequently, after months in prison, the three were acquitted through the efforts of their defense attorney, Clarence Darrow.

The *Appeal* made a major issue of the affair, and in one rather foolish countertactic became involved in difficulty itself. A former governor of Kentucky, William S. Taylor, at the time in Indiana, was wanted in his home state for questioning about a murder of a political opponent. The governor of Indiana refused to extradite Taylor to Kentucky. When there was no action taken against Idaho officials for their illegal "kidnaping" of Moyer, Haywood, and Pettibone, Warren of the *Appeal* advertised a reward for the kidnaping of Taylor and his return to Kentucky. To defend the victims of one kidnaping by urging another, to protest the breaking of the law in one case by urging its violation in another, was hardly good logic, but Warren did have a valid point. He wanted to show the world that in the eyes of the federal Department of Justice and the federal judiciary the kidnaping of labor leaders was condoned while the kidnaping of major party politicians was not. Warren proved his point. A federal grand jury indicted him for sending "scurrilous, defamatory and threatening" literature through the mails; nothing happened to the kidnapers of the WFM officers. In a long drawn-out case Warren was convicted and sentenced to six months' imprisonment and a fine of five thousand dollars. Happily, President Taft eliminated the sentence altogether and reduced the fine to a token one hundred dollars. Warren refused to pay even this sum, and nothing was ever done about it.[36] Here surely was a case of intelligent conservatism on the part of the Taft administration.

But despite its vigorous and incessant indictment of industrial capitalism, and its ability to keep the Socialistic chip on its readers' shoulders, daring the "capitalist oppressors" to knock it off, the *Appeal to Reason* was not of the left wing of the Socialist Party. In its spirit it was as radical as anything within the Socialist fold; in its thought it was not. The touchstone is the attitude of the *Appeal* toward the IWW. This Western newspaper never approved the Wobblies, although it at first tolerated them, and after De Leon got control of the organization in 1906 the *Appeal*'s opposition was blunt.

When the IWW was organizing at its first convention, the *Appeal* reported the news from Chicago well and with no editorializing. After the convention it carried an article by Debs, "Working Class Unionism," that was very enthusiastic about the IWW if not very enlightening. Immediately under the Debs article Warren wrote a reply to Debs, beginning, "I cannot share Comrade Debs' enthusiasm over the organization of the Industrial Workers of the World. . . ." Warren's reasoning was curious. He held no brief for the AFL; in fact, he thought no more of that organization than Debs did, and he recognized the superiority of industrial unionism over craft unionism. Warren argued that the basic problems that faced workingmen could be solved only by political organization, not economic organization, and that the new IWW might weaken the Socialist

Party by distracting members' minds from the essential problems of the day.

The *Appeal* slowly became more hostile to the Wobblies, and even before the IWW's second convention there was talk of a Wobbly boycott of the Girard newspaper because of Warren's view. But Wayland and Warren stoutly maintained that industrial union-ism was no business of theirs and that they would not for any cause divert their attentions from the political front. They supported Bill Haywood's candidacy for the governorship of Colorado in 1906 be-cause that was within their function, political action, but they would not support his IWW. After De Leon gained control of the IWW in 1906, the *Appeal* was critical and bitter as only belligerents in an SP-SLP (among radicals all leftist parties are known by their initials) fight can be: "De Leon and his fanatical followers . . . have worked themselves into a frame of mind bordering on, if not identical with, anarchy. They are disorganizers rather than organizers . . . . while the Socialist movement is bound by its principles to befriend any organization of workingmen that bears the brunt of battle in the war of the classes, it cannot afford to be led into a trap set by anyone who . . . seeks to control organized labor through a mob of dis-rupting anarchists. Down with De Leonism; up with Socialism!"

Wayland always asserted that he kept the *Appeal* out of factional disputes within the party. The *Appeal* staff was unquestionably sub-ject to much pressure to enlist in the intraparty wars. A Wichita physician once demanded the *Appeal* take sides, either for the "bourgeois Socialists" or for the "ones who demand a clean-up in the working class party." Wayland replied that the *Appeal* must keep "its face toward the enemy, and its prow headed straight for the Co-operative Commonwealth. . . . Shall the Appeal lend its aid to one faction—(and possibly the wrong one, as my judgment is no better than yours)—or shall it continue its work of tearing down the walls of capitalism?" Very possibly concern for his paper's circula-tion was a factor in Wayland's professed neutrality in factional battles, but, in any case, the *Appeal* did not become clearly identified with any wing of the party. It printed articles of the radical political actionist Debs regularly, was friendly with the hazily anarchosyndicalist Jack London, took pride in the municipal reforms of the conservative Milwaukee Socialists, and had an arrangement with Charles Edward Russell whereby Russell turned over to the *Appeal* material he could not use in the muckraking *Everybody's*.[37] The important thing about the *Appeal* was not its ideological position, which was vague, but its remarkable contribution in helping to build a strong Socialist movement in the Great Plains region.

And Socialism in the region from Texas north to Kansas was strong, surprisingly strong, considering the rural nature of the area. In Oklahoma the Socialists were nearly as strong as the major parties. In 1910 Oklahoma had more paid-up Socialist members than any other state in the Union, including populous industrial states such as New York, Massachusetts, Pennsylvania, and Ohio. In that year 5,842 Sooners paid their dues; in New York there were exactly eight hundred fewer dues-paying members. Six years later the Oklahoma Socialists were topped in total membership only by New York.[38] The Socialist vote in Oklahoma indicated even greater strength. In 1912 Oklahoma polled 41,674 votes for Debs, 16.5 per cent of the total votes cast for presidential electors in the state. An indication of good organization and party virility was its increased vote in the congressional elections two years later. In 1914, 52,963 Sooners voted the Socialist ticket, and in three counties the party polled one-third of the total vote. Surely the belief of orthodox Eastern Socialist intellectuals, typified by Hillquit's statement that the "present socialist movement largely depends for its support upon the existence of a numerous class of workers divorced from the soil," was not justified by the facts in Oklahoma.[39] That Hillquit could write such a statement not only reveals his ignorance of a significant movement within his own party; it also reveals the regional nature of American Socialism.

Socialist strength in Oklahoma was considerable because there the party was clever at adapting techniques and programs fitted to the local radical agrarian tradition and because it worked hard at political organization. After the 1912 election Oklahoma Socialist leaders went to the state election board and investigated the Socialist vote in every precinct of the state. They then went into each precinct and organized a party local, seeing to it that every precinct had a responsible chairman who would distribute literature and assign watchers and counters at the polls. This system brought Socialist-voting nonmembers into the party in all but two hundred of the state's 2,565 precincts, making Oklahoma the best organized state in the Socialist Party. Thus the Milwaukee system of organization was put on a state-wide basis, but equally important was the forging of a state program concerned with the real problems and issues of the state, not with abstract, and to the Oklahoma farmer, distant conflict of proletariat and bourgeoisie.

This state program was a blend of Socialism and Populism, constructed in a manner to appeal to the attitudes of Western farmers. The party made a strong bid for the farm tenant vote. Its literature made frequent reference to the plutocrats in the "electric light towns" and featured photographs contrasting the comfortable homes of the Democratic candidates with the miserable hovels of the tenants on these Democrats' farms. The platform had many planks appealing to the tenant farmer and small farm owners. The Socialists promised a law setting a maximum legal interest rate and invalidation of all contracts charging more than that rate; they promised state-owned grain elevators and warehouses, the state to lend money at low interest to pay off mortgages upon the presentation of warehouse receipts; they called for tax exemptions up to $1,000 for farm dwellings, tools, farm animals, and improvements; and they promised state insurance against pestilence, plant and animal disease, hail, flood, storm, and fire. The Socialists also instigated two state referenda designed to liberalize the election and voter registration laws. All these demands were firmly in the Populist tradition, and it must not be forgotten that Populism then was not long dead.

But Oklahoma Socialists did not lose sight of their more truly Socialist demands. In their platform they reaffirmed their allegiance to international socialism and to the Socialist Party of America. They did not conceal their ultimate purpose, "seizing the powers of govern-

ment of the state of Oklahoma and using such powers for the immediate betterment of the condition of the workers and eventually
bringing about a classless society." But their strength lay in their
immediate demands on state issues. Such demands were considered
conservative and in the long run self-defeating by some elements in
the party, but they did help to create a strong movement in Oklahoma; and, had they become law, the position of the tenant farmers
and poor freeholding farmers of the state would have been substantially improved. Furthermore, the spirit of the Oklahoma movement
—admittedly a vague and immeasurable quality, but a real one nevertheless—that the tub-thumping of the Socialist encampments and the
red ink of the *Appeal* evoked made for an atmosphere of unrest, class
consciousness, and militancy that was pregnant with promise of significant social change. When a small-town Democratic editor from
Oklahoma wrote to his party chief, President Wilson, that Oklahoma
Socialism was growing to alarming proportions and urged Wilson
to make agrarian reforms to combat Socialism, the country editor
knew whereof he spoke.[40]

The Socialists had no centers of significant strength in the South
other than Texas, Arkansas, Oklahoma, and Missouri, and these states
were as much Western as Southern. But in Louisiana there was one
very interesting little Socialist island. In 1912 Debs polled 5,249 votes
in Louisiana, one-fourteenth of that state's vote, and ran ahead of
William Howard Taft, the Republican candidate. The Debs vote
came almost entirely from the "hillbillies" and lumberjacks in the
yellow pine region, from Vernon and Winn parishes. The town of
Winnfield, in Winn Parish, elected the entire Socialist slate to local
offices. But the Socialists received almost no vote at all from other
parts of the state. In New Orleans they received only a few votes
and in the parishes in the alluvial plain almost none.

It is not surprising that the areas of Socialist strength in Louisiana were precisely the areas where the Populists a few years before
had had their main strength. These areas differed from the rest of the
state in significant ways. In the Populist-Socialist areas there were
fewer large landholders than in the rest of the state (the percentage

of farms over one thousand acres was smaller than the state percentage), there were considerably fewer Catholics, there was a higher rate of literacy, and the soil was less fertile.

Before 1912 Socialist strength in Louisiana had never been more than negligible, and never again after the elections that year were the Socialists strong. The reason for the temporary upsurge of Socialism in Louisiana was a violent labor dispute in the lumber industry. A strike against some of the lumber companies had begun in May, 1911, under the leadership of one Arthur Lee Emerson. During the strike many of the timber workers joined the IWW, and after Burns Detective Agency men ambushed a strike "speaking" at the little company town of Grabos in July, 1912, leftist sentiment among the strikers increased. Bill Haywood came into the area and campaigned for Debs, although Debs himself, probably acting upon the advice of conservative Socialists in New Orleans, known to the upcountry Socialists as "yellows," did not even stop in the strike area when he visited Louisiana during the campaign. Thus when election day came in 1912 it was against a background of violence and class conflict. By 1916 labor conditions in the local lumber industry had quieted somewhat, and the Socialists polled only 292 votes.[41] The whole labor upheaval in Vernon and Winn parishes was typical of the IWW; it followed the IWW pattern that had been set earlier at McKees Rocks, Pennsylvania, and Lawrence, Massachusetts. The Wobblies were good strikers and vicious battlers when class conflict was at white heat. But when passions had cooled and the trade union function had changed from striking to workaday, prosaic union maintenance, which involves a degree of class collaboration rather than class warfare, the IWW was inadequate. The Wobblies were always able to give a good account of themselves in industrial struggles even if they did not always win their strikes, but they were never able to maintain themselves during periods of relative peace.

In the Rocky Mountains and the Pacific Northwest the Socialist movement was dominated by revolutionaries who regarded the Oklahoma movement as effeminately mild. Here was the stronghold of

Bill Haywood and the IWW. Here was clearly the most radical section of the Socialist Party.

The term "anarchosyndicalism" is generally used to describe the philosophy of these left Socialists. It is not a very exact term because of the inevitable comparison with the anarchosyndicalism of Georges Sorel, the French author of *Reflections on Violence*. Haywood, for example, and Sorel are only very roughly comparable. Sorel, although no paragon of clarity, was much less confused in his philosophy than was Haywood. But there is no other word to describe this philosophy, and with this caveat it may legitimately be used. American anarchosyndicalism was a hodgepodge of several tenets: of distrust of anything not emanating from the proletariat, of Socialist revolution, of opposition to any reform within capitalism as constituting nothing but a delay in the revolution, of "direct action," as they euphemistically called sabotage and industrial violence, and of "one big unionism." At its clearest this philosophy was a plan for the organization of all labor into one vast and well disciplined union for the purpose of conducting a national and revolutionary general strike, the successful strikers then to establish a completely socialist economy with political power residing in the labor organization. This was the plan as outlined in Jack London's short story "The Dream of Debs," a title that would have been more accurate had it been "The Dream of London, 1909." Anarchosyndicalism in its hazier and more typical form was "Big Bill" telling a Cooper Union audience:

. . . the reason that I don't go into the halls of parliament to make laws to govern the working class is because the working class is working with machines, and every time some fellow has a thought, inspiration, the machine changes, and I don't know that laws can be made quick enough to keep up with the changing machinery. . . . I again want to justify direct action and sabotage. . . . I don't know of anything that can be applied that will bring as much satisfaction to you, as much anguish to the boss as a little sabotage in the right place at the proper time. Find out what it means. It won't hurt you, and it will cripple the boss.

That such contempt for law and political action as this was popular among the miners and lumberjacks of the Western mountains is not surprising when one considers society in that area. Here there were no niceties in industrial warfare. Capital developed figures like General Sherman Bell and labor developed figures like Bill Haywood. The alliance between capital and government was open and its power flagrantly used. Where a laborer's only contact with the state had been through a labor injunction, a trumped-up criminal indictment, or a trooper's bayonet, such contempt for the state and parliamentary action was to be expected of men of integrity. If many Western Socialists were tough, hard-bitten, and primitive, so were the conditions from which they came.[42]

In these Western states the Socialist vote was significant. In the election of 1912 Debs polled over 10 per cent of the popular vote of Washington, Idaho, Montana, Nevada, California (here, however, conservative Socialists were dominant), and Arizona. But the ultra-radical views of large numbers of these Western Socialists prevented their becoming a real political party or their using their strength to lasting advantage. In Washington, for example, when the Socialists elected a member to the state legislature, the state organization refused to allow the Socialist legislator to cooperate with the labor and farmer blocs; it declined to support an eight-hour-day law he sponsored and condemned him when he voted for a progressive for speaker on the grounds that he should have nominated and voted for himself. All this the Washington Socialists did because "the main function of the socialist party was to organize and get a strong dues-paying organization so when the crucial moment came they would be able to do the job and take possession of the industries." [43] Such is hardly the way to build a political organization. But then these Socialists had no intention of building a political party. To them the Socialist Party was an educational or propagandist agency, not a political group.

It is probable that the refusal of the Washington Socialists to support their legislator in normal political activities did not spring from any systematic, well thought out justification of radicalism but rather from distrust of anything that smacked of middle-class respectability. The lengths the Western radicals went to to demonstrate their "proletarianness" were sometimes absurd. At the 1912 national convention of the party at Indianapolis, for example, Jacob Panken, a New York City Socialist who later was to become a municipal judge, had agreed to eat dinner with the delegates from Oregon. None of them knew the city well, and they walked the streets looking for a likely restaurant. Panken saw one that looked good to him and suggested they eat there. The Oregonians vetoed the proposal on the grounds the place had tablecloths and was therefore bourgeois. The group ended up in a place called the Red Devil, chosen because of its crimson name, which was devoid of tablecloths and other bourgeois appointments. Thomas Sladden, at one time state secretary of Oregon, yielded to none in his devotion to the cult of the proletariat. This worshiper of the worker even removed the cuspidors from Oregon state headquarters when he took office on the grounds that these ungainly pieces of furniture were bourgeois and that real tobacco-chewing proletarians disdained such sissified conveniences.[44]

One other center of significant Socialist strength, California, remains to be described. Until 1909–1910 the California movement was sharply split between left and right, and the battles between the two groups were bitter. There was an unusual amount of confusion, unusual even for Socialists. After elections of state and local party officers both sides would claim the victory and set up dual organizations, each of which would proceed to expel the members of the other from the party. In the winter of 1909–1910 the conservatives won final control of the state organization. Until then the conservatives had controlled the Los Angeles area and the radicals the San Francisco Bay area. After the conservative victory J. Stitt Wilson, a Protestant minister, was elected mayor of Berkeley on the Socialist ticket, and he gave that university town a clean, reformist administration of the Milwaukee type.[45]

The high tide of California Socialism was the mayoralty election of 1911 in Los Angeles. The leader of the Socialists in Los Angeles was Job Harriman, a successful lawyer who had been Debs's running mate in 1900 and one of the most conservative leaders in the party. Except for Harriman's occasional genuflection toward the cooperative commonwealth, it was difficult to distinguish him from progressives of either of the two major parties. He was consistently on the most conservative side of Socialist Party intramural disputes. It is ironical that Harriman, of all Socialists, should have become identified in the eyes of the voters of his city with labor violence. In the fall of 1910 someone bombed the building that housed the ultrareactionary General Harrison Gray Otis's Los Angeles *Times*. The following spring James and John McNamara of the Structural Iron Workers Union, AFL, were charged with the dynamiting through indictment procedures reminiscent of the treatment of Haywood, Moyer, and Pettibone only a few years before. The labor and radical press came to the defense of the McNamara brothers, and the lines between labor and capital, conservatives and progressives, were taut when the time came for the Los Angeles primary elections. In the primaries Harriman received more votes than any candidate of the major parties, and the electorate approved two constitutional amendments supported by the Socialists. It looked as if the intensification of social conflict brought by the McNamara case would result in a Socialist victory in the Los Angeles general elections. Harriman himself ran on a civic reform platform and did not personally make the McNamara case part of his campaign, but there was no question in the minds of Los Angeles voters that a vote for Harriman was an expression of sympathy for and belief in the innocence of the McNamaras and that a vote against the Socialist candidate meant support of Harrison Gray Otis and an "open shop" city. Socialist campaign buttons bore the legend "McNamaras Not Guilty! Vote for Harriman!" Then on December 1, 1911, James McNamara, acting upon the advice of Clarence Darrow, his counsel, and Lincoln Steffens, went into court and pleaded guilty. That ended Socialist hopes for victory despite Harriman's last-minute disclaimers of relationship to the dynamiter. Still, on election day Harriman received 50,827 votes to his opponent's 87,165.[46] This was not quite the end of the Socialist Party in California—it elected two state legislators in 1914—but never again did the party in that state have the promise it had before the McNamara affair. Thereafter Californians tended to identify the Socialist Party with violence, despite the mildness of California Socialist leadership, and in the United States political identification with violence is fatal, even though, paradoxically, Americans are among the most violent people in the West European tradition.

These, then, were the regional organizations in the prewar Socialist Party, a typically American party in the sense that it extended from coast to coast, in almost all regions of the country, embracing a variety of social philosophies. Hillquit, Lunn, Maurer, Debs, Simons, Berger, Wayland, Haywood, and Harriman had little in common beyond the little red Socialist membership cards in their wallets. There were divisions and other aspects of the party not revealed in this regional overview of American Socialism which will be considered in the next chapter, but such a regional approach illustrates the fact that the Socialist comrades were strange bedfellows. Yet political parties in the United States are famous for bunking strangers together, even incompatible strangers, and the Socialists until World War I were above all a political party.

II

IMMIGRANTS, NEGROES,
INTELLECTUALS, MILLIONAIRES,
AND MINISTERS

A REGIONAL approach to the Socialist Party is necessary properly to understand that organization and the whole prewar radical movement, but there were significant aspects of the party that are not revealed by an examination of the various regional Socialist movements. Within the party were important differences in social class, in national origins, in race, in religious outlook, and in educational background, as well as in regional orientation, and these differences bore but little relationship to the party's geography.

The largest nonregional bloc in the Socialist Party consisted of the so-called foreign-language federations, organizations of non-English-speaking immigrants affiliated with the party. The great majority of the millions of immigrants who came to America in the great migration waves of the late nineteenth and early twentieth centuries either supported the major political parties or were not interested in political matters at all. The stereotype of the immigrant as a wild-eyed, bomb-throwing, flaming red has been shown to be a false one.[1] Yet there were immigrants who had been socialists in Europe, and these did not leave their socialism in their native land. The circumstance of living in a strange new land did not necessarily change the socialist immigrant's social and economic ideas and attitudes, and yet, except for the unusual newcomer who could read and speak English, there was no American socialist organization to which he could turn. The Socialists in time saw the opportunity presented by the immigrant radicals, and devised a scheme to bring them into the party.

Socialism had considerable strength among the Finns of the Pacific Northwest, the Duluth-Superior district along the Minnesota-Wisconsin state line, the upper peninsula of Michigan, and Massachusetts. In 1904 a few hundred Finns of socialist conviction joined the Socialist Party and organized themselves into the Finnish Federation. At first the federation received no recognition from the party. Individuals in the federation paid their dues directly to the party's local organization and, officially, had no different status in the party than any other member. Then in 1907 the Finnish Socialists asked the party to allow them to establish one of their members in the national office at Chicago to translate official actions of the party, such as the minutes of the National Executive Committee. The request was granted. At the party's next national convention, in 1908, the party passed a resolution declaring itself in favor of such affiliated foreign-language groups, but it did not set a definite policy for the establishment of other federations or for the mechanics of their affiliation until the party congress of 1910—called a congress instead of a convention because no candidates were nominated. Meanwhile the Lettish Socialists had made an arrangement with the party somewhat like the scheme of the Finns.[2]

The 1910 congress amended the party constitution to permit any foreign-language socialist group of five hundred or more members to affiliate by establishing a translator in the national office. The party agreed to pay the salary of the translator. Under this arrangement several immigrant groups formed federations and affiliated with the party. In 1911 the South Slavs, the Italians, and the Scandinavians affiliated with the party, the Hungarians and Bohemians joined in 1912, as did the Germans, Poles, Jews, and Slovaks in 1913 and the Ukrainians, Lithuanians, and Russians in 1915. In 1917, the year the United States entered World War I, there were 32,894 members of the various foreign federations. The total party membership that year was 80,126.

Some of these foreign federations established clubrooms and served as community social centers as well as political organizations. These community centers made money for the federations, and some of the federations became quite wealthy by Socialist Party standards. The Finnish Federation in 1913 owned sixty-five to seventy meeting halls, valued at about $600,000. It also owned a printing plant and a school, the Workers' College of Smithville, Minnesota, which cost the federation about $6,000 a year. The Bohemians of Chicago owned three buildings for which they had rejected an offer of $30,-000, and printing equipment worth $50,000.[3]

The language federations were as independent of the national Socialist organization as they wanted to be. Because of the language barrier, the party knew nothing more about the federations than the federations wanted the party to know. The translators in the national office were the only liaisons between the English-speaking and for-eign-language-speaking groups, and their position gave them unusual power. They became much more than official linguists; they came to fill a role similar to that of the state secretaries, issuing dues stamps to their federation locals, handling the federations' correspondence, and going on organizing tours. Although the translators received their pay from the party's national executive secretary, they were not party employees in the same sense as other workers in the national office. They were selected by the federations rather than by the party, and could be as cooperative or as independent of the rest of the national office personnel as they wished. Not surprisingly, there was frequent friction between the translators and their colleagues at Chicago.

This situation especially galled national executive secretaries when they considered that, although the national office paid the translators, many of the federations were in a better position to do so. In 1914 the various federations cost the party approximately $11,000. The party's net revenue from the federations was about 14 cents a year for each federation member, whereas the regular English-speak-ing party member contributed 60 cents a year to the national office.

In the spring of 1914 Walter Lanferseik, then the national secretary, recommended to the National Executive Committee that the federations be required to pay the translators' salaries and that the money the party thus saved be used to subsidize the weaker state organizations.[4]

It is probable that the party would have changed its arrangements with the language federations had it not been for a peculiar situation that arose in the Finnish Federation later in 1914. During a strike in the Michigan copper mines, radicalism of the IWW brand grew among the Finns. The federation's officers and the staff of *Tyomies*, the Finnish Socialist daily published at Superior, Wisconsin, fought the syndicalist faction without much success. The syndicalists even gained control of the newspaper for a brief period, and when the antisyndicalists soon removed them the syndicalists founded a rival newspaper, *Socialisti*, in nearby Duluth, Minnesota. The strike had seriously hurt the finances of *Tyomies*, and now the competition of a rival paper published just ten miles away threatened its very existence. The antisyndicalists had control of the federation's offices and used that power to expel all locals that refused to support *Tyomies*. But the expelled locals, although no longer in the federation, remained in the regular state and national organization because the state organizations took no action against them.

This put the National Executive Committee in a tight spot. It wanted to curb the independence of the language federations, yet to limit the power of the Finnish Federation at the moment would be to come to the aid of the expelled syndicalist locals. And the NEC certainly had no desire to help syndicalists. "If autonomous foreign groups [locals] are permitted to join the party like an English local, it becomes possible to annul and wreck the work of the regular foreign-speaking federations. Any kind of syndicalistic or impossibilist propaganda can be carried on, and there can be no local control, because the language becomes a barrier." Because of the language difficulty, only the federation could ride herd on the foreign-language-speaking syndicalists. It was necessary, therefore, for the federation to retain its power. Accordingly, the NEC resolved that "the decision of the Finnish Federation as to expulsion of locals or members shall be accepted by state, county and local organizations as final . . . . the Language Federations have full charge and jurisdiction in the organization of the language locals, and of all propaganda in the particular language." [5] Thus the federations remained all but autonomous, despite their expense to the party and despite the annoyance their sometimes uncooperative translators caused the national office.

Curiously, although it was the extreme left of the party that rankled most from the NEC's decision in the Finnish dispute, five years later the extreme left benefited from the outcome of the affair. Soon after the NEC made its decision in the case of the Finns, Charles E. Ruthenberg, leftist national executive committeeman from Cleveland, objected strenuously to the disposition of the case. He would have extended the party's discipline over the federations regardless of the consequences. [6] But had Ruthenberg's point of view toward the federations prevailed in 1914 and 1915, his work in leading some of the federations into the communist movement in 1919 would have been considerably more difficult. Such are the fortunes of politics.

On the whole question of immigration Socialists agreed no more than they did on other important issues of the day. The party found itself torn between two opposing principles. One of the basic tenets of socialism was the international solidarity of the working class. Class lines were supposed to be stronger than national boundary lines. Marx in 1848 had exhorted the workingmen of *all* countries to unite, for they had nothing to lose but their chains. Yet American union men had found they did indeed have something more to lose than chains. They had unions and the hope of better wages and working conditions to lose to the immigrant, who not infrequently was a peasant ignorant of trade unionism and willing to work for low wages. As he in time became a union man a new migration of "greenhorns" landed, and the process was repeated. Should American Socialists, then, adhere to the idea of the international solidarity of labor and welcome immigrants, or should they cooperate with the trade unions in attempting to pressure through legislation restricting immigration? Debates among Socialists on these questions were bitter, but they never resolved themselves into a clear-cut party position. The sum effect of the disagreement among Socialists over the immigration question was to make the party's official policy one that straddled the two positions.

Immigration from Europe was one of the relatively few things Debs and Berger could agree upon. Debs wrote, in his typically overripe prose, that if the party did not "stand staunchly, unflinchingly, and uncompromisingly for the working class and for the exploited and oppressed masses of all lands, then it stands for none and its claim is a false pretense and its profession a delusion and a snare." Berger, not unmindful of Milwaukee's large German and Polish population, wrote that when the revolutionary fathers of the United States welcomed the oppressed of Europe the immigrants "came and brought with them more of the spirit of liberty than some of the descendants of those revolutionary heroes like. Hence we have the spasmodic efforts to shut off immigration." Berger claimed "every decent immigrant brings with him labor power enough to supply many more mouths than his own by his industry, [and] all claims that he is a detriment to the country is [sic] poppycock." But immigrants from Asia were an altogether different matter. Asian "coolies," Berger wrote, constituted a real danger to the American trade unionist and his family's standard of living. In Kansas the *Appeal to Reason* had no use for immigrants of any kind, European or Asian. Capitalists, charged the *Appeal*, were conspiring "to bring in the lowest scum of Europe, that they may have cheap labor." Capitalists and their hired politicians, believed Wayland and Warren, had similarly sinister plans for importing cheap labor from Asia. "A workingman who votes either of the old tickets votes to be a slave and have Chinese and Japanese and pauper competition for a chance to earn a living." The party never reconciled these disparate views into an official policy. The history of the attempt to hammer out a policy acceptable to all is long and confused, but a brief account will suffice to point out the nature of the compromise.[7]

The delegates to the Stuttgart Congress of the Second International in 1907 thoroughly discussed the question of the international migration of labor and adopted a policy that recognized immigration as an international, rather than a national, problem. The Congress urged socialists of the nations that were sending forth large numbers of emigrants to build strong trade union movements to raise living standards, which would reduce the pressure for emigration and at the same time produce a trade union tradition among those who did emigrate. As for the nations receiving immigrants, the International recognized a distinction between natural and artificial immigration and opposed artificial immigration, such as contract labor. But the Congress condemned a nation's restriction of immigration on racial or ethnic grounds.[8]

Many American Socialists, probably a majority of them, favored the principles of the Stuttgart resolutions with one exception: they wanted no immigration of Asian workingmen—the "Mongolian hordes" and the "yellow peril," as the *Appeal to Reason* called them. At the 1908 convention the party adopted a resolution, after an extended debate—and Socialists frequently managed to slow down their proceedings with unbelievable parliamentary snarls—that recognized much of the Stuttgart position but avoided the question of Oriental immigration by stating that the whole matter of exclusion on a racial basis needed further study.[9] This resolution satisfied no one, and the subject came up again at the party's 1910 congress.

At this meeting the Committee on Immigration offered the delegates a majority resolution written by Ernest Untermann, Victor Berger, and Joseph Wanhope, and a minority report written by John Spargo. The majority report urged the exclusion of all Asian immigrants. Spargo's report followed the Stuttgart pattern except that he argued that, in principle, the American Party could if it wished be for immigration restriction on a racial basis. At the moment, however, Spargo argued, Oriental immigration was so negligible as to present no danger to American workers. From the floor of the congress Hillquit offered as a substitute still another resolution:

The Socialist Party favors all legislative measures tending to prevent the immigration of strike-breakers and contract laborers, and the mass importation of workers from foreign countries, brought about by the employing classes for the purpose of weakening the organization of American labor, and of lowering the standard of life of American workers.

The party is opposed to the exclusion of any immigrants on account of their race or nationality, and demands that the United States be at all times maintained as a free asylum for all men and women persecuted by the governments of their countries on account of their politics, religion or race.

The first paragraph of Hillquit's resolution was one that might have been written by an AFL convention; the second paragraph might have been written by an international congress of Marxists. What the whole resolution meant depended upon the interpretation of "mass importation." After a long debate this substitute resolution from the floor was passed by a close vote,[10] and Hillquit, ever the shrewd lawyer, had again effected a compromise within the party. There were attempts at later party conventions to adopt a new statement on immigration, but this Hillquit resolution remained the party's official position as long as the immigrants came to America in large numbers.

Neither was there agreement among Socialists on the question of the American Negro. Socialist opinions about Negroes ranged all the way from the militant views of William English Walling, a Socialist founder of the National Association for the Advancement of Colored People, to the white supremacy of Victor Berger. Berger was as blunt as possible in an editorial in his *Social Democratic Herald.* "There can be no doubt that the negroes and mulattoes constitute a lower race—that the Caucasian and indeed even the Mongolian have the start on them in civilization by many thousand years—so that negroes will find it difficult ever to overtake them. The many cases of rape which occur wherever negroes are settled in large numbers prove, moreover, that the free contact with the whites has led to the further degeneration of the negroes, as well as all other inferior races." Berger seemed not to be aware that his readers might infer that Negroes learned their presumed tendency to rape from contact with whites, but he did hold that the values of white capitalist America were responsible for "the barbarous behavior of the American whites towards the negroes." In America, Berger argued, people are judged by their wealth. Negroes are poor. *Ergo*, Negroes are inferior. "The utter degradation of the negro is . . . a part of this system." [11] If Berger seemed to be contradicting himself, he could reply that capitalist values only further degraded an already inferior people.

Berger's statement of white superiority was not official party policy, but he was close to the party's position in his argument that capitalism degraded the Negro. Until after World War I the Socialist Party as an organization did nothing special to better the position of the Negro in American society. The party held that the sole salvation of the Negro was the same as the sole salvation of the white: Socialism. Antagonism between the races was artificially introduced by capitalists to divide the working class. The Negro plank in the Tennessee Socialists' platform of 1912 was typical:

We recognize that the question of race superiority injected into the minds of the white wage-worker against the negro and other races is only a tactical method used by the capitalist class to keep the workers divided on the economic field. We therefore call upon the negro workers, and those of other races, to unite with the Socialist Party on the political field as the only avenue of abolishing wage slavery, and the solution of the race question. [12]

The *Appeal to Reason* hewed rather closely to the party position on Negroes, but it put forth another argument that was quite similar to the "black belt" program of the Communists years later. The *Appeal* told a Boston Negro who had inquired what Socialists would do for his race that after the establishment of the cooperative commonwealth Negroes "will have cities and plantations and shops in which there will likely be no white people except as teachers and other instructors. There will be black cities, but they will be as beautiful as those the whites live in." The *Appeal* used this plan of segregation, which it apparently considered benevolent, to answer Negro haters as well as Negroes. An Arizona reader of the *Appeal* inquired: "Do Socialists believe in miscegenation? Do they believe in social equality with the negro?" The reply was: "Socialists *do not* believe in a mixture of the races . . . . Socialists believe in justice to the negro, not in social, but in economic equality . . . . Socialism will separate the races." [13] The party itself never adopted such a segregationist position and did not practice segregation of Negroes within the party except in some, but not all, Jim Crow states.

The Socialist Party paid so little attention to the Negro that when the national office received a query about how many Negroes there were in the party and what their party status was no one knew the answer to the question. Fortunately for the historian, the party's information bureau director conducted a survey of Socialist Negroes by sending questionnaires to all state secretaries. All Northern state secretaries reported that there were Negro members in their states but that they were in regular party locals and that the records did not indicate a member's race. There was no way of knowing how many Negro party members there were in these states. The same situation existed in two Southern states, Louisiana and Kentucky. The only other Southern states with more than a handful of Negro members were Florida and Mississippi. Florida had segregated Negro locals. Mississippi's 150 Negro party members did not belong to party locals at all but were members-at-large, paying their dues directly to the state secretary. This was the scheme used in vicinities throughout the nation where there were fewer Socialists, black or white, than the five members necessary to form a party local.[14] How many Negroes there were in the prewar Socialist Party and exactly what role they played in the organization cannot be ascertained. But some things are certain: they were not important in the party, the party made no special effort to attract Negro members, and the party was generally disinterested in, if not actually hostile to, the effort of Negroes to improve their position in American capitalist society. An unsubstantiated but probably valid generalization is that in prewar white and capitalistic America, life for the Negro was as difficult as he could well bear, without adding a red stigma to his black skin; and for the white Socialist being a red was burden enough without also being for the blacks.

Yet two New York Socialist intellectuals, William English Walling and Charles Edward Russell, were among the founders of the National Association for the Advancement of Colored People, and if any one person can be said to be the person responsible for the founding of this militant organization for Negro rights it was Walling. He and his wife were visiting friends in Chicago when a race riot began in Springfield, Illinois, ironically the home of the Great Emancipator. The Wallings went to Springfield immediately, observed the strife, and returned to New York to launch a movement for the improvement of racial relations. Walling wrote two strong articles on the role of the Negro in America for a magazine of national circulation and began a series of meetings of pro-Negro humanitarians and intellectuals in his home from which grew the NAACP. When the NAACP secured W. E. B. Du Bois as editor of its magazine the *Crisis*, and thereby established a link with the Niagara movement among Negro intellectuals, the organization was well on its way to overthrowing the accommodation philosophy of Booker T. Washington and effecting a revolution in American Negro thought.

But Walling's views on the Negro had no hope of gaining wide favor in the prewar Socialist Party, and Negro leaders knew it. Du Bois had so little hope for the Socialists that in 1912 he resigned his party membership to support Wilson's presidential candidacy even though Wilson was reared in the South and had made only a most equivocal statement on Negro rights.[15]

As fighters for Negro rights Walling and Russell were a small minority in their party, but as middle-class intellectuals they were part of one of the most important groups in American Socialism. For an organization whose motto was "Workers of the World, Unite," the Socialist Party had an extraordinary number of members who were not of the working class. Socialist leadership particularly, as in many of the social democratic parties of Europe, was heavily weighted with lawyers, journalists, and teachers, many of whom had never earned a day's wages with the skill of their hands or the strength of their backs. The numbers and influence of middle-class intellectuals in a party which professed proletarian aims could not avoid notice, and the party viewed its intellectual members with a mixture of pride and embarrassment. One Peter Collins, a lecturer for a Catholic anti-Socialist organization called the Militia for Christ, made much of the importance of intellectuals in the party in his anti-Socialist propaganda. Unconsciously aping the extreme left of the party, and anticipating the arguments of the Communists in later years, Collins told his audiences that the Socialist Party was incapable of advancing the interests of workingmen because its leadership was not proletarian. A Socialist Party member wrote to the national office for statistics which he thought would give the lie to Collins. Carl D. Thompson's embarrassed reply was amusing:

. . . it is true that by far the larger proportion of those who have been instrumental in founding and developing the socialist movement have not been what are usually known as working men. They have in the large majority of cases been intellectuals and professionals.

But this is a strange turn that the opponents of socialism have taken of late. Formerly they upbraided us because the socialist movement was made up of ignorant, uneducated working class people, who had nothing, knew nothing and amounted to nothing. Now, all of a sudden, we are upbraided because our founders and leaders are men of unusual intellectual attainments, scholarship and training, and strangely enough, some of them actually men of wealth! We certainly have our opponents jumping sideways! [16]

The national office was doing no little bit of jumping sideways itself.

Many "intellectuals and professionals" in the party, as well as several nonmembers who were interested in Socialism, were organized into a smaller group within the party, the Intercollegiate Socialist Society. This organization, founded "for the purpose of promoting an intelligent interest in Socialism among college men and women, graduate and undergraduate . . . [and] the educated men and women of the country," offered Socialist intellectuals a vehicle through which they could identify themselves as a special section of the party. By bringing intellectuals together the ISS strengthened their role in the party, although this result was not calculated and probably not even conscious. The ISS itself never took part in Socialist Party matters, but at its meetings and in its activities Socialist

Party members with academic and scholarly interests were afforded an opportunity to talk over matters of party policy, in other words, to caucus informally. There was nothing unique about the intellectuals of the party doing this. Trade unionists in the party acted in the same way through their organizations.[17]

The ISS originally was the idea of Upton Sinclair. He talked over his brainchild with George Strobell, a well-to-do Socialist jewelry manufacturer and a brother-in-law of Henry Demarest Lloyd. Sinclair and Strobell got a rather illustrious group to join them in issuing a "call" for an organization meeting of the ISS. This group included Oscar Lovell Triggs, Thomas Wentworth Higginson, Charlotte Perkins Gilman, Clarence Darrow, William English Walling, J. G. Phelps Stokes, B. O. Flower, Leonard D. Abbott, and Jack London. At the organization meeting, on September 12, 1905, the group elected London president, Stokes, Sinclair, and Owen R. Lovejoy vice presidents, and Strobell, George Willis Cooke, Morris Hillquit, Robert Hunter, Harry W. Laidler, and Mrs. Darwin J. Meserole to the executive committee. Laidler, then a student at Wesleyan, was the only undergraduate to be elected an officer.

At first the ISS made little headway among college students or alumni. The idea of people who could afford college being interested in Socialism was new in America. Sinclair recalls with humor how alien the idea of collegiate Socialists was. "I remember calling up the secretary of some university club, to ask for the membership list, and I could not make him understand the strange name of our organization. 'Intercollegiate *Socialist* Society, you say?' The Catholic Anarchist League, the Royal Communist Club, the Association of Baptist Bolsheviks!" During the organization's early period Strobell and Rufus W. Weeks, a vice president of the New York Life Insurance Company, kept it going with financial contributions. Then, in the great upsurge of progressivism and radicalism just before World War I, the ISS grew quickly. In 1913 it could afford the publication of a quarterly magazine, the *Intercollegiate Socialist*. By a decade after its founding the ISS had chapters in sixty colleges and universities. There were chapters in the major New England colleges,

most of the state universities outside the South, and the more prominent Protestant denominational colleges. There were ISS chapters
on the campuses of the Republican Nicholas Murray Butler and the
Democrat Woodrow Wilson. The ISS even successfully invaded the
capitalist-hallowed halls of Andrew Carnegie's Institute of Technology.

The ISS and the League for Industrial Democracy—the ISS
changed its name after World War I—has attracted to it a great
number of brilliant minds. A very good college faculty could be
assembled from sometime ISS or LID members. Among those who
have been associated with the organization, besides those previously
mentioned are: Walter Agard, Roger Baldwin, Louis B. Boudin,
Randolph Bourne, Paul Blanshard, Bruce Bliven, Paul Brissenden,
Robert W. Bruère, Louis Budenz, Howard Brubaker, Stuart Chase,
Albert De Silver, John Dewey, Paul H. Douglas, Morris Ernst, Zona
Gale, Lewis Gannett, W. J. Ghent, Felix Grendon, Paxton Hibben,
Jessie Wallace Hughan, Ellis O. Jones, Horace M. Kallen, Edmond
Kelley, Florence Kelley, Freda Kirchwey, William Ellery Leonard,
Lewis Lorwin, Robert Morss Lovett, Alexander Meiklejohn, Broadus
Mitchell, A. J. Muste, Harry Overstreet, Ernest Poole, Selig Perlman,
Jacob Potofsky, Anna Rochester, David Saposs, Vida Scudder, John
Spargo, Charles P. Steinmetz, Ordway Tead, Alexander Trachten-
berg, Norman Thomas, Walter Weyl, Bouck White, Edwin Witte,
Helen Sumner Woodbury, and Charles Zeublin.[18]

The truly distinguished intellectuals in the ISS gave the Socialist
Party a luster, a certain aura of respectability, which was advanta-
geous to it, but unfortunately some of the Socialist intellectuals were
eccentric to the point that anti-Socialists could smear the party as
a collection of crackpots. Jack London is a case in point. He undertook a lecture tour under ISS auspices in the winter of 1905–1906
that aroused a great deal of editorial comment. London, who signed
his letters "Yours for the Revolution," took with him on this tour
a Korean valet, who dressed him for his lecture appearances in as
unproletarian costume as it was possible to devise. London addressed
his audiences dressed in a white flannel shirt with a rolling collar

that suggested a little boy's sailor outfit, a white silk tie, a black cheviot suit, and patent-leather pumps. London also frequently became involved in charges of plagiarism which appeared to be valid. On one occasion the New York *World* published in adjoining columns excerpts from a London article and the one copied from. Activities such as these certainly did not advance the party's interests. Neither did some of the antics of Upton Sinclair, whose health ideas were more than a little strange. Sinclair was associated with Bernarr Macfadden at Macfadden's sanitarium at Battle Creek and contributed many articles to one of the health faddist's physical culture magazines. When the muckraker David Graham Phillips was shot and killed by an apparently insane violinist, Sinclair expressed the opinion that it was not the six bullets in Phillips which killed him. The cause of death, according to Sinclair, was some beef tea that doctors gave the wounded writer.[19]

Probably many Socialists also agreed with W. J. Ghent that the presence of Bohemians in the party who got out little magazines like the *New Review* and the *Masses* did not aid Socialist fortunes. The *Masses*, which advertised, "The *Masses* Has a Sense of Humor . . . Enjoy the Revolution," drew special fire from Ghent, who was as clever a writer as there was in the Socialist movement. Ghent charged that the *Masses*, financed by "rich men and women of that nebulous middle world which lies somewhere between the Socialist movement and the world of bourgeois complacency," had converted no workers to Socialism and had presented nothing coherent to anyone. "It has found no trouble in mixing Socialism, Anarchism, Communism, Sinn Feinism, Cubism, sexism, direct action and sabotage into a more or less harmonious mess. It is peculiarly the product of the restless metropolitan coteries who devote themselves to the cult of Something Else; who are ever seeking the bubble Novelty even at the door of Bedlam." [20]

Perhaps it was the "cult of Something Else," perhaps it was a feeling of guilt brought by having plenty in the midst of poverty, perhaps it was a sincere desire to right the world's wrongs, but whatever their motivation there were comrades who were, in Thompson's phrase, "actually men of wealth." These "millionaire Socialists"—in popular parlance every Socialist with a comfortable income was a "millionaire"—were few, but the presence of only a few in a political organization dedicated to the abolition of the economic system in which these wealthy men made their money was bound to attract considerable attention. Among the wealthy Socialists were Gaylord Wilshire, eccentric California publisher of *Wilshire's Magazine*, promoter of dubious gold mine ventures, and the man for whom Los Angeles's Wilshire Boulevard is named; J. G. Phelps Stokes, of an aristocratic New York family and president of the Nevada Central Railroad, whose marriage to Rose Pastor, an immigrant cigar maker, got a great play in the sensational press; Joseph Medill Patterson, of the Chicago family that publishes the *Chicago Tribune* and the New York *Daily News;* and William Bross Lloyd, son of the millionaire author of *Wealth Against Commonwealth.* Probably only these could accurately be described as "millionaires." But others, such as Walling, Hunter, Weeks, Strobell, and Nelson O. Nelson, a St. Louis plumbing manufacturer, were comfortably well off.

"Millionaire" Socialists, as a group, played no important role in the party. There was no more agreement among them on proper party policies than there was among any random group of party members. Left wingers in the party have claimed the "millionaires" strengthened the party's Right because they were undeniably bourgeois, and right wingers have claimed they strengthened the party's Left because they could afford to be as radical as their whims dictated. Each argument has a semblance of truth. The whole matter of the "millionaires" has been overemphasized, both in the days when the party was strong and since.[21] Some of them, notably Walling, were significant as men of ideas, but as men of money they probably had no more significance than as curious exceptions to the principle of economic determinism and as subsidizers of needy Socialist endeavors. Certainly there was no clique of "millionaires" within the Socialist Party as there were cliques of intellectuals and Christian Socialists.

The term Christian Socialist is a vague one. Usually members of the Socialist Party were believers, in at least some degree, of Christianity or of Judaism. And many, perhaps most, Socialists had joined the party because capitalism had offended their Judeo-Christian ethics rather than because of any exposure to dialectical materialism. Practically all Socialists were in a sense Christian Socialists. The term has also been used in connection with the religious communitarians, such as the Oneida perfectionists or the Shakers. The term here shall be used only to describe ministers whose interpretations of the Christian life led them to join the Socialist Party, and members of such organizations as the Christian Socialist Fellowship, whether clergymen or laymen.

To say that practically all Socialists were in a sense Christian Socialists is not to say that they were fundamentalists in religion, nor church members, nor even churchgoers. In fact, many Socialists had rebelled against religious orthodoxy as they had rebelled against political and economic orthodoxy. Large numbers of Socialists were opposed to organized churches and to most ministers, who, they felt, served to buttress the capitalistic social order—as indeed many did. But to be anticlerical and religiously unorthodox does not necessarily make one less Christian in his ethics. One does not have to reject the Sermon on the Mount when he rejects organized religion.

The party itself avoided religious matters. There were anticlerics who thought the party should take a clear-cut position against organized churches, and there were devout party members who thought the organization should preach that only through Socialism could true Christian brotherhood be effected on earth. Until 1908 the party had nothing official to say about religion. At the convention that year the delegates adopted by a close vote, after a heated debate, an official disclaimer of Socialist concern with religious matters. These sentences were added to the party's Declaration of Principles: "The Socialist movement is primarily an economic and political movement. It is not concerned with the institutions of marriage or religion." (The reference to marriage was to combat the frequent anti-Socialist charge that Socialists advocated "free love.")

But for an organization that disclaimed concern with religion the party had within it an unusual number of ministers. In 1908 there were an estimated 300 Socialist clergymen. Among the ministers or former ministers in the party were such prominent Socialists as George D. Herron, J. Stitt Wilson, George R. Lunn, Winfield Gaylord, Carl D. Thompson, Walter Thomas Mills, Edward Ellis Carr, and Bouck White.[22] Many Socialists were sons or daughters of Protestant ministers. And the party, in its later days, of course, several times nominated Norman Thomas, a former Presbyterian minister, to be its presidential candidate.

By and large, Socialist clergymen were among the more conservative party members, but there were a few who were quite radical. One such radical was the flamboyant Bouck White, author of the hilarious *The Book of Daniel Drew,* a purported autobiography, and of the once very popular *The Call of the Carpenter,* which portrayed Jesus of Nazareth as a social revolutionist. White's radicalism embarrassed such relatively staid Socialists as Hillquit, Julius Gerber, once executive secretary of Local New York, and W. J. Ghent. Furthermore, many Socialists were uneasy about the presence of any minister in their party because the clerics hardly fitted the Marxist stereotype. White, minister of the Church of the Social Revolution in New York, became involved in a protest movement aimed at embarrassing the Rockefeller family for the Standard Oil Company's role in the "Ludlow massacre" in Colorado, in which thirteen members of strikers' families were killed by state militia. Upton Sinclair organized a group of pickets, wearing black bands of mourning, to parade around the Standard Oil Company building in New York. White invaded the Calvary Baptist Church, where the Rockefellers were members, with the announced intention of challenging its pastor, Dr. Cornelius Woelfkin, to a debate on the subject of the teachings of Jesus regarding men of great wealth. When White arose during the service to make his challenge, he was grabbed and dragged from the church by police and ushers. Subsequently he was convicted on a disorderly conduct charge and sentenced to six months on Blackwells Island, an unusually harsh sentence for such a charge. White was also an ardent opponent of war and nationalism, and, to demonstrate dramatically his contempt for nationalism and its symbols, he sometimes burned the American flag during his speeches.[23]

But White was an unusual Socialist clergyman. Most of them never organized anything like the Church of the Social Revolution nor burned flags. Most of them confined their leftist activities to reading such newspapers as the *Christian Socialist*, which had as its motto "The Golden Rule Against the Rule of Gold," and attending the annual conferences of the Christian Socialist Fellowship. This organization was founded by ministers and laymen in 1906 to spread Socialist principles, as they understood them, among church people, "to show the necessity of socialism to a complete realization of the teachings of Jesus; to end the class struggle by establishing industrial and political democracy, and to hasten the reign of justice and brotherhood upon earth." At its founding the Fellowship expressly pledged its support to the Socialist Party. This action was a departure from the earlier Society of Christian Socialists, founded in 1889, which did not as a group support any political party.[24]

Because of its emphasis on peace instead of struggle, on the brotherhood of man instead of class conflict, the Fellowship appeared to be more pallid than it actually was. If Fellowship members appeared sometimes to be incredibly sentimental, still they could engage in fierce fights within their own organization [25] and, as will be seen in the next chapter, in intraparty struggles.

Thus the Socialist Party in its heyday was composed of a little of everything—of recent immigrants and descendants of the *Mayflower*'s passengers, of tenement dwellers and prairie farmers, of intellectuals and unlettered sharecroppers, of devout ministers and belligerent agnostics, of syndicalists and craft unionists, of revolutionists and gradualist reformers. That such a mixture should explode occasionally is not surprising. The years 1909 to 1913 saw such an explosion.

III

PARTY BATTLES
1909–1913

To HAVE expected harmony in the Socialist Party, composed as it was of many diverse elements, representing all degrees of left-of-center opinion, would have been to expect saintly conduct from human beings. But people are not saints—perhaps people in politics miss the mark further than others—and political parties, by their very nature, are not harmonious. The conventions of political parties, any of them, are marked by conflict. At Democratic conventions there is frequently a large bloc that walks out of the convention hall or threatens to do so. At Republican conventions orators provoke their listeners to hiss and boo leaders of their own party as well as those outside the GOP. But only rarely do these family fights fail to end in compromise, handshakes, and a continuation of the uneasy alliances.

The family fights of the Socialist Party in its first decade or so likewise ended in compromise and a continuation of the uneasy alliance. Although the fights were hard ones, there were at the national level no secessions nor attempts to expel the opposition. There was one exception to this. In 1905 there had been an attempt to remove Victor Berger from the National Executive Committee because he had urged support for a Republican candidate for a judgeship. The National Committee voted to remove Berger, but after pleas for compromise a party membership referendum rejected his removal, and he was restored to his seat on the NEC.[1] Differences were compromised; the coalition was kept alive.

Then late in 1909 came a new party fight in which one small group, in its attempt to "capture" the party, departed from the recognized rules of intraparty conflict. This group did not restrict itself to the political weapons of open argument and appeal to the membership; it conspired, it plotted, it operated secretly. The secret plan was revealed and the attempted coup was unsuccessful, but the bad blood that remained after this controversy greatly diminished the Socialist Party's chances of long remaining the coalition of all the American left.

The fight began on November 19, 1909, when A. M. Simons, then editor of the *Daily Socialist* of Chicago, wrote a personal letter to William English Walling. Walling at that time was not a member of the party—he did not join until the following year—although he was greatly interested in its work and wrote for Socialist publications. Simons expressed dissatisfaction with the party's attitude toward the AFL. The Socialists, thought Simons, would never get anywhere politically so long as they were hostile to the trade unions and their leadership. The Chicago editor implied strongly that he favored the formation of an American labor party. "I do not like the English policy, but I say frankly it is better than the present Socialist Party." In denouncing the AFL's "pure and simple" labor philosophy and its leadership, the party had made itself, according to Simons, "a hissing and a by-word with the actual wage workers of America." The AFL, he recognized, was not without serious defects, and he asserted no one had denounced these defects more than he. He was "forced to recognize that it comes much nearer representing the working class than the S.P., and unless we are able to so shape our policy and our organization as to meet the demands and incarnate the position of the workers we will have failed of our mission." [2]

Just why Simons should have written such a letter to Walling at that time is difficult to understand. Simons certainly had very little reason to suppose that in Walling he would find one sympathetic to his ideas on the proper relationship of the party to the

AFL. It is true that Walling was always, before the time Simons wrote the letter and after, sympathetic to the AFL. Walling's position was curious. He himself was very critical at this time of the AFL's "bread and butter" unionism, of its political philosophy, or rather its lack of a political philosophy. Yet even when Walling was publicizing the cause of the revolutionists of czarist Russia, when he was writing on syndicalism, he felt "He must help labor become whatever it sought to become, to fulfill its aims and realize itself according to its own laws and ways. To have tried to do more would have been arrogance." Perhaps Walling reasoned that he as a middle-class person—his father had been a wealthy physician, his grandfather the Democratic vice presidential candidate in 1880, and he himself had enough inherited income to support his family without working—would be presumptuous in telling trade unionists how to conduct their affairs even if he disagreed with the way they were being conducted. Simons probably knew this attitude of Walling's. Furthermore, just eight months before Simons wrote the letter, Walling had published an article in a widely read Socialist magazine in which he argued that a political alliance of organized labor and the Socialist Party would not then be in the best interests of either. Walling's argument was complex. If in the 1908 elections the AFL had supported Socialist candidates, and the major parties had not put up fusion candidates in opposition, such an AFL-Socialist force could have elected only twenty or thirty congressmen. So few congressmen would be ineffectual in Washington, and their election would only cause an antilabor reaction in Congress and in the courts. Thus labor would not benefit from such a political alliance. The labor and Socialist movements, Walling wrote, must ultimately merge. But they should not merge until the Socialists have strength in all classes but the capitalist class, among "brainworkers," farmers, and unorganized labor. For the Socialists to merge with the trade unions before gaining such strength would not be in the best interest of the party or of the nation. Labor unions, wrote Walling, may take the leadership in the establishing of social democracy, "But the moment they begin to *monopolize* the movement to the *partial exclu-*

sion or *subordination* of unskilled labor, of the brainworkers and of the farmer working men, the fate of democracy is sealed." Thus such a political alliance would not benefit anyone.[3] Still, Simons wrote Walling the letter. He lived to regret it.

Walling launched an attack against Simons to prevent Simons from doing anything to change the party into a labor party or to modify Socialist hostility toward the AFL leadership. Not being then a party member, Walling could not fight Simons in meetings of any unit of the party. But he gave Gustavus Myers a copy of his letter from Simons and instructed him to read it at a meeting of New York Socialists. Myers read the letter, and Ludwig Lore, then editor of the New York *Volkszeitung*, joined Myers in denouncing Simons's ideas. In the words of one Socialist, the public reading of the letter caused a "near-riot."

Walling also publicly charged Simons of conspiring with Berger, Hillquit, Hunter, and John Spargo to capture the party's machinery in order to transform the organization into a relatively conservative labor party, a political wing of the AFL. In a mimeographed letter which he distributed widely among the Socialist membership, Walling accused these five men, all of whom were then members of the National Executive Committee, of conspiring "to perpetuate [themselves on the NEC], if possible, without regard to what action the party takes." Simons replied that Walling had distorted his letter by extracting parts of it out of context, and disclaimed all intentions of a conspiracy. "There was nothing whatever in the letter that I feared to have published. There was almost nothing that I had not said in print elsewhere." [4] But Walling refused to withdraw or modify his accusations.

Walling had no evidence in Simons's original letter upon which to base his charge of conspiracy, although he may have had evidence which he did not publicly disclose. But Walling, nevertheless, came fairly close to the mark with his accusation. One of the accused conspirators, Spargo, admonished Simons, "Surely, you ought to be careful as to whom you write, even intimating our plans!" Another of the accused, Hunter, wrote to Simons that he regretted he had not warned him of Walling's "present mental and moral irresponsibility." Walling seems to have had no evidence to support his inclusion of Hillquit in the accusation, and it is clear that at the time Walling made his charge Berger was not in league with Simons. After the charge was made, however, Berger came to Simons's defense. A letter from Berger to Simons, which the writer marked "Confidential," bears quoting because it clears Berger of Walling's charge, reveals the plan to carry the forthcoming NEC elections for the conservatives in the party, and indicates a great deal about the nature of the Socialist organization:

Confidential

MY DEAR SIMONS:—

I am informed that there is a cabal headed by William English Walling, . . . Charles Kerr and others. The purpose of this cabal is to oust the Social-Democrats from the National Executive Committee and to throw the Socialist party into the hands of the impossibilists.

I had not decided whether to accept the nomination to the National Executive Committee or not. It is a Sisyphus labor, and to a great extent it is more advisory than executive.

Of course under the present conditions in this country, this decentralization and state autonomy has been a good thing. Otherwise the party would have been torn with half a dozen splits during the last five years. There is, however, this disadvantage, that freaks, crooks, and charlatans can take shelter in the party. And these men now seem to think themselves strong enough to control the party. But an impossibilist party, such as they wish to create, would be an anomaly in the Socialist movement. If they succeed they will try to destroy the work which we have accomplished even in those places where we have been successful. . . .

I think we [Berger, Simons, Hillquit, Hunter, and Spargo] are none of us anxious for a re-election. But at the same time I believe that none of us have [sic] done or said anything which deserves that we should be knifed even by the impossibilists. The only explanation of the matter is the jealousy which men who do nothing feel for those who do their best to accomplish things. . . .

I hope you will use the Daily Socialist to the best advantage. I shall open up the columns of the Herald and Vorwaerts in this matter in the near future.[5]

The original issue in the controversy, the advisability of a labor party, was soon lost in the heat of the battle between the two groups that called each other "impossibilist" and "bourgeois reformer." Even Debs, who usually avoided intraparty feuds, got into the fight when he allowed Kerr to publish in his *International Socialist Review* a letter he had written to Walling. He commended Walling for his "uncompromising spirit and attitude" and warned: "If the trimmers had their way, we should degenerate into bourgeois reform." "I have been watching the situation closely and especially the tendencies to REACTION to which we are so unalterably opposed. The Socialist Party has already CATERED FAR TOO MUCH to the American Federation of Labor, and there is no doubt that A HALT WILL HAVE TO BE CALLED." Walling apparently thought Berger *et al.* planned to "cater" to all kinds of reformist groups. He wrote to the president of the National American Woman's Suffrage Association that she might be approached by some Socialists in the hope of getting her organization's support for a labor party. She should beware, Walling wrote, because Berger was actually not for woman suffrage and was "damning the woman suffrage movement with faint praise." [6] Walling was originally critical of Berger because he was too reformist; now he was critical of him because he was not strong enough in a reformist demand. The entire affair was becoming confused.

But the issue from which the controversy had arisen was not the important thing about the whole incident: the importance of the Simons-Walling affair was that the system of bargaining among the party factions had broken down. One faction had attempted to gain control of the party by means other than the system of open argument and compromise. Their opponents further to the left retaliated. Kerr, in writing to Louis Boudin, suggested organizing a Left Machine and promised to put Boudin's "name before readers of the *Review* in a way that may help you in getting elected" as a delegate to the Socialist International.[7] In any case, the whole issue of a labor party was an academic one for the Socialists. The anti-Socialist leadership of the AFL had no inclination to play politics with the

Socialists, no matter how palatable the gradualists and reformers might make the party for them.

Conservative Socialists had the advantage in the party elections to the NEC held early in 1910. The conservatives' first advantage was in their substantial control of the Socialist press. Simons edited the Chicago *Daily Socialist*, Berger published the Milwaukee *Social Democratic Herald*, and Hillquit's personal followers edited the New York *Call*. That left among the major Socialist publications the *Appeal*, which professed neutrality in intraparty battles, and the *International Socialist Review*, which was only a monthly. Another advantage of the gradualists, related to the first, was that they were better known nationally than their opponents. Of those on the extreme left of the party, only Haywood was a well known figure; of those who were on the party's left but who did not reject political action as did Haywood, only Debs, Kate O'Hare, and the *Appeal* men Wayland and Warren were nationally popular. None of these radicals was a candidate for the NEC in 1910. Four of the five Walling had accused were elected in 1910. Only Simons did not return to the committee. The other three elected were George Goebel, Lena Morrow Lewis, and James F. Carey. The elections were clearly a victory for the conservatives in the party, as were the elections later in the year for delegates to the International Congress. The eight International delegates elected in the party referendum, listed in descending order as to the votes they received, were: Berger, Haywood, Hunter, Hillquit, Lewis, Spargo, May Wood-Simons, and Luella Twining.[8] Of these, Haywood was the only leftist.

Although the radicals lost the elections they did not cease sniping at their more conservative comrades. Throughout 1910 Thomas J. Morgan of Chicago was a thorn in the side of the conservatives—"constructive" Socialists they liked to be called—with his little newspaper the *Provoker*. Tommy Morgan was an old-timer in the radical movement. He had been in the Knights, the Socialist Labor Party, the Populist movement, and the Socialist Party since its founding, and he had learned several rough-and-tumble tricks useful in intraparty fights. He now charged in his newspaper that Simons was using his position in the party for his personal financial gain and that Simons, despite his protests against violence as a means of ending capitalism, had hired thugs to aid the cause of the conservative Socialists in the Cook County (Chicago) local of the party. Simons, of course, denied the charges. When Morgan could not make such charges against Simons stick, he began to publish personal smears of J. Mahlon Barnes, then the National Executive Secretary and a conservative. Morgan charged Barnes with inefficiency, misuse of party funds, drunkenness, and sexual promiscuity with the girls who worked as clerks in the national office. These charges of immorality aroused many Christian Socialists against Barnes, and the NEC yielded to the pressure and ordered the election of a committee to investigate the charges and report on their validity. The committee, which was not composed exclusively of the party's conservatives, cleared Barnes and repudiated Morgan. The National Committee, in a mail poll, voted 39 to 2 to accept the report, 22 not voting. Barnes's opponents cried the investigation was a whitewash and demanded another. In August, 1911, the NEC brought Barnes and his critics together for a "trial." The NEC did not publish its findings concerning Barnes's morals and administrative efficiency, but it accepted Barnes's resignation, which action his critics interpreted as a vindication of their charges. John M. Work of Iowa was elected National Executive Secretary to fill Barnes's place.[9]

Meanwhile, other things were happening in the party that caused a change in the issues of the struggles between Left and Right. In the fall of 1910 the Milwaukee organization won the municipal elections, and Berger was elected to Congress for the first time. In 1911 Lunn won the mayoralty election at Schenectady. It began to appear to those who had wanted a labor party that one would not be necessary. In Milwaukee the Socialist victory had come with labor support, both electoral and financial;[10] it appeared that, in Milwaukee at least, labor was coming to the Socialists rather than the Socialists having to go to the AFL. Then, late in 1911, the McNamara confession precipitated a different party issue: sabotage and labor violence. Besides the McNamara case, the issue was brought to the fore by the Wobblies' free-speech fights in West Coast cities and by their great strike in the textile mills of Lawrence, Massachusetts. The IWW technique in the free speech campaigns was similar to one the Indian nationalists were to use against the British. When a city administration refused the IWW the right to conduct street meetings, and arrested those who went ahead, Wobblies would pour into the city, get themselves arrested for conducting street meetings, and fill the jails. Usually the city administration would relent when the jail became full of noisy and hungry Wobblies and when as many more were on the streets, itching for an arrest. Although the IWW was seven years old in 1912, the Lawrence strike made it nationally known for the first time. Lawrence was a wild and heated city during the strike. Two of the IWW strike leaders, Joseph Ettor and Arturo Giovannitti, were framed with a murder charge after a striker had been killed in a parade. When the Italian Socialist Federation dramatized the poverty of the strikers by organizing an exodus of the strikers' children from the city to homes of sympathizers elsewhere in the country, the Lawrence police tried to stop the movement with force. They attacked a group of children and their parents at the railroad station, clubbing both adults and youngsters. Dynamite was found in the city.[11]

All these events quickened the discussion in the party over violence in the labor and radical movements. What should official Socialist attitude be toward violence in labor disputes? Should Socialists use violence to bring the end of capitalism? Should Socialists obey laws, passed, enforced, and interpreted by defenders of capitalism, when these laws operated against the interests of the working class as Socialists understood those interests? It was the same kind of problem that had confronted the abolitionists before the Civil War. Should one accept the Fugitive Slave Act or should one agree with William Lloyd Garrison that there was a higher law? Socialists debated these questions at great length.

Early in 1912 Haywood and Hillquit, both members of the party's NEC—Haywood having been elected late in 1911—debated at Cooper Union the question "What Shall the Attitude of the Socialist Party Be Toward the Economic Organization of the Workers?" Attendance was limited to those who could show paid-up membership cards, and Abraham Cahan, publisher of the *Jewish Daily Forward,* so much wanted to hear the debate that he paid $17 back dues in order to attend. It was in this debate that Haywood urged his Socialist listeners to try "a little sabotage in the right place at the proper time." Debs, although usually more sympathetic to Haywood than to Hillquit, did not agree with Haywood on this point. Debs told his followers that he had no respect for capitalist laws that hurt the working class, but that he was opposed to sabotage and to violence as an instrument of policy because they did not really advance working-class interests. "I am opposed to any tactics which involve stealth, secrecy, intrigue, and necessitate acts of individual violence for their execution." Debs hoped the Socialist Party would clearly endorse his position. "I hope to see the Socialist party place itself squarely on record at the coming national convention against sabotage and every other form of violence and destructiveness suggested by what is known as 'direct action.' " [12] The next national convention did put itself on record against sabotage, but in a manner that Debs perhaps had not bargained for.

The 1912 convention met at Indianapolis, where the Socialist Party had been born eleven years earlier. In those eleven years the party had come a long way. There were delegations from every state except South Carolina, and from all the foreign-language federations. In May, the month of the convention, 100,845 members had paid their dues. The party was prosperous. It paid Pullman fares for the delegates from their homes to Indianapolis. This was the party of Debs, who after the great 1894 railroad strike had vowed never again to ride in a Pullman. But at this convention, when the Socialists were beginning to show political power, the differences that divided Socialist from Socialist proved to be so great that no party bands were elastic enough to keep all Socialists together.

The convention's tone was set by Karl Legien, a leader in the German Social Democratic Party and the German trade union movement who was in the United States on a lecture tour arranged by

Samuel Gompers. Legien brought the greetings of the German comrades and a warning against syndicalism. He told the delegates that the German party, the most successful Socialist party in the world, had "no room for sabotage and similar syndicalist and destructive tendencies." [13] The convention went on to adopt a platform and pass all kinds of resolutions without serious incident. Neither the party's conservatives nor radicals appeared to be running the show. Then, with the report of the committee on the party's constitution, the fireworks began.

The constitution committee recommended that Article II, Section 6 of the constitution, which had to do with eligibility for party membership, be amended. Section 6 had already provided for the expulsion of party members who opposed political action. Now the committee proposed that the section be strengthened by amending it to provide for the expulsion of any member "who opposes political action or advocates crime against the person or other methods of violence." Winfield R. Gaylord of Milwaukee, an eccentric former Congregational minister who rode around Milwaukee in a motorcycle with his sons in the sidecar, proposed from the floor of the convention a still different wording, and the committee accepted the change. The amendment now read:

Article II, Section 6. Any member of the party who opposes political action or advocates crime, sabotage, or other methods of violence as a weapon of the working class to aid in its emancipation shall be expelled from membership in the party. Political action shall be construed to mean participation in elections for public office and practical legislative and administrative work along the lines of the Socialist Party platform.

Debate over the amendment was hot, but Hillquit, a skillful parliamentarian, brought the issue to a vote as quickly as possible. One of the last harmonious acts of the party was the singing of the "Marseillaise" and the "Red Flag" while the vote was being counted. The amendment passed 191 to 90. Haywood took no part in the debate, but he told a reporter, "That looks like it was aimed at me." Big Bill, who had lost an eye in an industrial accident when still a boy, did not need perfect vision to see that.[14]

An analysis of the vote on the amendment does not reveal that the social class of the delegates determined their position on "direct action," if we consider occupation to be an index of social class. W. J. Ghent, who strongly supported the antisyndicalist amendment, listed the occupations of 84 of the 90 delegates who voted against the amendment. Only 28 of these were industrial workers. Forty-six of them had middle-class occupations, lawyers, editors, merchants, physicians. Fifty-two of those voting against the amendment held some kind of a party position. Ghent concluded from these figures that the middle-class representation at the convention had voted for syndicalism.[15] That the prosyndicalist delegates were middle-class is not denied, but so were the antisyndicalist delegates. Those who voted against the amendment were a rough cross section, occupation-wise, of the entire convention.

Immediately after the convention amended the party's constitution it set to work to nominate its candidates. Berger insinuated that Debs might not accept the nomination if offered it, but the chairman for the day, Lewis J. Duncan of Montana, a Debs man, set Berger and the delegates right on that point. There were two candidates for the nomination put up against Debs, Emil Seidel, mayor of Milwaukee, and Charles Edward Russell. Debs won easily; in a roll-call vote he received 165 votes to Seidel's 56 and Russell's 54. Seidel's vote was strong in Wisconsin, California, Missouri and, strangely enough, Oklahoma. Perhaps it was the close connection of Ameringer with the Milwaukee Germans that influenced the Oklahoma delegates for Seidel. Russell's vote came mainly from New York. The West and Midwest, except for California, Oklahoma, Missouri, and Wisconsin, were solid for Debs. Seidel was elected to the vice presidential candidacy over Dan Hogan of Arkansas and John W. Slayton of Pennsylvania.[16]

After the storm over the amendment to the constitution and the nominations, in the final stages of the convention, Hillquit managed to put through the appointment of his old friend J. Mahlon Barnes as campaign manager. This relatively minor matter was to become the root of a very bitter fight between the conservatives and the Left, whether syndicalist or radical parliamentarian. The whole Barnes affair had not been dead a year when it was revived. This time that gay cigar maker's morals were to be even more than before an issue of factional battles. The syndicalists were looking for a vulnerable spot in the conservative wing of the party. Nonsyndicalist radicals such as Debs, not being able conscientiously to disagree with the conservatives on the sabotage amendment, likewise were looking for some way to embarrass the Hillquit-Berger axis. Poor Barnes was caught in the middle.

The Christian Socialists objected to Barnes immediately. Edward Ellis Carr, in the *Christian Socialist*, dug up all the old charges against Barnes, and good Christian readers of that paper were aroused. There was even talk of another national convention "to straighten out matters." But the conservatives in the party, Barnes least of all, were not concerned with this reaction from the Christians. That was to be expected. But they were concerned when the party's radicals took up the anti-Barnes cry and goaded the Christians to hotter attack.

Late in June Barnes heard that the *International Socialist Review* was soon to publish an attack on him. Barnes went to see Kerr, publisher of the *Review*, to find out what he could. Kerr told him he was indeed going to attack the appointment, but he would not let Barnes see a copy of the article. Kerr asserted that he did not know who had written it, although he admitted that Haywood had "worked it over." Kerr was very frank with Barnes in telling him why he was objecting to the appointment. Barnes wrote to Hillquit about the interview:

He said it was not a personal attack and that he personally could think of no one who could perform the functions of the office as well as I; that it was just a matter of policy as against Hillquit's domination of the convention. He said that they were pursuing a consistent policy dating back to the Walling letter; that they are convinced you and Hunter were both in with Simons. He said that of course their people will vote with the Carr crowd, but for different reasons.[17]

Debs had already told Barnes he was disappointed in having him for his campaign manager, and Barnes suspected that Debs had written the *Review* article. He asked Debs if his suspicion were correct. Debs replied that he had not written the article, but that he knew about it and that he was not going to do anything to prevent its publication. His appointment, Debs wrote to Barnes, was "a mistake and an injustice . . . . it would revive the whole scandal and . . . be a most unfortunate thing for the party and everybody concerned. That was my opinion from the first and every passing day since has but served to strengthen it." But Debs was not angry with Barnes, whom he considered only a dupe; he was angry with Hillquit. He wrote that it was a pity that Hillquit, "a man who is so skilled in the trickery of capitalist politics was not a delegate at Chicago [site of the Republican convention] or Baltimore [site of the Democratic convention] instead of Indianapolis." [18]

Debs actually had good reason to object to Barnes as his campaign manager even if Barnes's reputation and morals had been above reproach and if Hillquit had had nothing to do with his appointment. In the campaign of 1908 the Socialists had chartered a train, which they dubbed "The Red Special," from which Debs conducted a strenuous campaign. In 68 days Debs addressed 550 meetings, speaking from early morning until late at night. His voice threatened to fail at one point, and Barnes, in the national office at Chicago, was notified to arrange for physicians and substitute speakers. Instead of consulting with Debs about substitutes, the normal thing for a party official loyal to his standard-bearer to do, Barnes telegraphed to Hillquit suggesting that he and J. G. Phelps Stokes, of all people, select the replacements.[19] Debs, however, may not have known of this. If he had he probably would have brought up the matter in 1912.

With the knowledge that their presidential candidate was also opposed to Barnes, Christian Socialists now intensified their drive against the campaign manager. Barnes was denounced as "a degenerate and a libertine unfit to serve the great cause of socialism in any capacity." Locals of the party here and there demanded Barnes's recall. Several Socialists wrote to Debs that they would leave the party if Barnes were allowed to remain.[20]

Defenders of Barnes charged that the radicals and the Christian Socialists used blackmail to keep their forces in line. They as-

serted that the radicals had charges of immorality worked up against
an NEC member and Debs, to be made public if either of them
showed signs of weakening in the war against Barnes.[21] The fight
against Barnes continued, whether or not there was any actual blackmail. Critics forced the NEC to meet and reconsider the Barnes appointment. Debs attended this meeting, although he was not an
NEC member, and made an impassioned plea for Barnes's dismissal.
At one time Berger had been willing to drop Barnes as too hot a
potato to hold,[22] but now he and Hillquit and their followers refused to yield or to compromise. Barnes stayed on.

As campaign manager Barnes did a creditable job—his abilities
were never in question—and the Socialists made their best electoral
record. Debs polled just under 6 per cent of the popular vote, a
percentage never reached before or since. But the party was beginning to come apart at the seams even as it was scoring its greatest
successes. The issue of violence, raised by Haywood and disposed of
by the adoption of the antisabotage amendment, had split the radicals
of the party. The conservatives, led by Berger and Hillquit, had
thereby increased their strength, and in their refusal to yield on the
Barnes issue they indicated they were going to use their newly acquired power as they saw fit.

Hillquit's opponents continued to strike at him through Barnes
even after the campaign. The party incurred a $12,000 deficit in
the campaign, and there were claims that the deficit was due to
Barnes's mismanagement. John M. Work charged that Barnes had
used the regular funds of the party, as apart from earmarked campaign funds, although this had been expressly forbidden, without
asking the NEC for permission until after the funds had already been
spent. The following year the radical Ohio state organization brought
formal charges of mismanagement against Barnes. It charged, among
other things, that Barnes had used the party's stationery and postage
to defend himself from his critics during the campaign. Ohio also
charged that the National Executive Committee, in allowing the
use of the front page of the January, 1913, issue of the official
Monthly Bulletin for an advertisement of Hillquit's *Socialism*

Summed Up, had shown undue favoritism in the interest of Hill-quit's royalties. A special investigating committee examined the charges and cleared everyone. The section of the committee report having to do with the advertisement for Hillquit's book, however, was something less than satisfactory. The committee reported that the space was taken for the advertisement because the national office had too large an inventory of the book and did not want to lose money on the volume. In any case, stated the investigating committee, Hillquit had waived royalties on the book. Since Hillquit declined royalties the Ohio charge that he had benefited financially from the advertisement was unfounded, but there was one matter the investigating committee did not explain. It did not explain the NEC's strange concern about a large inventory of *Socialism Summed Up* in January, 1913—strange because the book was not published until that month. The conclusion is inescapable that the NEC, or whoever was responsible for the advertisement, was interested in furthering the gradualist Socialist philosophy the book advocated.[23]

Immediately after the election conservative leaders of the party took steps to put the new antisabotage clause of the constitution into action. The New York state organization instituted a party referendum calling for the recall of Haywood from the NEC on the grounds that he had violated Section II, Article 6, as amended, at a public meeting in New York City early in December, 1912. This article, of course, provided for the expulsion of any member who advocated sabotage, not for his recall from a party position. Party members voted their mail ballots on this referendum in January and early February, 1913. They voted to recall Haywood from the NEC, 23,495 to 10,944. Only about 30 per cent of the members voted on the referendum, which is a small percentage but typical of Socialist Party referenda. Four years later less than 40 per cent voted on the even more important referendum concerning the party's position toward the war. A regional breakdown of the vote bears out the generalizations about the party made in the first chapter. The largest majorities against Haywood were in New York (3,431 to 875), Massachusetts (1,296 to 457), Pennsylvania (3,094 to 1,308), and

Wisconsin (1,697 to 244). Only ten state or territorial organizations voted no on the referendum: Alaska (47 to 37), Hawaii (11 to 1), Montana (436 to 245), Nevada (164 to 116), Oregon (323 to 321), Tennessee (112 to 84), Texas (551 to 162), Utah (90 to 70), Washington (768 to 528), and West Virginia (157 to 154).[24]

The recall of Haywood was the only use the Socialist Party made of the antisabotage clause of its constitution. Mass expulsions of individuals would have called for machinery the party did not have. But Haywood's recall was sufficient to rid the party of most of its syndicalists. Haywood himself dropped from the party,[25] as did many of his followers.

Historians, however, have exaggerated the numbers of members who left the party after the adoption of the antisabotage amendment and the recall of Haywood. That there was a decline in party membership and that much of the decline is attributable to the party's antisyndicalism is not disputed, but the decline was not so great as has been asserted and the reasons for it were not entirely due to the Haywood affair. The average monthly membership in 1911—that is, the average number of dues stamps sold each month during the year—was 84,716. Membership rolls grew during the first four months of 1912, from 121,862 in January to 135,436 in April. There was a drop to 100,845 in May, before the convention and the adoption of the antisabotage amendment. The rolls were swollen above normal in March and April because state secretaries made a special effort to get all affiliated persons paid up in their dues since the size of a state's delegation to the national convention was determined by its number of paid-up members. The rolls then grew during the campaign, a natural development, reaching 127,966 in October, 1912. In January, 1913, when the referendum on Haywood's recall was being voted upon, there were 100,550 paid-up members, and in February there were 110,002. After Haywood's recall there was a decline each month until June, 1913, when 80,795 Socialists bought their dues stamps. Thereafter the membership increased each month until October, when it stood at 96,620. The average monthly membership for the year 1913 was 95,401. Carl D. Thompson, one of the party's most conservative members, was surely much too sanguine when he entitled his 1913 manuscript on party membership "Bigger, Better and Stronger Than Ever," but assertions that the party declined "more than 50,000 members" from June, 1912, to June, 1913, which would be roughly a 50 per cent decline, or that "another 40,000" left the party in the four months after Haywood's recall, are nearly as wrong. Nor can the decline in membership be attributed entirely to the fight against the syndicalists. The first several months of the Wilson administration saw a spate of social legislation, and the reform aspects of Wilsonism attracted many conservative Socialists who were willing to accept something a great deal short of the cooperative commonwealth.[26]

Nonsyndicalist radical Socialists had been caught in a box by the whole matter of Haywood and syndicalism. As political actionists they were opposed to syndicalism, although they had no use for the tame gradualism of those who were the syndicalists' loudest critics, either. They opposed the use of violence as an instrument of class warfare and the glorification of "direct action" because such tactics were not effective in a society where employers could rally greater physical force and because they were not popular among a working class that held attitudes toward private property developed in an agricultural age. They opposed the tactics of the syndicalists on pragmatic grounds, not because these tactics offended middle-class values. Yet by cooperating with the gradualists in amending the constitution to expel syndicalists, and by condoning the logical next step, the removal of Haywood, the radicals had upset the delicate balance of power among the party's factions to their own disadvantage.

The Hillquit-Berger axis now controlled the Socialist Party, and the organization drifted steadily in the direction of conservatism. By 1916 even Simons could comment, with some justification but also with ill grace considering his background, that the party was "today little more than an organized appetite for office—a Socialist Tammany, exploiting the devotion of its members instead of the funds of corporations, for the benefit of a little circle of perfectly

honest, but perfectly incompetent and selfish politicians." Debs, seeing the direction of the drift, threatened to retire and then did so—
for two months, which was as long as that fighter could keep quiet.
When Debs went back into action, he announced that although he
still opposed sabotage and violence he was for rescinding Article II,
Section 6. His ostensible reasons were that the amendment was
restrictive of the free speech of the party members and that its
adoption was "seeking favor in bourgeois eyes," but he probably
actually had in mind the restoration of the old balance among the
party's factions. He even went so far as to propose amalgamation
with the hated Socialist Labor Party, a move that probably would
have served to strengthen the Socialist Party's radical wing.[27]

But the two socialist political parties never united, and the antisabotage clause remained in the Socialist Party constitution until
1917, when the party quietly dropped the bars against syndicalists
in the hope of gaining some support in their battle for preservation
against the war spirit. By 1917 Socialists found it difficult to get
excited over the question of syndicalism anyway. As with most basic
problems, which are not really solved but merely replaced by other
basic problems, the importance of syndicalism waned during the first
Wilson administration and a new problem confronted American
Socialists. The party was now concerned with the World War.

IV

SOCIALISTS FACE THE WAR
IN EUROPE
1914–1917

IN the late summer of 1914 Americans were stunned when they read
in their newspapers that war was beginning in Europe. One by one
the European nations declared war upon one another. First it was
some obscure Balkan countries, about which most people in the
United States knew little and cared less. Then Austria and Germany,
then Russia and France, and finally England. Americans were bewildered by the rapid passage of events. What did this war mean for
the United States? Could the United States stay out of it? How could
such a terrible thing happen in this civilized and enlightened twentieth
century, so full of hope and promise?

American Socialists were just as confused about the European
War as the rest of the people. Embroiled in its own internal struggles for party power, concerned mainly with purely domestic problems, and having the faith of a younger brother in the socialist parties
of Europe, the Socialist Party was poorly prepared for the outbreak
of war.

There was, of course, a Marxian theory of the causes of war that
the Socialists could fall back on to explain the European situation.
The theory, briefly, was that a capitalistic economy must, in the very
nature of things, expand in order to continue to exist. In time, the
potential for economic expansion within a nation becomes so small
that the economy must expand beyond its national boundaries or,

in other words, become imperialistic. When two or more capitalistic, imperialistic national economies come into serious enough conflict over commonly desired opportunity for exploitation, the result is war. This theory should have been known to all decently read Socialists, but when the National Executive Committee met to issue its first statement on the European War in August, 1914, it was so surprised and confused that it neglected this theory and wrote a proclamation that, but for one paragraph, might have been written by any peace group.

The Socialist Party, said the NEC, is opposed "to this and all other wars, waged upon any pretext whatsoever," because war is a "crude, savage, and unsatisfactory method of settling real or imaginary differences between nations, and destructive of the ideals of brotherhood and humanity to which the international Socialist movement is dedicated." The proclamation urged President Wilson to use the good offices of the United States in every way possible to bring an end to the war, and suggested specifically that he immediately begin negotiations for mediation. Any group opposed to war could have said as much. In only one particular did the NEC statement differ from the thought of any non-Socialist opponent of war. The NEC blamed the start of the war on the European "ruling classes" and pledged its support to "the Socialist parties of Europe in any measures they might think it necessary to undertake to advance the cause of peace and good-will among men." [1]

But right there, for American Socialists, was the rub. The socialists of Europe had not prevented war; indeed, most of the European socialists were actively supporting their nations' war efforts. With the exception of a few men like Liebknecht in Germany, Jaurès in France, and Mann in England, the constituents of the International were as bellicose as the "capitalist parties." At many congresses of the Second International delegates had vociferously stated their opposition to war. No Socialist had been for war before it came, but come it did and the strong socialist parties of Germany and France had not stopped it. How to explain this situation was beyond the understanding of the American Socialists. "We do not imagine for a moment that a single German Socialist actually wanted War any more than we believed the English, French, and Belgian comrades wanted War. Just the same . . . in spite of the strong anti-military sentiment of the French Socialists, in spite of the anti-war propaganda of the English movement, above all, in spite of the 4,500,000 voting Social Democrats in Germany, we find the working classes of Europe flying at each other's throats." Considering this record in Europe, "it is time that we took stock of ourselves. We must know just how much froth there is upon the beer." [2]

There was quite a bit of froth. A sizable minority of Socialists, mostly intellectuals, were for the Allied cause from the beginning. They were not for war per se and they regretted the war had come; but they argued now that it had come it should be fought through to its conclusion and, they hoped, German militarism crushed. This group grew in size and its point of view became more pronounced as time went on. The arguments by which these pro-Allied Socialists arrived at this position were several.

The most abstract of these arguments was offered by William English Walling, among others. Walling, taking a position upon some kind of Marxian Olympus from which he could view in proper perspective the actions of mortal men, saw the conflict of England and France with the Central Powers as one between capitalism on the one hand and a semifeudal, militaristic precapitalism on the other. Only a highly developed capitalism, he argued, could prepare the way for socialism. Therefore, it was in the interest of Socialists that German militaristic semifeudalism be crushed. He did not bother to explain how this precapitalistic Germany had developed the strongest socialist movement in the world. Later Walling came down from his Olympus and saw the European conflict as a rather simple battle between freedom and democracy in the English-French camp and black reaction on the other side. Identifying Germany as the enemy of freedom and democracy, he said during the campaign of 1916, ". . . it is worth any sacrifice whatever in blood or money to prevent these forces from receiving a set-back in 1917 at the hands of the identical reactionary powers they overthrew in 1648, 1776, and

1848." Walling's old enemy A. M. Simons wrote, ". . . the war is
steadily becoming a conflict between progress and reaction." J. G.
Phelps Stokes, the Socialist railroad president, and John Spargo
echoed these sentiments.[3]

Another defense of the pro-Allied position was to point out the
German invasion of Belgium, the atrocities there, and the sinking of
the *Lusitania*. A. M. Simons went so far with this argument, even
before America entered the war, as to call the Socialists who disagreed
with him "pro-German." Other pro-Allied Socialists argued that the
Allied cause was righteous and that the socialists of France and England were justified in supporting the war because the German Social
Democratic Party had betrayed them. In August, 1914, Georges
Clemenceau, who of course was not a socialist, published in *L'Hu-
manité* an article with this thesis. Robert Rives La Monte, an associate
editor of the *International Socialist Review* who was then in France,
sent the Clemenceau article to his magazine with the note: "I agree
fully with Clemenceau. The German comrades have been weighed in
the balance and found wanting." The chief editor and publisher of
the magazine, Charles H. Kerr, who was usually on the extreme left
within the party, translated the Clemenceau article and published it
without further comment.[4] One last argument against neutrality, a
curious one seldom advanced at all and never made explicit, was that
a government at war must, in order to win, adopt "state socialist"
measures to rationalize and make efficient its economy. Walling in his
The Socialists and the War included a whole section called a "Summary of the Revolutionary State Socialist Measures Adopted by the
Governments at War." While the measures described were certainly
"state," few would consider them "socialist" and even fewer would
consider them "revolutionary."

This, then, was the froth, but there was much more strong and
heady antiwar brew beneath it. A majority of the American Socialists,
as well as nearly all the party's top leadership, was strongly opposed
to the war. After its initial surprise, the party recalled its Marxist
learning. Debs saved some of his most vitriolic prose for his antiwar editorials, such as "Never Be a Soldier." Hillquit was unalterably

opposed to the conflict. In reply to the pro-Allied Socialists he wrote that American Socialists should not take sides in the war at all. "The ghastly carnage in Europe has no redeeming features. It is not a war for democracy, culture, or progress. It is not a fight for sentiments or ideals. It is a cold-blooded butchery for advantages and power, and let us not forget it—advantages and power for the ruling classes of the warring nations." And in Milwaukee, Berger and most of his followers were so opposed to the war that A. M. Simons constantly called them "pro-German." He claimed even that Milwaukee Socialists "rejoiced" when the *Lusitania* was sunk and that Socialist school children "celebrated" the disaster with songs.[5]

Although most Socialists were agreed in their opposition to the European War and wanted it to come to a quick end, they did not know what to do to stop the bloodshed. Indeed, there actually was little they could do. What efforts American Socialists made were marked with dissension and inefficiency. In September, 1914, the national executive secretary of the party, Walter Lanferseik, a usually efficient Kentucky businessman, sent a cable to the socialist parties of ten European nations over his, Berger's, and Hillquit's signatures, urging these parties to persuade their governments to accept mediation by the United States. Lanferseik apparently took this action completely on his own. Hillquit knew nothing of the cable until he read about it in the press, and, although he was sympathetic to the suggestion of mediation, he was understandably considerably irritated with the way Lanferseik had handled the matter.

A few days later the National Executive Committee proposed to the European parties an international socialist conference to be held in Washington to study ways and means to bring an end to the war. The officials of the parties in the belligerent nations were not interested in the proposal, but the socialists of European neutral nations were receptive to the idea if the conference would be held in Europe. The NEC approved and promised to send six delegates, but only if the meeting were postponed until mid-January, 1915. When it appeared that the proposed conference would not have delegates from any of the parties of belligerent nations, the American party lost its enthu-

siasm for the project and appropriated travel funds for only one delegate, Hillquit. Hillquit was quite disgusted with the failure of his party
to cooperate fully in a conference it had suggested, but when Camille
Huysmans, head of the International Bureau, wrote to him that European socialists considered mediation a hopeless cause and recommended canceling the conference altogether, Hillquit, too, retreated
from the idea. Officially, at least, the conference was still scheduled
to open at Copenhagen on January 15th, but Hillquit did not sail even
though the NEC had not officially relieved him of his assignment.[6]

With the bad taste of the ill-fated Copenhagen conference still
in their mouths, the American Socialists were asked to pay up their
International dues. The International Bureau notified the NEC that
it owed a special assessment for expenses incurred in connection with
the meeting of the Second International which had been scheduled for
Vienna in August, 1914, but which had been called off when war
broke out. The American party also owed back dues for 1914 and
current dues for 1915. This, coming just after the International had
demonstrated its futility as a peace agency, was too much for the fru-
gal souls on the NEC. The NEC voted to pay the special assessment
of $136 since it was a debt incurred when the party still had faith in
the efficacy of the Second International. But a tie vote on the motion
to pay the back dues for 1914 prevented action on that count, and the
NEC voted unanimously to pay no dues for 1915.[7] With this action
the Socialist Party of America severed its connection with the Second
International and tacitly gave up its effort to bring the European War
to a quick, negotiated close.

From that time on, American Socialists concerned themselves
with preventing the entrance of the United States into the conflict
rather than attempting to end the war in Europe. The Socialist Party
made just one more effort to effect peace negotiations, but this did
not come until the United States had declared war. In May, 1917, the
Second International called a conference to meet in Stockholm to discuss how to end the war. The Socialist Party appointed Morris Hillquit, James H. Maurer, and Algernon Lee as delegates to this con-

ference, but the United States Department of State, citing the Logan Act of 1799 as authority, denied the delegates passports.

After the Socialist Party dropped out of the Second International, individual Socialists continued to hope for a negotiated peace and occasionally made public pleas for immediate peace. For example, in February, 1916, Debs was hopeful there would soon be a decisive battle or campaign which would make peace overtures opportune. He urged the people of the United States to support such peace negotiations in every way possible should they develop.[8] But the efforts of the Socialists as a party to end the war were over; the problem now was to keep the United States out of it.

Socialists were not alone in their desire to keep the United States out of the war. Indeed, President Wilson, in order to promote neutrality, had urged Americans to be neutral in spirit as well as in deed, and his record of having kept the country neutral was to be partly responsible for his reelection in 1916. There were several organizations whose purpose it was to preserve the peace, such organizations as the American Peace Society, the American Union Against Militarism, the Women's Peace Party, the Emergency Peace Federation, and the Carnegie Endowment for World Peace.[9] There was hardly a program to preserve neutrality advanced by any Socialist that was not held in common with one or more of these peace societies or their members.

But there were important differences between the Socialists and the peace societies. The main difference lay in their analysis of the basic causes of the war, and this difference was enough to prevent close cooperation. The peace societies, which were thoroughly capitalist and middle-class in their orientation, could not agree that "This is a business men's war, worked up and encouraged by merchants and manufacturers who lust for more markets, more spheres of trade influence, more land and men to exploit. National differences, racial hostilities, all are mere superficial factors." And the Socialists held the peace societies in very low regard. A left-wing Socialist declared, "Peace societies are nothing more or less than schemes whereby certain parasites of the present system amuse themselves or gain a livelihood," and the conservative Socialist W. J. Ghent was equally bitter. Ghent especially resented the pacifist charge that the European socialists were responsible for allowing the war to start. "Yes, the Socialists could have prevented or stopped the war. They didn't, and so they deserve the maledictions that are showered upon them. Especially do they merit the reproaches of the Christians, . . . of pastors and priests, . . . of Syndicalists, . . . of anti-militarists, anti-nationalists, anti-governmentalists and anti-parliamentarians, also, since all of them over there are at the front, shouting and shooting and bayoneting for *la patrie* or *vaterland* or the United Empire." [10]

One of the programs to ensure neutrality shared by many Socialist and non-Socialist opponents of war was the proposal of an embargo against all the belligerent countries. The Socialists had a slogan, "Starve the war and feed America," and non-Socialists agitated for an embargo to an extent sufficient to cause Congress and President Wilson for a while seriously to consider the plan. But an embargo would not be truly neutral. Britannia ruled the waves in fact as well as in song, and an American embargo would only apply against the Allies what the British navy had already applied against the Central Powers. German agents, therefore, actively worked for an embargo. Resentment of German influence and the opposition of business caused the peace societies to retreat from an embargo. Socialists likewise dropped their agitation for an embargo, because, as Debs put it: "We are neither pro-German nor pro-Ally. We are Socialists." The Socialist platform in 1916 contained specific suggestions to keep the peace, but an embargo was not one of them.[11]

Although he continued publicly to advocate neutrality, President Wilson toward the end of his first term inaugurated an armament program that came to be known as the "preparedness program." Why it was called the preparedness program rather than preparation can be understood only by a generation that a few years later rejected normality for President Harding's "normalcy." Building military might became very popular as preparedness parades marched in the streets, and some schools inaugurated military training in the curriculum. The Socialists were all but unanimous in their hostility to preparedness, and there was great opposition to the program among the non-Socialist peace organizations. Debs, speaking for most Socialists, declared that preparedness would "transform the American nation into the most powerful and odious military despotism on the face of the earth," and charged that President Wilson in advocating armament had deserted his principles under the influence of Wall Street. When a Philadelphia Quaker organization asked Debs to express his opinion on military training in the schools, Debs replied he "would no more teach school children military training than teach them arson, robbery, or assassination." Socialist opposition to preparedness was so strong that when Charles Edward Russell made a public statement in favor of the program, the only prominent Socialist ever to do so, he probably lost the 1916 presidential nomination of the party. Late in 1915, at the convention of the Intercollegiate Socialist Society, Russell declared, "I believe that America ought to be prepared to defend itself as the last bulwark of democracy." This speech made Russell very unpopular in his party. It was a mark of Debs's fairness that he defended Russell even though he disagreed with him thoroughly. "There is no instance in American politics where a man in order to be true to his own conscience deliberately forfeited the nomination for the presidency of the United States. . . . Such men, however mistaken, are all too rare in the world." [12]

One proposed tactic to preserve peace unique to the Socialists was the threat of a general strike in the event of a declaration of war. This proposal was advanced by only a small minority of Socialists, at least publicly. It was the pet idea, logically enough, of William D. Haywood. At the 1910 meeting of the Second International, Haywood had been the only American delegate to vote for the unsuccessful motion of the French leader Jaurès for a general strike against war, and in 1914 he still declared such a revolutionary strike to be "the only guarantee of peace." [13] But there was never any possibility that the party would adopt such a radical measure as part of its antiwar program. The syndicalist aspects of the proposal were contrary to the views of the groups that dominated the Socialist Party. Besides, for the Socialists to have called upon the American worker to meet a declaration of war with a general strike would have been more than a little ridiculous in view of the relatively weak position of the Socialists in the trade unions and the eagerness with which the AFL's leadership, and probably its rank and file, accepted the war once it came.

One last proposal of the Socialists to keep the United States out of the war was the demand that a national referendum be held before a declaration of war. This was the pet idea of Allan Benson, whose star rose in the Socialist world when he began to write antiwar editorials for the *Appeal to Reason*. Until Benson's writings appeared in the *Appeal* he was an unknown in the movement, but such was the circulation of that newspaper and the popularity of Benson's antiwar articles that the party in 1916 nominated him for the Presidency. The suggestion of a referendum on peace or war was not exclusively a Socialist proposal—William Jennings Bryan advocated the principle in a speech at Madison Square Garden in February, 1917—but the Socialists emphasized the idea more than the peace societies, and gave it an unusual twist. Benson not only demanded the referendum; he demanded that those who voted for war in such a referendum be the first to go into the army—although he never explained how this could be done and retain the principle of the secret ballot—and he was so taken with the idea that he informed the party's national office that it was the only plank in the Socialist peace program he would work for. Some Socialists pointed out that although they favored direct legislation and were opposed to entering the war, they considered the Benson suggestion unworkable. Hillquit called the idea "perfectly wild." But these counsels did not prevail; the platform of 1916 contained the demand "That no war shall be declared or waged by the United States without a referendum vote of the entire people, except for the purpose of repelling invasion." [14]

The Socialists were so attracted to the direct-legislation principle that late in 1913 they decided by a referendum vote of four to one to nominate their national candidates in 1916 by party referendum rather than at a national convention. Early in 1916 such a nominating referendum was held. Debs refused to be considered for the nomination, partly because of his poor health, partly because of his wife's wishes, and partly because he thought it time for a younger man to make the appeal to the electorate. The conservatives in the party who had tried to keep the nomination from Debs in 1912 were thus relieved of their problem in 1916, and at least one of them was most unrestrained in his jubilation. The candidates for the nomination were Benson, James H. Maurer of Pennsylvania, and Arthur Le Sueur of Minot, North Dakota, and vice president of the People's College of Fort Scott, Kansas. Benson received a small majority in this three-cornered race; Maurer was a fairly close second, and Le Sueur a very poor last. George R. Kirkpatrick of Newark, New Jersey, a vigorous antiwar speaker and pamphleteer and a teacher at the Rand School in New York, defeated Kate Richards O'Hare for the vice presidential nomination.[15] Benson's strength in the referendum was greatest in the Western states, where the *Appeal* had its greatest circulation and influence.

Benson ran his campaign mostly by newspaper, and he was primarily concerned with opposition to preparedness, which perhaps played right into the hands of the advocates of preparedness. At any rate, Ralph M. Easley, an official of the National Civic Federation and a strong supporter of the preparedness program, was happy that Benson and the *Appeal* were so adamantly opposing preparedness because he expected that their opposition would frighten off major party opponents of preparedness, who would be uneasy about agreeing publicly with these radicals. "To my way of thinking, to place the anti-preparedness elements in the band wagon with 'The Appeal to Reason' would be helpful."

Allan Louis Benson, born November 6, 1871, at Plainwell, Michigan, was a journalist who had become rather successful in his field before he became a Socialist. An editor of the Detroit *Times* and later of the Washington *Times*, he became converted to Socialism by the singular method of reading an encyclopedia article written by an English Fabian. Benson ran a miserable race in 1916, receiving only 585,113 votes, only about two-thirds as many as Debs had polled in the last election. In only one state with significant Socialist strength, Oklahoma, did Benson do better than Debs had in 1912, and in Indiana he ran behind the rest of his ticket.[16]

Benson's poor showing, however, was not altogether his fault. The party itself had become weaker since 1912. With the expulsion of the syndicalists in 1912 and 1913, with the loss of prestige suffered by the European socialists' failure to prevent the war, and with the loss of some supporters to the progressivism of Wilson, the party membership rolls were about 35,000 names shorter than they had been in 1912.

The desertion of some Socialist voters to Wilson was curious. Some decided to support Wilson in the belief that it was worth abandoning hope of the whole loaf to get a half-loaf or even a few crumbs. Others, holding a similar belief, voted for Wilson thinking that a Socialist vote under the circumstances was a luxury, reasoning that it was wiser to vote for the lesser of the two major-party evils that had a chance of election victory.[17]

Still others, employing an argument that defies logical analysis, rebuked the Socialists for being too conservative, and then supported Wilson. John Reed, for example, voted for Wilson in 1916, convinced that "People like Hillquit, Berger, Spargo, et al. . . . are unbelievable smug fakers, and London's conduct in Congress was a joke." Gustavus Myers, critical historian of the great American fortunes and of Tammany Hall, wrote that as an idealist he must abandon the Socialists for the Democratic Party, which included some of the great American fortunes and all of Tammany. And A. M. Simons, author of the provocative *Social Forces in American History*, in criticizing the party's growing conservatism and political expediency, suggested that perhaps one could do more for Socialism outside the party than within it. In a wonderful tirade, Simons charged that the Socialist Party was out of touch with such movements as John Dewey's "pedagogical revolution," that it was pro-German, and that it allowed "itself to be dragged at the heels of the brewery and saloon forces." [18]

Felix Grendon, in a letter to the editors of the *New Republic* in answer to Simons's article, pointed out the faulty logic of this argument. As for Simons's criticism of the Socialists for accepting the support of non-Socialists, Grendon asked Simons: "Well, what did he expect [the Socialist Party] to do, during an election? Put on its best Sunday pose, raise its Marxian eyes to Heaven, and piously assure the nearly converted Socialist that it humbly commends him to the Republican or the Democratic fold whose leaders it modestly hopes will carry out the Socialist program better than its own leaders can do?" And as for the assertion that "the best place to work for Socialism is outside the Socialist Party," Grendon asked another pointed question. "A Socialist, leaving the party because it is not radical enough, joins the Wilson Democrats. Suppose his new companions fall short of the radical mark. Will he then enlist in the Colby Progressives, next with the Perkins wing of the Republicans until, in a climax of revolutionary progress, he rises to Taft and Smoot's Old Guard?" [19] But in the rising tide of nationalism, as American intervention approached, such counterarguments had small effect. The drift of conservative Socialists to Wilson continued.

Events in Washington and Europe moved swiftly after the counting of the votes in the fall of 1916. By late winter it appeared the Socialists in America would soon be faced with the problem their European comrades had faced: What to do when the nation declares a war which, in the Socialists' analysis, was brought by the capitalism they condemned? Should Socialists stick to their earlier convictions and fight against the war as they had fought against the coming of it? Should they lie low and try to ride out the storm as inconspicuously as possible? Or should they give the war effort at least partial and critical support and try to get what gains they could for Socialism? In March, 1917, after the German navy had resumed unrestricted submarine warfare, the Socialist Party called an emergency convention to decide just what the party's policy should be in the event America abandoned neutrality.[20]

By the time the nearly two hundred delegates to the special Emergency Convention met at the Planters Hotel in St. Louis, they were confronted with war as an accomplished fact. The President and Congress had beaten them by just one day. Congress passed the war resolution with an easy majority, but with nothing like the enthusiasm and unanimity of the war vote in 1941. Congressmen were under tremendous pressure from both sides, and one member of the House, looking back at those early spring days of 1917 several years later, wrote that had it not been for "Wilson's forceful and persuasive message, I am not sure that a majority could have been obtained for [the war] declaration." But unanimous or not, the St. Louis convention was confronted with war as a fact.

The delegates to the convention were a good cross section of the Socialist Party. The charge later made that they were wild-eyed aliens or Irish nationalists more interested in England's than in Germany's defeat was utterly without foundation. An examination of the list of delegates shows that an overwhelming majority of them were American-born. Less than a dozen were of German, Austrian, or Irish birth. Moreover, the composition of the convention was largely middle-class. Only about one-half of the delegates were farmers or workers, although many of them had worked with their hands in their younger days.[21] The delegates represented a home-grown variety of radicalism.

The convention quickly decided that the best way to formulate their position was to elect a War and Militarism Committee to conduct hearings and receive all the delegates who wanted to state their views. The committee elected was well balanced regionally and ideologically, representing all areas of Socialist strength and all shades of opinion. The colorful Kate Richards O'Hare of St. Louis was elected chairwoman. The fourteen other members of her committee were: Morris Hillquit, Algernon Lee, and Louis B. Boudin of New York City; Dan Hogan, Socialist newspaper publisher of Huntington, Arkansas; C. E. Ruthenberg and Frank Midney of Ohio; Victor Berger of Milwaukee; Kate Sadler of the state of Washington; Patrick Quinlan of New Jersey; Job Harriman of California; John Spargo of Vermont and New York City; Maynard Shipley of Maryland; George Spiess of Connecticut; and Walter P. Dillon of New Mexico.[22] Most of the week at St. Louis was taken with this committee's hearings and the drafting of its reports.

The committee soon learned that a great majority of the delegates were opposed to the war very strongly and in favor of opposing its conduct regardless of the consequences. There were very few delegates who held that the party should support the United States in "crushing Prussian militarism" in order to advance democracy. The majority agreed the war did not merit Socialist support; but being Socialists, and therefore, paradoxically, aggressively individualistic, they differed very articulately as to the reasons why they condemned it. Many delegates held that the party should oppose every war; others held that the party should oppose every imperialist war, classified the World War as such a conflict, and therefore were against it. Still others held that the party should oppose the war as one of aggression but that it should support it should the United States be invaded. The Southwestern Socialists, fearful of a Mexican alliance with Germany, were the ones who held this position. They were unalterably opposed to the European War, but many of them agreed with Dan Hogan, who said, "If those damn greasers come across the line we'll get our guns and shoot." [23]

The War and Militarism Committee submitted three reports to the convention. The majority report, written by the strange combination of Hillquit and Ruthenberg and signed by nine other committee members, was a stinging indictment of the war. The report proclaimed "unalterable opposition" to the war and called upon the "workers of all countries to refuse support to their governments in their wars" because "wars of the contending national groups of capitalists are not the concern of the workers." This war, the committee majority maintained, "cannot be justified even on the plea that it is a war in defense of American rights or American 'honor.' Ruthless as the unrestricted submarine war policy of the German government was and is, it is not an invasion of the rights of the American people as such, but only an interference with the opportunity of certain groups of American capitalists to coin cold profits out of the blood and sufferings of our fellowmen in the warring nations of Europe." After condemning the war as neither one to destroy militarism nor to promote democracy because neither aim could be achieved by force of arms, the majority report listed seven plans of action for Socialists to pursue: (1) "Continuous, active, and public opposition to the war, through demonstrations, mass petitions, and all other means within our power"; (2) opposition to military conscription, sale of war bonds, and taxes on the necessities of life— "We demand that the capitalist class which is responsible for the war pay its cost"; (3) "vigorous resistance" to all measures curtailing freedom; (4) "Consistent propaganda against military training and militaristic teaching in the public schools"; (5) extension of the Socialist program of education for the workers in an effort to shorten the war and establish a lasting peace after the war; (6) "Widespread educational propaganda to enlighten the masses as to the true relation between capitalism and war, and to rouse and organize them for action, not only against present war evils, but for the prevention of future wars and for the destruction of the causes of war"; (7) a demand for the restriction of food exports and the socialization and democratization of the industries concerned with the production, transportation, and distribution of food and necessities so as to protect the "American masses from starvation." [24]

Louis B. Boudin wrote a minority report, signed also by Kate Sadler and Walter Dillon. Boudin, a hairsplitter without peer in a party which had many masters of the art, wrote a report that in its analysis of the situation differed only very slightly from the majority report. Most of his report was word for word the same as that of Hillquit and Ruthenberg. He added only the argument that America's entry into the war could not be justified on the grounds of democracy or protection of small nations because the administration had kept a neutral position when Germany invaded Belgium, the only time when such a claim might have been made. In one important respect, however, Boudin's report dissented from the majority's document. Boudin suggested no plans of action such as the seven points in the majority report; he was satisfied to state his opposition to American participation in the war and keep quiet. This, then, was the middle-ground position.

The third report bore only the signature of its writer, John Spargo, a bristling little English immigrant. Spargo maintained:

"Now that war is an accomplished fact, . . . we hold that it is our Socialist duty to make whatever sacrifices may be necessary to enable our nation and its allies to win the war as speedily as possible." He recommended, however, that Socialists demand the preservation of civil liberties, a $5,000 limit on personal income, a referendum before any draft act, government cooperation with labor unions, and the government ownership of railroads, mines, and war industries. These demands were not altogether radical and unorthodox. The State Senate of Wisconsin had already passed a resolution urging federal adoption of some of them.[25]

The majority report carried easily on the convention floor. One hundred and forty delegates voted to support the militant antiwar position; thirty-one voted for Boudin's centrist report; only five voted for Spargo's call to go along with Congress and the administration. The convention, however, had no final authority to declare the party's position. The party constitution required that the recommendations of the convention be put to a referendum of all paid-up party members. The convention voted to exclude Boudin's report from the referendum on the grounds that it did not differ vitally from the majority report. This action was of dubious constitutionality. Party rules dictated that a proposal must be signed by at least one-fourth of the convention delegates to be on the referendum ballot. Spargo's report had only five supporters and could not, therefore, be voted on in the referendum. Since a referendum with just one proposal, the majority report, would be undemocratic, enough opponents of Spargo's report signed it in order to get it on the referendum ballot.[26]

In the national balloting it was demonstrated that the Socialist Party was strongly antiwar. The membership adopted the majority report, known subsequently as the St. Louis Proclamation, by a vote of about three to one.[27] Opposition to the war brought a temporary unity to the Socialist Party. All of the party's major newspapers and magazines were vigorously against the war. The right-wing Hillquit and the left-wing Ruthenberg had collaborated in the drafting of the Proclamation, a collaboration that would be wondered at within just two years. The conservative Victor Berger signed the Proclamation and urged others to vote for it, although he thought the language of it too extreme. Debs, who as usual had not attended the party's convention, wrote a strong article urging his followers to vote for the majority report.[28]

Although some Socialists later wavered in their opposition to the war, as events in Europe changed, the American Socialists, when confronted with war, had remained closer to the orthodox Marxian position of opposition to capitalism's wars than had any of the strong European socialist parties. This fact may indicate a laudable fidelity to principle, but there are other and less noble factors to be considered too. For one thing, the strong European socialist parties had as the basis of their strength the trade unions, which were generally prowar, and these parties had to compromise their principles to retain their labor support. If the American Socialists, weak because they never had such a strong relationship with organized labor, had possessed a comparable labor strength in their party, they too might have not been so militantly antiwar. Certainly American organized labor, both leadership and rank and file, with very few exceptions, gave the American war effort unqualified support.

Perhaps, too, the stand of the American Socialists might have been different if they had known what was to happen to them during the conflict. The Socialist Party in April, 1917, did not know what it was to be a dissenter in a total war. The Spanish-American War, a three-month affair, had been too short completely to unleash the intolerance that wartime nationalism evokes. In all previous wars of the United States there had been a considerable part of the population in opposition to war, large enough and well organized enough to survive the conflict and to retain strength. Neither did the Socialists know just what degree of madness a war-enraged people is capable of. The Socialists of the United States were soon to know.

V

MAKING THE WORLD
SAFE FOR DEMOCRACY
1917–1918

AN overwhelming majority of Socialist Party members were strongly opposed to the war and were committed to agitation against it, but there was a group of Socialist intellectuals, men of some prominence in non-Socialist circles, who dissented from their comrades' position. The defections of these Socialist intellectuals made only a negligible dent in the party numerically, but because of their prestige and the publicity given in the daily press to their leaving the Socialist Party to support the war it appeared to non-Socialists that the party was suffering a rather severe split. When a Socialist laborer or farmer decided to swim against the current and oppose the war with his comrades—and thousands of them took this decision—editors of daily newspapers saw nothing newsworthy in their action; but when a Charles Edward Russell or a William English Walling left the Socialists and supported the war newspapers took notice. John Spargo, who was not so well known as some of the other prowar intellectuals, even made the front page of the *New York Times* when he charged soon after the declaration of war that in adopting the St. Louis Proclamation the Socialist Party was "essentially unneutral, un-American, and pro-German." [1]

When men like Russell, Walling, Spargo, A. M. Simons, W. J. Ghent, Allan Benson, Upton Sinclair, J. G. Phelps Stokes, and Gustavus Myers deserted the Socialist cause, they deprived the party of some of its aura of respectability and widened the gap between progressives and radicals. The gap was further widened by the movement to the right that progressive Democrats took during the war years. The effects of this division of the left-of-center forces are difficult, perhaps impossible, to document, but it seems quite probable that it was a major factor in the failure of progressive political action during the next several years and in the failure of liberals to prevent the reactionary trend in America just after the war.

The degrees of apostasy among the prowar Socialist intellectuals varied. Perhaps the greatest apostate was A. M. Simons, once considered to be in the left wing of Socialism. Simons became Director of the Bureau of Literature of the Wisconsin Loyalty Legion, a 200 per cent patriotism organization, and used that position for vehement attacks upon his former comrades. He charged Victor Berger, with whom he had worked on the *Milwaukee Leader* before the war, of accepting subsidies from German agents to run his newspaper and of slanting the *Leader*'s reports of the war news to favor the Germans. And the Socialist Party in opposing the war, Simons wrote, "has betrayed not only socialism but its own membership and its very cause and today stands in opposition to democracy." A Milwaukee friend of Simons, Winfield Gaylord, a former Socialist state assemblyman, supplied the federal government with Socialist documents and letters which he thought proved the party "treasonable." [2]

Gustavus Myers was another former Socialist who associated with an anti-Socialist patriot organization during the war. Soon after the United States entered the war, Myers wrote to President Wilson suggesting that the Socialists' "dangerous and insidious propaganda be exposed." Wilson put Myers in touch with George Creel, chairman of the Committee on Public Information, who got Myers a job with the League for National Unity. This organization was headed by Ralph M. Easley of the National Civic Federation, who was one of the most vigorous anti-Socialists in the country. Myers was offended when he heard that his former comrades had "been talking about how 'Myers sold out.'"

Others did not become officials in patriotic organizations, but some of them were no less active in attacking their former political bedfellows. Walling became alarmed at what he thought to be pacifist sentiment in the columns of the staid New York *Tribune* and wrote to Theodore Roosevelt urging him to use his influence to put an end to it. He wrote such savage charges of pro-Germanism among the Socialists in his home-town newspaper at Greenwich, Connecticut, that the editor of the conservative little sheet felt compelled to label the charges as "exaggerated." Walling's close personal friend J. G. Phelps Stokes was violent not only against the Socialists but against major-party politicians who he did not think were up to his prowar standards. He wrote letters to the Vice President and the Speaker of the House urging congressional investigations into the possibly treasonable activities of Senators Robert M. La Follette, Asle J. Gronna, and William J. Stone and Congressmen William E. Mason, Frederick A. Britten, and John M. Baer. If found guilty of treason, presumably by committees of Congress, he recommended immediate and drastic action: ". . . if any are guilty, let the guilty be shot at once without an hour's delay." [3]

John Spargo, ever an erratic person, in a letter of resignation from the party which he made public, declared he hesitated to use the term "pro-German" in referring to the Socialists. "I have hesitated to use that term and hasten to add that I do not think that there has been (except in a few unfortunate instances) any conscious advocacy of the German cause, as such." He perhaps hesitated, but he did not stop. A few months later there was no hesitation as he wrote pamphlets with such titles as *The Pro-German Cry of "No Indemnities,"* in which he spoke of "the infamy of the spokesman of American Socialism [Hillquit] upholding the impudent claims of the guilty Hohenzollern dynasty."

Charles Edward Russell used his voice and pen against the Socialists also. He was reported to have said in a public address at Madison, Wisconsin, that "the Socialists who are opposed to the war are dirty traitors [who] should be driven out of the country." Years later Russell still believed "a majority of our members sympathized with Germany and hoped she would win." Russell was, however, on the whole less vociferous in his denunciations of the Socialists than Spargo, Walling, or Stokes. After the war he worked to release from prison all those who had been incarcerated for their antiwar activities, and early in 1919 he urged President Wilson to prevent Debs's imprisonment. Allan Benson joined Russell in this appeal. Benson had left the party after the referendum on the St. Louis Proclamation, less than a year after he had run for President on the Socialist ticket.[4]

W. J. Ghent chose a colorful way to leave the party. Having already committed himself to support of the war in the pages of his *California Outlook*, Ghent resigned from the party when it adopted its antiwar position. He wrote to his old friend Morris Hillquit why he could not support the party's position on the war and closed the letter in this fashion:

> You are my enemy and I am,
> Yours,
> W. J. GHENT

Ghent gave the war constant support, but he was not emotional in criticizing the Socialists even when he wrote editorials on what he called their "disloyalty." [5]

Upton Sinclair, one of the most prolific writers of all time, resigned from the party to support the war, but he was very strong in his opinion that the federal government should not in any way abridge civil liberties during the war. He believed that Socialists had a right to oppose the war and that the government was defeating the ends it supposedly was fighting for when it stifled criticism. His was one of the most tolerant voices in the prowar chorus.[6]

Defections such as these by Socialist intellectuals hurt the party's reputation more than it diminished the strength and antiwar militancy of the party itself. More serious in its effects was the change in policy made by the *Appeal to Reason* late in 1917. The *Appeal* was at first militant in its opposition to the war, but its antiwar tone was much less pronounced after the postal authorities held up its

June 30, 1917, issue. Late in 1917 Louis Kopelin succeeded Fred Warren as editor, and from then on the *Appeal* was for the war. Kopelin wired to President Wilson, "I am on your side," and informed his readers: "Strange as it may seem a destructive war is bringing constructive social effort to America. . . . We are living in a time when society is ready to listen to the argument of efficiency and economy for the common good." [7]

The prowar Socialists organized themselves into a society called the Social Democratic League of America. This organization, which Hillquit cynically but correctly called "an organization of leaders without followers," never became more than a paper organization. In the summer of 1917 the Social Democratic League tried to make common cause with the remnants of the Progressive Party, which Theodore Roosevelt left stranded in 1916, the Prohibitionists, and some woman suffragists. Representatives of these groups met in New York early in July, 1917, and drafted plans for the organization of a new political party which would not be "in any sense a 'peace party' or a 'war party'" but which would "struggle for political and industrial democracy." This group held its first national conference in Chicago in October, 1917, where it took the name National Party. Its platform, the work of a most diverse group including Charles A. Beard, A. M. Simons, John Spargo, J. G. Phelps Stokes, J. A. H. Hopkins, and Frederic Howe, was a progressive but certainly not a radical document. Politically, the National Party was for woman suffrage, direct legislation, the short ballot, proportional representation, better absentee voting provisions, and prohibition; economically, it was for the extinction of land monopoly, public ownership (the party did not use the term *socialization*) of railroads and public utilities, abolition of grain speculation, extension of postal savings services, old-age pensions, better factory inspection, and abolition of child labor.[8] This organization, which never survived its infancy, is no more than a footnote in the history of progressive political action, but it does serve to illustrate the political and economic principles of some of those who abandoned the Socialist Party in 1917, principles which were more progressive than radical.

The defection of intellectual and progressive Socialist Party members did not hurt the party's numerical strength. Walling, Ghent, Russell, and the others left the party very soon after the declaration of war, and as late as the end of 1917 the Socialist Party was as strong as, if not stronger than, it had been at the first of the year. There were some significant shifts in Socialist strength—the power of the party in the West declined and the New York organization became stronger—but the over-all influence of the party was about the same. It was not until the mob persecutions, the governmental prosecutions, and the suppression of Socialist newspapers in 1918 that the party began to wane.

In the fall of 1917 Morris Hillquit, running for mayor of New York City on the Socialist ticket, received the largest vote any Socialist candidate for that office had polled before or since. Hillquit received 145,332 votes, placing third in a four-cornered race. He was only slightly behind John P. Mitchel, the Fusion candidate, and nearly one hundred thousand votes ahead of the regular Republican candidate, William F. Bennett. The Tammany candidate, John F. Hylan, won the election easily.[9] The vote for Hillquit was an increase of more than 400 per cent over the vote Russell had polled as the Socialist candidate in 1912. And this remarkable vote was achieved over the opposition of some of the biggest names in American politics.

Theodore Roosevelt, always happy to strike blows against Socialists and their cause, took the platform against Hillquit. He referred to Hillquit as a "Hun . . . inside our gates." Charles Evans Hughes during the campaign referred to Hillquit as "unpatriotic" and "treasonable." Clarence Darrow, upon the advice of President Wilson, exploited his popularity on the lower East Side to work against the Socialist candidate. Hillquit's former comrades Russell, Stokes, and Henry Slobodin were against him in the campaign. But the efforts of these people were of little effect. Perhaps a greater handicap to Hillquit was the presence at all of his public meetings of stenographers from the United States district attorney's office, who took notes to be examined for possible violations of the Espionage Act. Hillquit, a lawyer, was careful in his criticisms of the war never to say anything that would prompt an indictment.[10]

Hillquit's vote was heaviest in the neighborhoods that were dominated by first- and second-generation immigrants, especially immigrants from eastern Europe.[11] The significance of this immigrant support is difficult to determine. It may have been that eastern European immigrants were more against the war than the general population; it may be that this group, being poor, was attracted to Hillquit's municipal program, summarized by the slogan "The City for the People," which included a demand for city-owned public housing projects. It may be only that these people were attracted to Hillquit personally because he himself was a Russian Jewish immigrant who could speak their language. The ferment of social revolution in Russia may have been a factor, although America did not receive the news of the Bolshevik Revolution until after the election. At any rate, Hillquit's popularity in these immigrant neighborhoods alarmed some people, who urged that the flame under the "melting pot" be made a little hotter.

Debs, in writing an editorial on the municipal elections of 1917, had good reason to gloat. The Socialist Party, supposedly dead because of its opposition to the war—that was the impression left by the daily press—had enjoyed signal success. In the nation's largest city it had elected ten state assemblymen, seven aldermen, and a municipal judge, in rolling up its big vote for Hillquit. In fifteen selected Northeastern cities the Socialists had polled 21.6 per cent of the total municipal vote. Debs's prediction turned out to be far wrong; but it is understandable that he should write in December, 1917: "The tide has sharply turned. The Socialist party is rising to power. It is growing more rapidly at this hour than ever in its history." [12]

New Yorkers might give a heavy vote to an antiwar Socialist, but they tried no overt revolution, they refrained from attempting to stop the war by violence. There was just one case in the nation where a group of Socialists revolted against the war. This was the extremely naïve and altogether fantastic Green Corn Rebellion in Oklahoma.

The terrible poverty of the tenant farmers in the cotton area of the South Canadian Valley of Oklahoma made the area ripe for radicalism, and Socialists were thick in this district of poor, sandy farms. The poverty of the people there approached that of Asia. Nearly all the radicals were sharecroppers, slaves to the cash crop demanded by their landlords. Those who did own their own farms were heavily in debt to local banks, which charged from 20 to 40 per cent interest. General stores made loans too risky for the bankers to make and charged even higher rates of interest. The strength of Socialism in this area alarmed conservatives, and they had good cause for alarm. In three of these poor counties, Seminole, Hughes, and Pontotoc, the Socialists had polled slightly over one-third of the vote in the congressional elections of 1914. The Socialists there were a real third party, having their share of local offices.

Yet these Socialists had no real understanding of their party or of what it stood for. They were Socialists because the party was the only political organization that gave these sharecroppers a thought except during the hot summer days of the primary elections. They were certainly not good social democrats; there was a strain of anarchosyndicalism among them, or at least a hazy philosophy of violence. In the years just before the war two secret radical organizations, the Working Class Union and the Jones Family, established themselves in this district. The Working Class Union had been founded by a Dr. Wells Le Fevre of Van Buren, Arkansas, in 1914. (This little Ozark community, curiously, was a center of ultraradicalism. Thomas J. Hagerty, an unfrocked priest who had helped found the IWW, had once had a parish there.) The WCU's official organization, such as it was, was relatively mild in its radicalism, but its very loose organization allowed the WCU locals to follow any doctrines they pleased. The locals in the South Canadian Valley district were filled with flaming radicals who gave recruits an oath of secrecy on a six-shooter and a Bible. The Jones Family was a similar,

but smaller and entirely home-grown, organization. These two organizations had no connection with the Socialist Party whatsoever,
and most of their members were not paid-up Socialists. These poor
farmers voted Socialist, but they were too poor to pay party dues
regularly, low as the dues were.

Farmers in this area not only embraced a radical domestic program; they were emphatically antiwar. "Alfalfa Bill" Murray had
been defeated in his race for Congress there in 1916 because of his
strong prowar stand. These farmers thought they had voted for
peace when they helped to elect Woodrow Wilson, whom they
called "Big Slick," a nickname that probably failed to bring a smile
to the lips of that stiff-necked Presbyterian; they deeply resented
the declaration of war and the passage of the draft act. Prowar
propaganda had not reached them. Being only barely literate if literate
at all, they did not read newspapers to any significant extent, and
there had been no war speeches in the area. Deeply disturbed by
what they considered Wilson's breach of faith, and resentful of the
possibility of being drafted, although they would have probably
eaten better as soldiers than they did as civilians, these angry farmers
decided to take overt action. It is not surprising that the one violent
antiwar incident involved farmers. There is a tradition of angry farmers resorting to violence when no other course seems possible that
extends back as far as the days of Shays's Rebellion and the "claims
clubs" of frontier squatters.

Their plan was to assemble at some central place at an appointed hour, scour the country getting more recruits for their rebellion, march to Washington, seize the government, and stop the war.
Having only the murkiest sort of notion about where the nation's
capital was, they planned to march all the way and to subsist on green
corn and barbecued steer, taken from the countryside as they went
along. They believed the rumors, which were absolutely without
foundation, that similar revolts were being organized elsewhere and
that there were 190,000 Wobblies in Chicago ready to lead a march
of the industrial workers.

The Socialist Party organization in Oklahoma had no connection at all with the rebellion. In fact, regular Socialists in the state who had heard of the proposed revolt counseled against it. But the rebels regarded this discouragement as inconsistent with the stated antiwar position of the party.

The rebellion began on the night of August 3, 1917. Two days later it was virtually over, the poorly armed and bewildered radicals being easy prey for the sheriff's posses that quickly organized in the towns. Nothing at all worked out according to the rebellion plans. Even the detachments dispatched to blow up bridges and pipe lines failed miserably to make their dynamite effective. Civilian posses captured all the rebels in a few days, and it was not necessary even to call upon the state guards or the army. Military law was never declared.

In the reaction against the rebellion Socialists who had had no connection with the revolt at all, even one former county commissioner who hid during the excitement—not from the sheriff, but from the rebels—were hunted down and arrested.[13]

The rebels were tried in federal court under the Espionage Act and found guilty. Most of them received suspended sentences upon the promise to return to their farms, but five years later eight of the leaders were still serving long sentences in the federal penitentiary at Leavenworth, Kansas. One of these was a former Baptist minister who had been expelled from his church because of his radical activities.

The Green Corn Rebellion killed the Socialist Party in Oklahoma. Discredited in the eyes of revolutionists by the utter failure of the revolt, split into "yellows" and "reds" by the refusal of the party organization to support the rebellion, and cowed by the conservative reaction that frequently follows unsuccessful experiments in ultraradicalism, the Oklahoma party, once the strongest in the nation, dwindled away to nothing. Indeed, employing a strategy that hindsight can see was foolish, an emergency convention of Oklahoma Socialists dissolved the state organization entirely on the grounds that their action would help to prevent the prosecution in the trial of Victor Berger and other party officials, then going on in

Chicago, from establishing a connection between the party's anti-war statements and an overt act.[14]

But evidences of party strength, such as the municipal elections of 1917, and of radical militancy, such as the Green Corn Rebellion, were not to last throughout the war. As the months of war wore on, as the war-inspired nationalism became more intense, Socialist strength declined before the onslaught of hostile public opinion.

Although the federal government was by no means a bulwark for the preservation of civil liberties, mob action and the anti-Socialist measures of state and local officials probably hurt the party more than Congress and the administration. Patriotic organizations roundly damned all things "un-American" without ever defining the term very precisely. The kind of mentality that renamed sauerkraut "liberty cabbage," that sang a dreadful song called "I'd Like to See the Kaiser with a Lily in His Hand," that deleted the study of the German language from school curriculums—or even allowed students to work off their German credits by raising war gardens—or that defaced with yellow paint the homes of suspected German sympathizers made a very dangerous environment for Socialists. Socialists everywhere had difficulty renting halls for their meetings, had their meetings broken up by local police, encountered physical violence at the hands of patriotic vigilantes, and suffered economic discrimination from anti-Socialist employers.[15]

Socialists had no recourse in law against mob action, for the law itself was being amended so as seriously to restrict Socialist action. Very soon after the declaration of war seven states passed acts abridging freedom of speech and press, and although the federal government adopted such a law in June, 1917, states continued to enact such measures. It was the federal laws, however, which inhibited Socialists the most. The Espionage Act, which became law on June 15, 1917, granted the federal government the power to censor newspapers and ban them from the mails, and made the obstruction of the draft or enlistment service punishable by fine of up to $10,000 and twenty years' imprisonment. Additional powers of censorship were given in the Trading-with-the-Enemy Act of October 6, 1917, and the amendment to the Espionage Act of May 16, 1918, sometimes called the Sedition Act, made even attempting to obstruct the draft a felony. Socialists were frequently to run afoul of these laws.

Although prosecutions of individuals deprived the party of some of its leaders and inhibited the actions of others, the Socialist movement was probably impaired more by Postmaster General Albert S. Burleson's denial of full mailing privileges. The law empowered the Postmaster General to withhold from the mails newspapers which contained material considered to be in violation of the Espionage Act, but it did not explicitly grant the power to deny a newspaper its second-class mailing privileges on these grounds. Nevertheless, Burleson assumed this power and eventually the Supreme Court upheld him.[16] By the time the Court acted the war had been over for two years, and there would have been no practical difference if it had rebuked Burleson.

Less than a month after the passage of the Espionage Act Burleson revoked the second-class mailing privileges of the *American Socialist* of Chicago, the party's only official paper, for advertising a pamphlet, Irwin St. John Tucker's *The Price We Pay*, which linked American participation in the war with House of Morgan loans to the Allies. The *New York Call* had to pay full first-class postage after November 13, 1917, and conceivably Burleson had a personal motive in revoking the cheap postage rates of the *Rebel*, the organ of the Tenant Farmers Union edited by "Red Tom" Hickey. Hickey had been very critical of the way Burleson treated the tenants on his Texas farms. But the Post Office Department went one step further, and probably an unconstitutional step, when late in 1917 it ceased to deliver even first-class mail to the *Milwaukee Leader*. Thereafter, the *Leader* received mail only through its employees' homes.[17] By the end of the war nearly every Socialist newspaper and periodical had run afoul of Postmaster General Burleson. The Western and rural Socialists suffered more from Burleson's policies than their urban comrades. Door-to-door deliveries and newsstand sales were impossible outside the big cities, and where population was sparse and Socialists even sparser the Socialist newspaper was frequently the only connection a member had with the national movement. Thus Burleson's actions, coming at the same time as the collapse of the party in Oklahoma and the defection of the *Appeal to Reason*, which circulated mostly in the West, helped to cause the decline of the Western and rural wing of the party. Since the party was at the same time growing in the Eastern cities, the composition of the organization was changing considerably.

President Wilson consistently supported the actions of his Postmaster General and, in effect, gave him a free hand. During the Hillquit campaign in 1917 Herbert Croly, author of *The Promise of American Life*, wrote to the President criticizing Burleson's policies. He argued that suppression of the Socialist press was creating Socialist support in New York City, and urged a policy of persuasion instead of one of suppression. Burleson's action, Croly wrote, "tends to create on the one hand irreconcilable pacifists and socialists who oppose the war and all its works, and a group of equally irreconcilable pro-war enthusiasts who allow themselves to be possessed by a fighting spirit and who tend to lose all sight of the objects for which America actually went into the war." President Wilson assured Editor Croly that censorship was to him a matter of great concern, but that after conferences with Burleson he believed his Postmaster General to be "inclined to be most conservative in the exercise of these great and dangerous powers." For Wilson to have believed any differently about Burleson would have required a reversal of his opinion. In September, 1917, when sending back to Burleson a memorandum on "Rules of procedure for the exclusion of illegal matter from the mails under the Espionage Act," Wilson had attached this note: "I must admit that I haven't been able to read all of the enclosed, but you know that I am willing to trust your judgment after I have called your attention to a suggestion." Many prowar former Socialists and several non-Socialists objected to Burleson's interpretation of the Espionage Act. The Hearst columnist Arthur Brisbane had been fearful of this sort of censorship before the Espionage Act was passed, and out in Washington a body of farmers met in their school building to condemn Burleson's revocation of second-class mailing privileges as a dangerous infringement of civil liberty.[18]

Socialists ran afoul of the Department of Justice as well as the Post Office Department. Here the Socialists were more the victim of zealous district attorneys, nationalistic juries, and war-warped judges than they were of Attorney General Thomas W. Gregory. Gregory consistently showed more restraint and judiciousness than his Cabinet colleague and fellow Southerner Burleson.

There shall be no attempt here to narrate the many prosecutions of Socialists under the Espionage Act. A few of the major cases will indicate the nature of the problems the Socialists encountered with the Department of Justice and the courts.

One of the early cases of a Socialist under the Espionage Act was that of Kate Richards O'Hare, the wife of the St. Louis Socialist editor Frank O'Hare, and a very active Socialist agitator in her own right. Mrs. O'Hare had made an antiwar speech in North Dakota in the summer of 1917, for which she was indicted, tried, found guilty, and sentenced to the penitentiary. In passing sentence upon Mrs. O'Hare, the trial judge made a statement which indicates the degree to which the war spirit had entered the courtroom: "This is a nation of free speech; but this is a time of sacrifice, when mothers are sacrificing their sons, when all men and women who are not at heart traitors are sacrificing their time and their hard earned money in defense of the flag. Is it too much to ask that for the time being men shall suppress any desire which they may have to utter words which may tend to weaken the spirit, or destroy the faith or confidence of the people?"[19] Apparently uttering words tending to "weaken the spirit" of the people was as much under the ban as obstructing the draft.

In March, 1918, Rose Pastor Stokes got into trouble when she made a mildly antiwar speech in Kansas City before the Woman's Dining Club. Mrs. Stokes, along with her husband, J. G. Phelps Stokes, supported the war at first, but after a few months she changed her mind. The Kansas City *Star*, in publishing an interview with Mrs.

Stokes, got her statements garbled and printed that she was for the war. Mrs. Stokes, more interested in accurate reporting than fearful of the district attorney, wrote a letter to the editor of the *Star*, which he published. In this letter she complained that her remarks had been misinterpreted, and that she did not support the war. She used the sentence, "No government which is *for* the profiteers can also be *for* the people, and I am for the people, while the government is for the profiteers." An indictment was brought against Mrs. Stokes, and after the case was heard the trial judge, in his charge to the jury, held that if the jurors thought her statement about the government and the profiteers had produced a temper and spirit that would "tend naturally and logically to interfere," then Mrs. Stokes was guilty. The jury thus estimated the effect of her remark and found her guilty.

But to imprison Mrs. Stokes for her letter was not enough. George Creel, the head of the Committee on Public Information, sent President Wilson a clipping from the Kansas City *Post* that demanded an indictment of the managing editor of the *Star*, Ralph Stout, for publishing Mrs. Stokes's offending letter. Wilson agreed with the *Post* and Creel. He wrote to his Attorney General, "Don't you think there is some way in which we could bring this editor to book?" Gregory replied with a long and patient letter pointing out that there was no case against Stout.[20]

There were other prosecutions of Socialists. Early in 1918 Victor Berger, Adolph Germer, the party's national executive secretary, Irwin St. John Tucker, and J. Louis Engdahl, among others, were found guilty in federal court at Chicago of obstructing the draft and enlistment services. Their conviction was later set aside by the Supreme Court on the grounds that the trial judge, Kenesaw Mountain Landis, had been prejudiced during the trial. The editors of the *Masses*, the Marxist literary magazine, were twice brought to trial under the Espionage Act. In each case the jury could come to no agreement and the indictment was eventually dismissed.[21] This was one of the very few Espionage Act cases that did not result in conviction. Over one hundred members of the IWW, including Haywood, were found guilty in a mass trial at Chicago, and there were numerous other cases involving little known members of the Socialist Party. But the most important case of all, and one which well illustrates the operation of the administration and the courts during the war, arose from the speech Eugene V. Debs gave before the Ohio State Convention of the Socialist Party at Canton in June, 1918.

Debs's Canton speech when read today does not seem to be a strong criticism of America's role in World War I. He spoke of wars in general: "The master class has always declared the war; the subject class has always fought the battles. The master class has had all to gain and nothing to lose, while the subject class has had nothing to gain and all to lose—especially their lives." [22] But the atmosphere that Sunday afternoon in Canton was full of tension, and Debs's Socialist listeners recognized the implications of his remarks for the current war. The United States Attorney for the Northern District of Ohio, E. S. Wertz, had stenographers taking an account of Debs's speech, and representatives of the American Protective League, a semiofficial patriotic and war organization that worked closely with the district attorney in northern Ohio, went through the crowd checking draft registration cards. [23] These ardent nationalists of the American Protective League heard Debs severely criticize the prosecutions of Socialists under the Espionage Act and heard him challenge the Department of Justice to the effect that if Rose Pastor Stokes was guilty he was also.

Wertz sent a copy of the Debs speech to the Attorney General at Washington pointing out passages he thought to be in violation of the law and asking for advice about possible prosecution. Wertz interpreted the Espionage Act very broadly. "You will note the sentence on page 16, to the effect that the I.W.W. in its career has never committed as much violence against the ruling class as the ruling class has committed against the people. This, of course, is the kind of criticism of the government of the United States which I believe Congress intended to forbid by its enactment of the amended Espionage Act." The Attorney General and his advisers

mulled over the Debs speech for three days and then discouraged
Wertz about prosecuting Debs; but they did not forbid prosecution:

Coming then to the question of whether Debs' speech does violate that
law, the case is not without serious doubts. In the opinion of the Department, most of the passages marked by you, in and of themselves, do not
violate the law. For instance, criticism of the courts of their administration of the war laws can hardly be called an attack on the "form of
government of the United States. . . ." Abuse of the actions of plutocrats of this country, real or imaginary, can hardly be brought within
any of the express provisions of the Espionage Act. There are certain
passages, however, some of which you have marked, which, taken in
connection with the context, might be held to have crossed the line between lawful and unlawful utterances. . . . These parts of the speech,
taken in connection with the context, bring the speech close to, if not
over, the line, though the case is by no means a clear one. All in all the
Department does not feel strongly convinced that a prosecution is ad-
visable.[24]

The Department of Justice was reluctant to bring poor cases into
court; it did not want acquittals under the Espionage Act. But it
failed to consider that with the spasm of patriotic, nationalistic fervor
that gripped the country, there was no such thing as a poor case
against a Socialist. It was nearly impossible for a radical to get an
acquittal.

Wertz, understanding public opinion better than his chiefs in
Washington, got a grand jury to indict Debs. During the trial Debs
offered practically no defense at all. Perhaps he was even seeking imprisonment. He told the jury: "I have been accused of having ob-
structed the war. I admit it. Gentlemen, I abhor war. I would oppose the war if I stood alone. . . . I wish to admit everything that
has been said respecting me from this witness chair. I wish to admit
everything that has been charged against me except what is embraced
in the indictment. . . . I cannot take back a word. I can't repudiate
a sentence. I stand before you guilty of having made this speech . . .
prepared to take the consequences of what there is embraced." The
jury of course found Debs guilty, and the trial judge, D. C. Westen-

haver, sentenced Debs to ten years' imprisonment. Before the sentencing Debs made a little speech to the court, one sentence of which has been widely quoted. ". . . while there is a lower class I am in it; while there is a criminal element, I am of it; while there is a soul in prison, I am not free." [25]

Debs's attorneys appealed the case to the Supreme Court. By the time the Court gave its opinion in the Debs case, Justice Holmes had already enunciated his "clear and present danger" doctrine. But in delivering the opinion of the unanimous Court against Debs, Justice Holmes made no mention of his previously stated doctrine and did not go behind the verdict of the original trial, in which there was no reference to the "danger" of Debs's speech. Justice Holmes accepted the original verdict as proof that Debs had intended interference with the war and that interference was the effect of his words.

After the Supreme Court had spoken only President Wilson could have prevented Debs from going to prison. Frank P. Walsh, a progressive, and the former Socialists Allan Benson and Charles Edward Russell urged Wilson to grant a respite to Debs. Wilson, then in Paris for the peace conference, replied that he doubted "the wisdom and public effect of such an action," but that if his new Attorney General of about one month's tenure, A. Mitchell Palmer, consented to a respite he would grant it. It is probable that Wilson would have been extremely surprised had Palmer consented, considering Palmer's antiradical activities during his first year as Attorney General. Palmer, who was then more concerned with rounding up radicals and sending them to jail than he was interested in mercy to Debs, did not hesitate in cabling to Wilson that it was "imperative that no respite or clemency be shown at the present time." [26] Thus Debs went to prison five months after the war was over for making a speech which the Department of Justice itself had not been convinced was in violation of law.

It seems clear that Attorney General Gregory and his immediate staff were much closer to an attitude of restraint and a judicious interpretation of the law than were the United States Attorneys in the various court districts. Gregory and his staff were aware of the dangers implicit in the Espionage Act. Gregory's Chief of the Bureau of Investigation even wrote, "The meetings engineered by the Socialists are now covered throughout the United States without any specific instructions and I think there is need rather for more caution than more vigorous efforts in the matter of handling Socialistic gatherings." [27]

It seems clear, too, that Gregory's respect for legal process and civil liberty was greater than President Wilson's. It was Gregory who reminded Wilson of legal process when Wilson wanted to indict the managing editor of the Kansas City *Star*. Several times Gregory advised restraint. Once, forgetting his academic days and the lessons he had once taught on the nature of the federal structure, Wilson sought ways to prevent the duly elected mayor of Michigan City, Indiana, an enemy alien, from taking office. [28]

But if the top echelon of the Department of Justice exercised restraint in handling the Socialists, others did not. Among the vigorous opponents of the Socialists during the war were Samuel Gompers and his American Federation of Labor. Soon after the United States declared war, a group of Socialists and pacifist progressives organized the People's Council of America for Democracy and Peace. This organization advocated a negotiated peace on terms which Wilson later embodied in his Fourteen Points. The AFL soon thereafter formed an organization with a similar name, the American Alliance for Labor and Democracy, to counteract the influence of the People's Council. Samuel Gompers was chairman of the American Alliance. In the fall of 1917 the People's Council made plans for a convention in Minneapolis, and the American Alliance promptly went to work to prevent their meeting. The Gompers group sent its secretary, Robert Meisel, to Minneapolis to rent all the available halls so that the People's Council would have no place to convene. After many difficulties and amidst considerable confusion, the People's Council managed to hold a half-day convention in Chicago. Even the money available to the American Alliance was not sufficient to preempt every meeting hall in the nation. It has been charged since, apparently with some foundation, that the Gompers group received money from Wilson's "secret fund." [29]

Here and there in the AFL were Socialist Party members in positions of authority and responsibility. One of these was James H. Maurer, president of the Pennsylvania State Federation of Labor since 1912. Maurer's opposition to the war was a thorn in the side of the AFL hierarchy, and at the 1918 convention of the Pennsylvania AFL the hierarchy was determined to remove him from office. It sent to the convention at Pittsburgh a group of men from outside the state to work against Maurer and his reelection. But the men sent by the Washington office of the AFL failed in their purpose; Maurer was reelected by the convention by a three-to-one vote. Maurer had more than the usual motivation in desiring victory in the election; a federal agent was at the convention who had orders to serve a warrant for Maurer's arrest should he not be reelected. [30]

By the time of Maurer's reelection in May, 1918, the complexion of the Socialist Party had changed considerably from what it had been at the beginning of the war. The party had declined in the rural West and had grown in the Northeastern cities. The old pre-war internal balance of power was gone, and the new forces of power within the party were never to come into balance for the party split into communist factions the year after the war. The growing urban centers of Socialist strength by no means saw eye-to-eye ideologically. The party's leadership in New York, Chicago, Milwaukee, and Pennsylvania was conservative, gradualist, evolutionary, revisionist, almost reformist. The leadership in Ohio, Michigan, and some of the language federations was radical, extremist, revolutionary, simon-pure Marxist. To use their own terms of approbation, the former were "yellows" and "trimmers," and the latter were "reds" and "impossibilists." The lines, of course, were not this clearly drawn; there were dissenters from the leadership's philosophy in each camp. The declining Western wing of the party, the section that once had spoken through Debs, the O'Hares, the *Appeal to Reason*, and the *National Rip-Saw*, had occupied an ideological middle ground. Agreeing with the conservatives, for the most part, in the matter of political action as against physical violence and revolution, this Western wing had also agreed with the radicals in their militancy and their romantic spirit. The war and its accompanying repressions thus tended to divide the party, strengthening the extremes and weakening the middle. The Russian Revolution was in time to intensify this polarization, but the revolution's first effect was to prompt Socialists to reexamine their position toward the war.

The revolution of the Mensheviks evoked surprisingly little comment among American Socialists, perhaps because the news of it, which was inadequately reported, reached America about the same time as the declaration of war. But the Socialists were quite stirred by the Bolshevik Revolution in the autumn of 1917. All wings of the party hailed the revolution in its first months. Only the Left retained its enthusiasm for the Bolsheviks, but at first even the extremely right-wing Louis Waldman thought of the Bolshevik upheaval as an ". . . awakening to freedom and to self-government."

At about the same time that Americans were beginning to become aware of the significance of events in Russia, President Wilson, in a series of speeches, announced his war aims. These Fourteen Points were quite in keeping with the thought of many Socialists about the postwar world, except, of course, that the Socialists went further than Wilson and urged democratic socialism in all nations as the only reliable foundation for permanent peace. The differences between Wilson and the Socialists as to war aims were differences of degree, not of kind. Debs wrote that Wilson's Fourteen Points were "thoroughly democratic and deserve the unqualified approval of everyone believing in the rule of the people, Socialists included." [31]

Germany's continued attacks on Russia after the revolution and the American peace program gave many Socialists a different outlook on the war. The Socialist aldermen of New York City, elected in 1917 on an antiwar platform, supported the third Liberty Loan drive in April, 1918. The Socialists' only congressman, Meyer London of New York, spoke at war-bond rallies. The neophyte Socialist Norman Thomas in a letter to Lillian Wald reflected the views of many Socialists:

Frankly my own feeling with regard to the war is undergoing something of a change. On religious grounds I am still obliged to think that war is a hideously unsatisfactory method of righteousness but the Russian situation and the progressive abandonment of imperialistic aims by the Allies under pressure from the President and British Labor remove the reproach of hypocrisy from us. Meanwhile the German people seem to be more completely under the dominance of their cynical Junker class than I had thought. Things change so fast that one is at a loss what to think. I wish Mr. Wilson could have taken the liberal stand he now has last summer.[32]

National Executive Secretary Adolph Germer had heard estimates that 95 per cent of the Russian Jewish Socialists of New York wanted to change the St. Louis platform now that Germany had continued her attacks on Russia. He thought this estimate high and he was not for significant revision of the party's official position on the war, but he did "believe that we ought to change our method of approach somewhat and . . . make it very clear that we are heartily in favor of encouraging unrest and strikes in the central empires and that we would like to have the Government open its channels for such activity in charge of the Socialist Party." Late in February, 1918, the Bohemian Socialists of Chicago passed a resolution urging the party to reverse itself completely and declare in favor of war on the Central Powers. The Illinois party, meeting in May, defeated a resolution calling for support of the war by only four votes. Former Socialists urged the party to swing to a new official position. Carl D. Thompson, who had been expelled from the party in 1915, led a campaign among the party membership urging it to abandon its antiwar position. Thompson declared, "Whatever may have been the causes that led up to the war, whatever the aims and purposes of those who started it, an entirely new situation confronts us now." Even Debs, just before making his speech at Canton that was to cost him thirty-two months in prison, told a reporter that "in the light of the Russian situation I think we should put forth a restatement of the aims of the Socialist Party." [33]

But even though a considerable group within the party was for at least amending the St. Louis Proclamation, actually to do so was another matter. Holding a national convention of the party was out of the question because of the likelihood of interference from vigilantes, local police, or Department of Justice agents. The party did the next best thing. It called a joint meeting of the National Executive Committee and the state secretaries to be held in Chicago, at party headquarters, in August. Even this meeting had Department of Justice observers. The meeting failed to accomplish anything important. The conflict between the Left and the Right within the party was already destroying its powers to move. The Chicago meeting quickly degenerated into a three-day quarrel between the left and right wings, which must have puzzled the Department of Justice men in attendance, and no action was taken on amending the St. Louis Proclamation. It is doubtful that the party's constitution could have been interpreted to sanction such a meeting's amending a statement written by a national convention and adopted by a party referendum. The Chicago meeting did endorse the Bolsheviks and remind the public that Socialists had been opposed to the Kaiser longer than the major parties had—the *Appeal to Reason* had always referred to him as "Crazy Bill"—but the official antiwar statement of the party remained unchanged.[34]

Finally, in the fall of 1918, the Allied Armies began to force the Kaiser's armies back, and mutinies and strikes broke out behind the German lines. On November 11th the German government agreed to an armistice, and the four-year-old war was over. American Socialists had little reason to celebrate on November 11, 1918. The war and the war temper had not killed the party, but it had left it much weaker than it had been two years before. Numerically, the party had not declined very much. From an average monthly membership of 83,138 in 1916 the party rolls had dropped only to 80,126 in 1917 and to 74,519 in 1918.[35] And membership was to increase by about 65 per cent in the first half of 1919 from the impact of the eastern European revolutions. But the membership statistics were deceptive. The party's press was impotent, many leaders were in prison or on their way there, internal strife was more intense than it had ever been before, relations with organized labor were more strained than before the war, and the hostility of large segments of the public was greater than ever. Furthermore, the Western element of the party, which had been more squarely in the American tradition of indigenous radicalism than other sections of the party and which had served as an adhesive in the Left-Right fissure, was now in about the same weak and disorganized condition it had been in at the turn of the century. The days of the Socialist encampments on the Western plains were over. No longer would Oklahoma small-town merchants find it commercially expedient to display the red flag in their store windows. In her Leavenworth cell Kate O'Hare heard the news of Debs's sentence to Atlanta, and at Girard, Kansas, the presses of the old *Appeal* were now putting out Little Blue Books for E. Haldeman-Julius.

American Socialists would have had even less reason to celebrate the Armistice could they have seen what the immediate future held for them. The worst was yet to come. The nationalistic frenzy that had been calculatingly fostered by the Creel Committee was not to be turned off as easily as it had been turned on.

During the war prosecutors and persecutors of Socialists justified their actions on the grounds that Socialist opposition to the war endangered the nation. After the war no such justification on the grounds of national self-interest existed, but there was no pause in the drive to stamp out the Socialist movement. After November, 1918, the more unrestrained members of the American Right persecuted Socialists merely because they were Socialists, and the end of the war intensified, rather than diminished, antiradical hysteria.

Reactionaries in the great postwar red scare were incredibly crude and blunt. They felt no need to be subtle, to employ finesse, in what they considered their crusade for Americanism. Nothing could be cruder and franker than an advertisement Pacific Northwest businessmen ran in the Tacoma *Leader* and the Seattle *Post-Intelligencer*. "We must smash every un-American and anti-American organization in the land. We must put to death the leaders of this gigantic conspiracy of murder, pillage and revolution. We must imprison for life all its aiders and abetters of native birth. We must deport all aliens." Socialists, Non-Partisan Leaguers, "closed-shop unionists," Syndicalists, "agitators," "malcontents"—all these "must be outlawed by public opinion and hunted down and hounded until driven beyond the horizon of civic decency."

Nor was there much that was original in the red scare. The old clichés, uttered loudly and frequently, were sufficient. Senator Atlee Pomerene, coauthor of a law that drove a wide hole in the antitrust laws, urged that Debs be required to serve his full prison term in a letter to Wilson's secretary that bristled with phrases like "the better element of this Country" and "law and order." A Cleveland Republican lumber dealer and past international president of Rotary, in a letter with the same object, deplored Debs's alleged lack of "love or respect for our flag," expressed confidence in President Harding's "ONE HUNDRED PERCENT AMERICANISM," and stated his belief that "America was intended to and shall forever be an Anglo-Saxon Nation." [36]

But if the anti-Socialist propaganda was trite, if it was crude, even if it was only barely literate, it was nevertheless effective. Reactionaries could see their efforts bearing fruit in numerous state laws and federal executive actions. Many state legislatures passed what were euphemistically known as criminal syndicalist laws, acts that outlawed agitation for revolution, at the same time, paradoxically, that they were requiring that public-school teachers of history present the American revolutionists of the eighteenth century in a most favorable light. The United States Chamber of Commerce lobbied in many legislatures for a sedition act which would make it criminal to utter remarks that "tended" to incite violence. [37]

No longer was there restraint in the handling of radicals by the top figures in the Department of Justice. In March, 1919, A. Mitchell Palmer succeeded Gregory as Attorney General. Thereafter the Department of Justice was at the fore in the antired crusade. Palmer's main qualification to be Attorney General of the United States was that he had helped get the nomination for Wilson at the 1912 Democratic convention. After Palmer graduated from Swarthmore College —he was a Quaker all his life—he had "read law" in a small-town attorney's office and had never been exposed to whatever re-spect for constitutional legal process might have been taught in a law school. Secretary of Labor William B. Wilson cooperated with Palmer by zealously deporting alien radicals. So many radicals were deported on the *Buford* in December, 1919, that the press dubbed the ship the "Soviet Ark."

There was a new organization in America in 1919 that played no small role in the anti-Socialist campaign—the American Legion. Within a year after the war to save the world for democracy ended, two thousand Legionnaires marched in parade on an auditorium in Reading, Pennsylvania, where a Socialist group proposed to hold a meeting. Marching at the head of the parade were the mayor-elect of the community and three ministers of the gospel. In Hoboken, New Jersey, in November, 1919, the mayor yielded to the pressure of two local American Legion posts and denied the local Socialist Party a permit to hold a public meeting.[38] Incidents like these were repeated all over the United States.

In such an atmosphere as this it was not surprising that the anti-Socialist sentiment was even stronger than the Anglo-American tradition of representative government. There were at least three denials of that tradition in the years just after the end of the war. When Congress met in a special session in April, 1919, the House refused to seat Victor Berger, who had been duly elected by his district in Milwaukee. There was no claim that his election had been irregular. He was denied his seat because he was convicted of vio-lating the Espionage Act. At the time he was out of prison pending his appeal to the Supreme Court. A special election was held in Berger's congressional district in December, 1919, and Berger won again, this time against a fusion candidate. But again the House refused to seat him. In November, 1919, five state assembly districts in New York City elected Socialists to represent them at Albany. A special legislative committee was appointed to investigate the qualifications and eligibility of the five, which were in question only because they were members of the Socialist Party. The special com-mittee recommended the five Socialists not be seated, and the Assembly sent them back to New York City. The New York State Bar Association appointed a committee composed of Charles Evans Hughes, Ogden Mills, and Joseph Proskauer to plead for the seating of these duly elected assemblymen, but even such a distinguished trio as this was unable to persuade the Assembly. Finally, there was another similar case in New York, which was the center for such unrepublican activity possibly because it was almost the only place in the country that elected Socialists. In November, 1919, two New York Socialists, Algernon Lee and Edward F. Cassidy, were elected to municipal office, but by a process of masterly inactivity and other dubious ruses they were prevented from taking their offices until two years later, only two months before their terms were to expire.[39]

The postwar antiradical hysteria waned considerably after the election of 1920, and Socialists again began at least to be accorded their civil rights. But by that time the Socialist Party was no longer potent enough to give nightmares to even the most apprehensive conservative. By the election of 1920, under the impact of events in central and eastern Europe, American Marxists had divided beyond the point of ever being susceptible to reunion, and Socialist faced Communist through an atmosphere of mutual distrust, suspicion, and hate.

VI

SOCIALIST VERSUS COMMUNIST

1919

WHILE the Socialists were suffering from attacks by conservatives in the months just after the Armistice there was an internal fight in the party that was to have a more permanent detrimental effect on the Socialist cause than the great red scare. Hysterical antiradicalism abated somewhat in the early months of the Harding administration, but the split of the Communists from the Socialist Party remained. Public opinion was sufficiently calm by the end of 1921 for President Harding to release Debs from prison without bringing overwhelming abuse upon his head. But the radical movement Debs had left over two years before was now divided into two hostile camps which fought each other with the intensity they had formerly reserved for capitalists.

Reactionaries and extreme revolutionaries analyzed the postwar American scene quite similarly, although each group would have scoffed at the suggestion that its outlook was akin to the other's. One feared a revolution; the other hoped for one. But they agreed in that each considered a revolution a real possibility. Where the conservatives saw the strike of the steelworkers as a facet of an international revolutionary conspiracy, the Left Wing Socialist saw it as an uprising of the proletariat, a beginning of "revolutionary mass action." Where conservatives saw the sinister and subtle hand of the Kremlin in the Boston police strike, the revolutionists saw even the Cossacks becoming imbued with the spirit and idea of the class struggle.

The whole development of the Left Wing Section of the Socialist Party and subsequent formation of rival leftist parties are understandable only when it is noted that the extreme Left believed a revolution in America was imminent. Revolutionists and evolutionists had worked together in the Socialist Party for years—not harmoniously, it is true, but together—when no one thought seriously that America would soon be at the barricades. It is likely that the two groups would have continued together in the same organization had not the revolutionaries after the Bolshevik Revolution had the illusion of imminent American revolution. These revolutionaries, having seen Russia in a matter of months emerge from a near feudalism to communist revolution, believed that the more highly developed United States was on the very brink of revolution. John Reed told Roger Baldwin, who was on his way to jail as a conscientious objector, that the workers would arise and free him long before his sentence ended, and other Left Wingers were more hopeful even than Reed.[1]

In coming to this conclusion Reed and his colleagues ignored a great many differences in American and Russian conditions. The war in Russia had ruined the national economy; in America it had brought an economic boom. In Russia the peasants were clamoring for land reform; in America the farmers were marketing two-dollar wheat. In Russia the army was mutinous, ready to use its arms in revolutionary struggle; the American soldier wanted, above all, to go home and get out of uniform. The Russian trade unions were underground and revolutionary; the American trade unions were politically conservative and striving for respectability. The political traditions and the economic conditions of the two countries were so different that really to believe America in 1919 was soon to be the scene of revolution required either a hysterical fear of change or a hopelessly romantic and hopeful view of the revolutionary potential of the American people.

The Socialists who formed an organized caucus within the

party, the Left Wing Section of the Socialist Party, and who later bolted completely to form the Communist and Communist Labor parties had their origins in the revolutionary wing of the party. Their condemnation of gradual evolution into socialism, their disapproval of social reform within capitalism, and their opposition to parliamentary socialist action were positions they had long held. But not until after the Russian Revolution were their differences with more conservative comrades much more than academic. They now thought they saw in the success of the Bolsheviks a demonstration of the validity of their revolutionary position, and with their hallucination of imminent revolution it was logical that they immediately either convert the Socialist Party to a revolutionary position or organize a new group along revolutionary lines. Given their assumption of a revolution in the near future, it was consistent that they should do all in their power to stop the party's emphasis on political action and to discard the "immediate demands." The Left Wing had an exaggerated idea of how conservative the rest of the Socialists were,[2] but their position was, on the whole, a logical extension of their assumptions.

There were more than ideological differences between the Left Wing and the dominant Socialist group. Personality conflicts sharpened the division, and there was a significant ethnic difference between the two. The rank and file of the Left Wing and later of the two Communist parties came largely from the language federations. Immigrants from eastern Europe were naturally more sensitive to events in their home countries than older-stock Americans, and in the months just after the end of the war the various Slavic federations grew tremendously. From the 74,519 members for the year 1918, the party's membership lists grew to 108,504 just before the split the following summer, and of this total membership 57,248, or 53 per cent, were in the language federations.[3] For the first time in the history of the party, English-speaking members were in a minority. These new Slavic members were to have an overwhelming majority in the Communist Party in its early days and a significant membership in the Communist Labor Party. The leadership of the

Left Wing, however, was not very different from the Old Guard as to national origin and social position. Indeed, the charges of the Left Wing, that the Old Guard was bourgeois, were ridiculous when it is recalled that it had leaders such as the well-to-do John Reed, a former Harvard cheerleader, and the millionaire William Bross Lloyd.

Although the leadership of neither group was more proletarian than the other, there were important differences between them. With few exceptions, the Left Wing leaders had never held positions of importance in the party, and the Old Guard accused them of being motivated by personal desires for party influence. There were more important differences of personality. Although the Old Guard had a full quota of colorful personalities, there was not as much romanticism in it as there was in the Left Wing. In a list of twentieth century American romantics, John Reed could not be denied a place near the top. His impulsive, wild, undisciplined spirit at times made him an absurd figure. Once at a committee meeting of Left Wingers he presented a wild plan for storming the Atlanta Federal Penitentiary to free Debs, and he put his case with such vigor and sincerity that for an hour the committee listened to every detail. The story reveals as much about the committee as it does about Reed. An equally romantic character was "Big Jim" Larkin, an Irish Marxist who had had a fabulous career in the Irish nationalist movement. At meetings of Irish-Americans Larkin used to bare his enormous chest to show a religious medal and declare that there was no philosophical conflict between Catholicism and communism.[4] Soaring spirits such as these could never be happy in an organization dominated by such steady, stodgy, stuffy leaders as Victor Berger and Morris Hillquit. There was also a bohemian quality to many in the Left Wing—particularly the *Liberator* and *Masses* group—which never blended well with the more orthodox manners of the Old Guard. The Left thought the Right was hopelessly bourgeois, and the Right thought the Left's radicalism was more glandular than philosophical.

Although the conflict between the Left and the Old Guard did not become serious until after the end of the war, their relations were quite strained even a few months before the Armistice. The

Joint Conference of the National Executive Committee and State Secretaries in August, 1918, which was supposed to reexamine the Socialist position on the war, came to nothing because of constant bickering between the radicals and the Old Guard. It was the plan of the conference for each state secretary to report on the party's activities in his state, but many of the state officials who represented leftist elements took the opportunity to attack the National Executive Committee's general conservatism. The leftist Ohio secretary took all his allotted time to declare that the national organization's support of the Bolsheviks was disgustingly timid and that the party should adopt a revolutionary program to prepare American workers for the world revolution. Joseph Coldwell, radical state secretary of Rhode Island, taking a trick from major-party politicians who find themselves out of control of the federal government, argued that the party's power should be decentralized and that legislative power should be taken from the National Executive Committee and granted to the state secretaries. This proposal set off an argument between the Left and the Old Guard, whose position was stated by the secretaries of Illinois and Indiana, Oliver C. Wilson and William H. Henry, that quickly degenerated into name calling and irrelevant issues.[5]

It was not until the fall, however, that the Left began actively to organize against the Old Guard. On November 7, 1918, the Slavic federations of Chicago formed the Communist Propaganda League, and about a week later the Lettish Federation of Boston issued the first copy of its radical periodical *Revolutionary Age*. For the editorship of their journal, which was later to become the official organ of the Left Wing Section, the Letts selected Louis Fraina, one of the most controversial and mysterious figures in the whole radical movement. Fraina had just demonstrated his ability as a communist polemicist with his *Revolutionary Socialism*.

The unusually able and energetic Fraina, although he had been a radical for some time, was too young in 1918 to have established much of a reputation in the Socialist movement. His initiation into radicalism was with the Socialist Labor Party, and he was reputed to have been one of De Leon's favorites, but sometime before the United States entered the war he left that party to join the Socialist Party. His star quickly rose after he became editor of *Revolutionary Age*, and he was perhaps the most effective member of the Left Wing Section in bringing the final party split. In June, 1920, nearly a year after the party split amidst inspired confusion at Chicago, Santeri Nuorteva, an official in the Soviet Bureau in New York City, accused Fraina of being an agent of the federal Department of Justice. The Communist Party put Fraina on "trial" and cleared him of the charges, but many Old Guard Socialists believe yet that Fraina was a police agent whose mission was to divide the entire radical movement and thereby reduce its effectiveness. About two years after the "trial" the Communists charged him with absconding with some Third International funds and organizing a communist opposition group in Mexico. The entire and true story of Fraina remains a mystery, but it is clear that, whatever his motives, his activities were a factor in the disruption of the American Left.[6]

On February 8, 1919, *Revolutionary Age* published a Manifesto and Program of the Left Wing, and a week later the radicals of New York City organized the Left Wing Section of the Socialist Party. This organization within an organization soon had its own press, its own officers, and its own dues system. The manifesto denounced the Socialist Party for failing to convert the World War "into a civil war—into a proletarian revolution," labeled the Socialist leaders "social patriots," and called for "mass action of the revolutionary proletariat" to overthrow the capitalist state and erect a government "of the Federated Soviets." Their program set forth what they considered the proper tasks of the Socialist Party: organization of "Workmen's Councils"; worker control of industry through worker soviets; repudiation of all national debts; expropriation of all banks and railroads and the socialization of foreign trade. They further demanded that the Socialist Party abolish its "immediate demands," that it "agitate exclusively for the overthrow of capitalism, and establishment of Socialism through a proletarian dictatorship," and that it affiliate with the Bolsheviki and the German Spartacans.[7]

Although the Left Wing Section had only about one hundred members when it started, its tactics and its exploitation of the sympathy most American Socialists held for the Russian revolutionists soon had the party in New York split wide open. Meetings of Socialist locals in the city became little more than squabbles between the Left Wing and the regulars. The Left Wingers worked as a unit in meetings: no Left member introduced motions without instruction from the steering committee appointed for the meeting, the Left voted in a solid bloc, and it confused parliamentary procedure by frequent calling of points of order, roll calls, and divisions of votes.

These tactics enabled the Left Wing to "capture" enough locals so that by April it could finance a Left Wing newspaper, the *New York Communist*. John Reed as editor and Eadmonn MacAlpine as associate editor used the paper to attack the regular organization, and the Old Guard fought back by starting the *New York Socialist*, in addition to the *Call*, which had been going for years. Both newspapers were vitriolic in their attacks. A low point in the feud came when Reed and MacAlpine, in retaliation against the action of Rand School officials in banning distribution of the *Communist* in their building, put out a fake edition of the *Socialist* and circulated it there.[8]

The Left Wing Section gained control of several New York locals, but the Old Guard dominated the state committee. When that committee held its annual meeting at Albany in April, it adopted a resolution stating it was "definitely opposed to the organization calling itself the Left Wing Section of the Socialist Party," and it instructed its executive committee "to revoke the charter of any local that affiliated with any such organization or that permits its subdivisions or members to be so affiliated." Thereafter, locals that openly ratified the Left Wing Manifesto and Program or used their funds for Left Wing agitation were summarily expelled, and the state organization reorganized the local around the Old Guard minority within it. It became apparent to the Left Wing leadership that to capture the party it had to have control at the top as well as at the membership level.[9]

The Left Wing, therefore, concentrated on winning the annual spring elections to the National Executive Committee. The New York Left Wing, together with the seven language federations that had ratified the Left Wing Manifesto and Program, agreed to vote as a bloc on the slate it had selected. The election was to be conducted in the same way as a party referendum, the ballots to be distributed to the party locals on the basis of their paid-up membership and the locals to tabulate their vote and report the results to the National Executive Committee.

The campaign was unusually heated, bitter, and personal, but behind the personal attacks were significant differences of principle and policy. Although the basic issues—evolution or revolution, political democracy or proletarian dictatorship, parliamentary action or "revolutionary mass action"—were seldom debated on their merits, these differences were fundamental and important.

The Left Wing continued to attack the party's war activity, charging that the Socialist leadership had given the St. Louis Proclamation only lip service and that the party's inactivity had caused it to fail to grasp a revolutionary opportunity. To this the Old Guard replied that it had stood uncompromisingly against the war and that any label of "social patriot" should go to those Left Wingers who had begun to support the war when Germany attacked Russia after the armistice of Brest-Litovsk. Old Guard defenders pointed out that most of the Socialists who had received long prison terms were not in the Left Wing and declared that if the party's antiwar activity was not what it should have been it was because of governmental repression and not because of lack of militancy.[10]

The Left Wing charged also that the Socialist leadership was in alliance with the anti-Bolsheviks of Europe. Leftist editorials frequently called the party leaders the American counterparts of Ebert, Scheidemann, Noske, Denikin, and other European antirevolutionary leaders. These editorials even asserted that the members of the

National Executive Committee, if given public power, would murder their Left Wing comrades. The Left Wing, identifying itself with the Bolsheviks and the German Spartacans, identified its opponents with the enemies of European communism. This charge was without justification, and the Old Guard was quick to point out that it had consistently supported the Bolsheviks, condemned the Ebert-Scheidemann government of Germany, and opposed intervention in Russia. The Old Guard did not like the Bolshevik methods and did not think they were adaptable to America, but it did not support the anti-Bolsheviks.[11]

A corollary of this charge was the Left Wing's assertion that the Socialists had refused to join with the Bolsheviks in an international organization and had instead supported the Berne Conference, an attempted revival of the old Second International dominated by the British Labor Party and the German "majority" socialists. Again the Left Wing's charges were unfounded. The American party had decided to send delegates to the Berne Conference and had conducted a referendum to elect delegates. Socialists who later became Left Wingers when the movement was organized had been candidates for election as delegates, but none of them was elected. The State Department had refused passports to the elected delegates, and the National Executive Committee had had to appoint delegates who were acceptable to the Wilson administration. By the time these delegates had received their passports, the Berne Conference had already met and taken a position the National Executive Committee did not like. The committee then sent but one delegate, James Oneal, whose only mission was to inform the conference of the position of the American party, which was that it would not affiliate with any international organization that excluded the Bolsheviks. The Berne meetings were over by the time Oneal arrived in Europe, and he had refused to go to the one session he could have attended, a special meeting of a commission of the Berne Conference at Amsterdam. The American party had not joined the Third International, but it had no connection whatsoever with the anti-Bolshevik Berne Conference.[12]

Still another point of conflict between the two groups was the question of amnesty for war political prisoners. The Old Guard proposed to work with pacifist and civil liberties organizations in the campaign for amnesty, and the National Executive Committee made plans for a national amnesty convention of all groups, Socialist or not, interested in the freeing of imprisoned conscientious objectors and political prisoners. The Left Wing condemned the proposed convention as a dangerous cooperation with bourgeois forces of reaction and declared that the only proper way to free the prisoners was through revolution. The language federations that had gone into the Left Wing (the Hungarian, Lithuanian, Lettish, Russian, Polish, South Slavic, and Ukrainian) distributed a resolution they had adopted against the amnesty convention among Socialist locals all over the country, urging that other units of the party also refuse to support the plan. This opposition to the national amnesty convention within the party and a raid by Department of Justice agents, who seized all the amnesty literature, led the party to drop the project.[13]

After the balloting for the new National Executive Committee was over, but before the old committee had had time to meet, tabulate the returns from the locals, and announce the results, the Left Wing Section of New York issued a call for a national meeting of Left Wingers to be held in New York City beginning on June 21. The meeting was necessary, according to the "call" for the conference, to discuss "the conquest of the party for revolutionary Socialism" and to decide "ways and means to prevent the party aligning itself with the International of the social-patriots of the Ebert-Scheidemann gangsters and the wavering center."[14] If the feeling that such a meeting was necessary implied an admission of defeat in the National Executive Committee elections, no such admission was expressed explicitly. But while the Left was strengthening its organization the Old Guard was not idle; the party leadership was about to counterattack.

It was customary for the National Executive Committee to do most of its business by mail and telegram, but the committee held that a meeting was necessary to discuss the crisis in the party's ranks. The decisions the committee made at its meeting in Chicago in the last week of May, 1919, were perhaps the most important ones that body ever had to take. Only ten of the fifteen members attended the meeting, since two of them were in jail or defending themselves in court and three were ill. The most important absence was that of Morris Hillquit, who was at Saranac recovering from tuberculosis. Just two of the committee members, L. E. Katterfeld and Alfred Wagenknecht, were in the Left Wing; the Old Guard had almost complete control of the party at the top.

The first question the committee discussed was what to do about the seven Left Wing language federations, the radical immigrant organizations within the party that were in more or less open revolt against the party. Owing to the precedent set in the Finnish controversy in 1914, the federations were outside the disciplinary powers of the state organizations, and nothing had been done about their rebellion before the National Executive Committee met. The committee, by a straight factional vote of eight to two, decided to suspend the seven offending language federations from the party. Although the way was left open for the federations to plead their case for reinstatement before a national convention of the party, the suspension amounted to expulsion, for no one seriously expected the rebellious federations to make themselves acceptable to the Old Guard majority. If a political party can stretch its constitution in the same way as the federal government, there was constitutional justification for the National Executive Committee's action. But the suspension was certainly unprecedented. The committee majority stated these grounds for their action: the seven federations, in actively opposing the national amnesty convention, had assumed the power to reverse the decision of the National Executive Committee, next to a national convention the supreme authority of the party; the suspended bodies had conducted a campaign against the party in its press with the ultimate objective of destroying the party; and, in joining the Left Wing Section, the seven federations had violated that section of the party constitution that forbade "fusing, combining, or compromising with any political party or organization," a provision that had been inserted to prevent local Socialist groups from combining with non-Socialists in local contests. This suspension affected 25,000 to 30,000 Socialists, few of whom were ever recovered for the party. Here and there a state organization offered to accept individuals or even locals from the suspended federations on the condition that they sever all connections with their federation and subscribe to the principles and constitution of the Socialist Party. But the few federation members who were not already in the Left Wing were alienated by what they considered the NEC's high-handed action, and few accepted the offer.[15]

The National Executive Committee next considered the case of the Michigan Socialist organization, which, although it had not joined the Left Wing, had in a recent state convention inserted into its constitution a provision which made any Michigan Socialist who advocated the "immediate demands" of the national platform liable to expulsion from the state organization. The convention had also passed a resolution urging party speakers to take a firm and hostile attitude toward religion, which was in opposition to party policy for reasons of political discretion even though many Old Guard leaders were personally opposed to organized religion. On the motion of Committeeman Seymour Stedman, the National Executive Committee voted seven to three to revoke the charter of the Michigan state organization and to reorganize the state along lines more in keeping with the Old Guard point of view. The vote was seven to three instead of a straight factional eight to two because one Old Guard member argued that the committee had as yet no official information on the action of the Michigan convention.[16] Although the action of the Michigan convention was in direct opposition to the national platform of the party, and although Michigan's action put those who supported the national platform out of the party, the National Executive Committee's expulsion of Michigan in time turned out to be a mistake from its own point of view. It later developed that the Michigan Socialists were not nearly so radical as their convention action indicated. Two Left Wing Michigan leaders, Dennis

E. Batt and John Keracher, had pushed the antireform measure through the convention, and it is not unlikely that the Michigan organization would have stayed in the party when the communist split finally came if it had not been for the NEC's quick and drastic action. But because of the expulsion Michigan Socialists quickly went to the most radical faction of the Left Wing, only to discover soon that their new comrades were considerably too radical for their taste.

In the disposal of the language federations and Michigan questions the committee had suspended or expelled about 30,000 to 35,000 Socialist members, and the Left Wing would have considered the committee's action a declaration of war if it had stopped at that. But the most drastic action was yet to come in the committee's decision on the recent elections for a new committee.

A check of the reported vote from the locals showed the Left Wing candidates for the National Executive Committee had won a sweeping victory, but some of the members of the committee had heard "rumors" of fraud in the election, particularly in the voting in the language federations. They had, accordingly, asked the Executive Secretary, Adolph Germer, to ask the language federations for the ballots. Only a few of the federations complied. The committee reported there were gross irregularities in the ballots it had seen— voters had signed their names to ballots that had already been marked, some ballots had been marked to indicate how the member should vote, some locals had not tabulated the vote accurately—and the committee assumed there were even greater irregularities in the ballots that had not been sent to national headquarters. The committee consequently, again by a vote of eight to two, declared the election null and void and ruled that the new National Executive Committee should be elected by a special Emergency Convention to be held at Chicago beginning August 30.[17]

The day after the National Executive Committee closed its meetings, the Socialists of Massachusetts met in convention. The Left Wing members of the National Committee sent a telegram to the convention informing the Massachusetts Socialists that the National Committee majority had "autocratically held up the national referendums to perpetuate themselves in office" and asking the Bay State comrades to "Help us reverse these outrageous actions." This was the first news of the nullification of the election to reach the membership, and the information did not sit well with the Massachusetts Socialists. Their convention quickly voted to send two delegates to the National Conference of the Left Wing, which had been called to meet at New York on June 21st. When this motion passed, sixty-eight Old Guard delegates bolted the convention and asked the National Executive Committee to recognize them as the Socialist Party of Massachusetts. The National Committee was quick to comply. When the news from Massachusetts reached Committeeman Hogan at his home in Arkansas, he wired a motion to national headquarters to the effect that the Massachusetts charter should be revoked and that Executive Secretary Germer should immediately reorganize the state. Within three days a majority of the National Executive Committee telegraphed their approval of the motion to Germer, and one more state was out of the Socialist Party.[18]

Between these expulsions and the meeting of the Left Wing in New York on June 21st, the Left Wing worked frantically against the National Committee. The Ohio party, which was dominated by the Left Wing, organized a press service to present its point of view, and Local Cuyahoga County (Cleveland) tried to institute a party referendum to reverse the National Committee's action in suspending the language federations and expelling Michigan. The local's officers distributed hundreds of mimeographed seconds of their motion for a referendum among other party locals, urging that other party units also work to annul the leadership's actions. The National Committee delayed action on the proposed referendum until early July, when it defeated the motion to put Cleveland's motion to a referendum on the grounds that the motion contained editorial comment, which was forbidden by Article 13, Section 3, of the party constitution. The Left Wing now cried that the Old Guard's practice of democracy was not equal to its profession of democratic principles; the Old Guard replied, through Executive Secretary

Germer, that the editorial comment had been placed in the motion purposely, with knowledge that it was unconstitutional, so that the National Committee would not send the motion to referendum and the Left Wing could charge the committee with autocratic proce- dure.[19] Paradoxically, throughout 1919 the Old Guard, which ex- tolled political democracy, resorted to monolithic tactics, and the Left Wing, which scorned political democracy as "bourgeois," con- demned the Old Guard for being undemocratic.

When the National Conference of the Left Wing opened in New York on June 21, there were ninety-four delegates in attend- ance, representing twenty states, although most of the delegates were from the seven suspended language federations or Michigan, Massachusetts, Ohio, or New York. The conference began conserva- tively enough when it elected its chairman, William Bross Lloyd, the wealthy son of the author of *Wealth Against Commonwealth*.[20] But the conference soon showed its revolutionary character when it adopted the report of the labor committee, written by John Reed. "The purpose of the left-wing organization is to create a revolu- tionary working-class movement in America, which, through the action of the working masses themselves, will lead to workers' con- trol of industry and the state, as the only means of expropriating capitalist property and abolishing classes in society . . . . the work- ers can only win the state power by extra-parliamentary action, which must have its basis in the industrial mass action of the workers."

The delegates agreed on their ultimate purpose, but there was little agreement as to method. The language federations and the Michigan delegation, being already outside the Socialist Party, wanted the immediate formation of a communist party. The others wanted to remain within the Socialist Party to try to win control of it at the Emergency Convention, to begin at Chicago on August 30. This group, led by Reed and Fraina, argued that forming a separate party immediately would antagonize Socialists who, although out of sympathy with the National Executive Committee, wanted to pre- serve the party's unity. They agreed, however, that if they failed to get control of the convention they would then organize a new party. The conference defeated the motion to organize a new party immediately by fifty-five to thirty-eight, whereupon thirty-one delegates from Michigan and the language federations bolted the meeting.

Those who remained called another conference to meet in Chicago concurrently with the Emergency Convention of the Socialist Party. Meanwhile, the direction of the Left Wing Section was to be in the hands of a National Council composed of I. E. Ferguson (national secretary), John Ballan, Maximilian Cohen, Benjamin Gitlow, James Larkin, C. E. Ruthenberg, and Bertram D. Wolfe. The conference made the *Revolutionary Age*, which had been started by the Lettish Federation, whose delegates had just bolted the conference, the official organ of the Left Wing, and they allowed that periodical's editors, Fraina and MacAlpine, to remain.

Within three weeks after the close of the conference the seceders announced in *Novy Mir*, the Chicago publication of the Russian Federation, the formation of the Communist Party of America and called the new party's first convention for Chicago on September 1st. They stamped the Left Wing majority as "centrists, struggling for a false unity," and declared that remaining within the Socialist Party for the rest of the summer would only postpone the revolution. Fraina, in the *Revolutionary Age*, defended the decision not to split from the Socialist Party immediately and predicted that no good would come from the alliance of the language federations and what he called the "Michigan Mensheviks," but soon thereafter he, Ferguson, and others of the National Council of the Left Wing deserted that organization and went over to the new Communist Party. Reed, MacAlpine, and Gitlow stuck to their decision to try to capture the Socialist Party.[21]

During the late spring and early summer the Left Wing had been doing its utmost to get possession of the ballots that had been cast in the election for a new National Executive Committee. By mid-July it had returns from twenty-six states and the District of Columbia, which, the Left Wing declared, showed that its candidates had won the election by a large margin. L. E. Katterfeld, Left Wing member of the regular National Executive Committee, then submitted a motion that the "new" National Committee meet in Chicago and instructed Executive Secretary Germer to wire the motion to the men whom the Left Wing had declared elected. Germer refused, and thereafter he stayed in the national headquarters twenty-four hours a day, suspecting that the Left Wing had plans to take over by force. The Left Wing did not try to storm the national office, but on July 26th the Left Wing candidates met in Cleveland, proclaimed themselves the "real National Executive Committee of the Socialist Party," and reinstated all the groups that had been expelled or suspended, some of whom had already formed a new party. The "New" National Committee elected Alfred Wagenknecht as its Executive Secretary.

Thus, by August 1, 1919, there was the confusing spectacle of four executive committees. In the order of their establishment they were: the regular National Executive Committee of the Socialist Party, with control of the national office in Chicago; the National Council of the Left Wing Section of the Socialist Party, with headquarters in New York; the executive committee of the newly formed Communist Party of America, the alliance of language federations and Michigan "Mensheviks," with headquarters in Chicago; and the "new" National Executive Committee of the Socialist Party, declared valid by the Left Wing, with headquarters in Cleveland. Fortunately for the historian of Socialist politics, in mid-August this last group gave up the game they were playing and again turned their attention to capturing the Emergency Socialist Convention, just two weeks away.[22]

While the short-lived "new" National Executive Committee was operating from Cleveland, the old committee in Chicago was active. On the motion of Fred Krafft of New Jersey, the National Committee put the Ohio Socialists among the exiles of Michigan, Massachusetts, and the language federations. The grounds for this action were the same as for the Massachusetts expulsion: affiliation with the Left Wing Section, plus a charge of financial irregularity.

To finance the approaching Emergency Convention, the National Committee had announced a special assessment of the membership through the sale of convention stamps, these special stamps to be pasted in each member's membership book along with his dues stamps. The proceeds of the sale of these stamps were to be sent to the national office, there to be divided equally among the Emergency Convention delegates for their expenses. A convention of Ohio Socialists had instructed their treasurer to keep the proceeds of these stamps and to divide the money among the Ohio delegates. Again, the expulsion motion contained an order for the Executive Secretary to reorganize the expelled state.[23]

The last week in August, 1919, saw all varieties of Marxists converging on Chicago to hold national conventions. The Socialist Old Guard and the Left Wing were going to battle each other for control of the Emergency Convention, to be held in Machinists Hall, beginning on August 30th. The seven language federations, the Michigan "Mensheviks," and several dissenting Left Wingers were going to the first convention of the Communist Party of America, beginning on September 1st in the hall of the Chicago Russian Federation, by then called Smolny Institute out of respect for their Soviet comrades. Chicago had not seen such confusion as was about to occur since the great railway strike in 1894.

On Friday night, August 29th, the Left Wing met in caucus on the ground floor of Machinists Hall, which it had rented for such purposes. The Socialist Party had rented the auditorium on the second floor. The fifty-two Left Wingers in this downstairs billiard and bar room made their plans for capturing the convention that was to meet the next morning. They elected Ruthenberg, who logically should not have been at the meeting since he had signed the call for the Communist Party convention, Gitlow, Katterfeld, and Reed to a steering committee, which they agreed should make all the decisions on the convention floor, and they agreed to vote as a unit on all matters. They adjourned after agreeing to be in the convention hall upstairs by nine-thirty the next morning, before the convention was scheduled to start.[24]

Unfortunately for the Left Wing, the secretary of the caucus left his notes for the minutes on a table in the barroom. The janitor of the building, who was also the bartender and a friend of Executive Secretary Germer since the two had been coal miners together in the Southern Illinois field, found these notes and, recognizing their value, turned them over to Germer. Germer had the notes mimeographed and distributed among the Old Guard delegates so that whatever advantage the Left Wing's secrecy afforded was destroyed.

Sometime during the evening before the convention a reporter from the *Chicago Tribune* interviewed Alfred Wagenknecht, who had been Executive Secretary of the Cleveland National Committee and who was slated to have that office again should the Left Wing win in the convention. Wagenknecht told the reporter that the Left Wing was organized so that, if necessary, it would "take over the convention by storm." The reporter relayed this information to a city detective, and the next morning a detail of Chicago police was in the convention hall.[25]

The Old Guard had appointed Julius Gerber of Brooklyn as the head of a small squad to go to the convention hall early Saturday morning to see that only accredited delegates took seats on the convention floor proper and that visitors and contested delegates stayed behind a railing that divided the gallery from the main part of the auditorium. When Gerber and his squad arrived they found that John Reed and several other Left Wingers had already taken seats in the front of the hall. Reed was the only Left Winger present whom Gerber knew, and Gerber told him that he must move to the area behind the railing since Reed's seat was contested. Reed's seat was in doubt because the party constitution required that convention delegates must have been party members for at least three years, and Reed had not joined the party until the summer of 1917. Indeed, he had voted for Wilson in 1916. Reed refused to move, and when Gerber tried forcibly to put him behind the railing the two began fighting. Reed stayed on the convention side of the railing.[26]

National Committeeman George Goebel ran the one block

down South Ashland Street to national party headquarters and told
Adolph Germer of the presence of the Left Wingers. Germer went
to the hall and told Reed he must move. Again Reed refused, jumped
on a chair, and told the assembled Left Wingers: "Don't go out.
Make the police put you out." Germer asked the sergeant in charge
of the police detail to put out the Left Wingers, and the sergeant,
probably quite bewildered by the whole affair, decided to clear
everyone from the hall and begin anew. While the police were clear-
ing the hall, L. E. Katterfeld, Left Wing member of the National
Committee, remarked that things could not have worked out better
from the Left Wing point of view. After the hall was cleared only
those delegates whose credentials had been countersigned by Germer were allowed on the convention side of the railing.[27]

When the big, raw-boned Germer, one of the few leaders in
any wing of the radical movement who looked like an artist's conception of a proletarian, could finally call the convention to order,
the first order of business was the election of a chairman and convention committees. For chairman the Old Guard nominated Seymour Stedman, a Chicago attorney who had been active defending
Socialists in the war cases and who was a member of the National
Committee, and the Left Wing named Joseph Coldwell of Rhode
Island. The futility of the Left Wing hope of capturing the convention became apparent when Stedman won the election 88 to 37.
The Old Guard likewise won the elections to the important Committee on Contests, which would judge whether or not to seat delegates whose credentials were doubtful. Until Monday, September
1st, the deliberations of this committee were the focus of the convention.

The delegates whose seats were contested, all of them from the
Left Wing, met with the Committee on Contests, and the committee
considered each case on its own merits. Fourteen of the twenty-nine
contested delegates won seats. The Ohio delegation appeared before
the committee to claim its seats, but it quit its cause before the case
was decided.

It soon became obvious to the Left Wing that it would not have a majority of the convention even if it won all the contested seats. Accordingly, and consistent with their preconvention plans, Joseph Coldwell announced on Sunday afternoon, before the Committee on Contests had considered all the cases, that all Left Wing delegates were to bolt the convention. Some of them rejected the decision and stayed to fight it out on the convention floor; by Sunday evening only twenty-six delegates had left.[28]

On Sunday night the bolting delegates, the Ohio delegation, and some Left Wingers from the convention gallery met in the downstairs billiard room. Reverting to their old tactic of claiming to be the "real Socialist Party," this downstairs group declared their meeting to be "on behalf of the newly elected Executive Committee of the Socialist Party." This tactic, used for about five weeks earlier in the summer, was this time to be used but two days. Marguerite Prevy, the presiding officer, and William Bross Lloyd, the sergeant at arms, had little success in keeping the meeting orderly. When C. E. Ruthenberg, still around Machinists Hall, although he logically belonged out at Smolny Institute, moved that the group's first action should be to consider unity with the Communist Party, whose first convention was to begin the next morning, the meeting broke into a noisy dispute that lasted until one o'clock in the morning. John Reed argued that the downstairs group was the real heart of the American communist movement and that, instead of considering unity with the language federations at Smolny Institute, the language federation should join their group. Louis B. Boudin asserted that the leaders of the Smolny Institute group had sabotaged every revolutionary movement they had ever been in and that the wisest procedure was to ignore them. After hours of heated argument, the downstairs convention appointed a committee to confer with the Communist Party, but it did not commit itself to a merger.[29]

The next morning the Communist Party convention at Smolny Institute got off to an exciting start with a raid by the Chicago police, who tore down decorations and placards and arrested Dennis E. Batt of Michigan. Rose Pastor Stokes protested, crying: "They are arresting our comrades. Three cheers for the revolution." A police sergeant, probably unaware that he was speaking to the wife of a railroad president, told her: "Shut up. It's always a woman that starts the trouble." But a police raid could not dampen the revolutionary spirit of this convention. It continued with its meeting, which soon developed into a row over what to do about the committee from the downstairs convention. I. E. Ferguson, former secretary of the Left Wing National Council, introduced a resolution that they meet with the delegation from the downstairs convention with a view to unification of the two groups. Louis Fraina spoke for the resolution, but a majority of the delegates agreed with Nicholas Hourwich, who argued that the downstairs convention was too conservative for the Communist Party's consideration. The convention defeated the resolution 75 to 31. The next day the English-speaking groups, most of whom were from Michigan, forced reconsideration of the question by resigning as a body from the convention committees and by threatening to bolt entirely. The convention agreed then to appoint a committee to confer with the committee from the downstairs convention, but the two groups could not agree until a year later, when they founded the United Communist Party.[30]

The Michigan delegation rebelled again over the adoption of a party program. The language-federation majority favored a program that sharply denounced any kind of political action and that called for a dictatorship of the proletariat. With this the "Michigan Mensheviks" could not agree. They had parted company with the Socialists over the question of reforms within capitalism, and they were by no means ready to reject political action altogether. They also rejected the dictatorship of the proletariat. When their efforts failed to get the convention to amend the phrase to "dictatorship of the majority," they refused to take part in any more convention votes, although they did not bolt. This was the beginning of still another split. A few weeks after the convention the Communist Party expelled the Michigan group, which then formed the Proletarian Party.[31]

Meanwhile, the downstairs convention, failing to reach any agreement with the Smolny Institute crowd, moved out of its bil-

liard room to the IWW hall on Throop Street, there to form a new
party which took the name Communist Labor Party. The Communist Labor Party convention was to be scarcely more harmonious
than the proceedings in Smolny Institute or Machinists Hall. The
chief controversy in this convention was a plank in the platform
committee's report that urged the workers to join with the Communist Labor Party "in the political field." John Reed argued against
this recognition of political action, as did most of the leaders who
had been in the Left Wing since its organization. Joseph Coldwell,
however, said that if he were against political action "he would do
the sensible thing—resign from a political organization and join the
I.W.W." Some of the delegates had never been in the Left Wing
and had left the Socialist convention only because they thought the
Socialist Party's conduct had been too arbitrary and drastic. These
delegates agreed with Coldwell, and when the revolutionists defeated the political action plank 41 to 28, many of them bolted for
the second time within a week. When Louis B. Boudin bolted the
convention he fired a parting shot with which many a bewildered
Socialist might have agreed: "I did not leave a party of crooks to
join a party of lunatics." [32]

With most of their dissident elements gone, the Communist
Laborites in the convention went on to write a platform not very
different from the program the Communist Party was putting together at Smolny Institute. The Communist Labor Party declared its
intention to affiliate with the Third International, declared that it
was in the midst of "the period of the dissolution and collapse of the
whole system of world capitalism," prohibited any association with
any political groups not wholeheartedly for the "revolutionary class
struggle," and committed itself to "only one demand: the establishment of the dictatorship of the proletariat." But despite the similarity of the programs of the Communist and Communist Labor
parties, personal animosities and mutual distrust kept the two groups
at each other's throats for months to come.[33]

At the time of the Armistice in November, 1918, the Socialist
Party had been the big tent of American radicalism, having inside it

everything from the Bolshevism of a Fraina to the municipal reform of a Berger. By the end of the conventions at Chicago the following summer, there were three parties where there had been one before, none of them very strong and all competing for the loyalties of working-class Americans, who for the most part ignored all of them. The Socialist Party was still the strongest party on the American Left despite its losses, and this organization, the parent of them all, was changing too, as was evidenced by the actions of the Emergency Convention after the various kinds of communists had left.

VII

FROM LEFT TO RIGHT

1919–1925

WHILE Left Wing seceders were organizing new parties and issuing revolutionary manifestoes in other parts of Chicago, the Socialist Convention in Machinists Hall was behaving in a rather unpredictable manner. Instead of taking a swing to the right, as might be expected now that it had lost its most radical elements, the Socialist convention was putting together as militant a program as the organization had ever had in its prewar days.

The Wisconsin delegation was the furthest right in the Emergency Convention, but it was not a very active force. Victor Berger was thoroughly disgusted with the course Socialist politics had taken and had given up hope for the party. "What the outcome of our convention in Chicago will be," he wrote ten days before the convention, "I don't know and I don't care—because Wisconsin is in a good position to go it alone for a while, and to form a new center for crystallization." [1] More interested in local than in national Socialist politics, Berger and his followers did little to restrain their more radical comrades.

The large New York delegation was more radical at this convention than it had ever been before, and, although Hillquit was still at Saranac Lake recovering from tuberculosis, it reflected its leader's views. Hillquit in 1919 was not nearly so conservative as the Left Wing declared. When the Left Wing Section was formed in February, Hillquit remained quiet for weeks despite National Secretary

Germer's urging to attack the Left. He even criticized his party for lack of militancy. His biographer tells us that "Hillquit did not view the split with too great concern. . . . For the time being, he was tolerant of the Bolshevik tactics in Russia." When Hillquit finally did go into combat against the Left Wingers in an article, "The Socialist Task and Outlook," for the *New York Call,* he made no vicious attack on them. He did not criticize the Bolsheviks nor defend the European parties in the Berne Conference. He called upon Socialists to be more militant, and declared that his opposition to the Left Wing was "not because it is too radical, but because it is essentially reactionary; not because it would lead us too far, but because it would lead us nowhere." Putting his finger on an important aspect of the Left Wing movement, he wrote that it was "a purely emotional reflex of the situation in Russia." [2] The position of Hillquit's followers in the Chicago convention was similar: opposition to the Left Wing, but increased militancy for the Socialist Party.

The New York delegation, and a smaller and more radical group led by John Louis Engdahl, former editor of the *Daily Socialist* of Chicago, demanded that the National Executive Committee explain in detail its actions in expelling three state organizations, suspending seven language federations, and nullifying the election for a new National Executive Committee. Engdahl refused to accept as final the explanations the committee made in its prepared report to the convention, which, incidentally, Hillquit had not signed.[3]

The National Executive Committee, accordingly, went into greater detail on each of the suspensions and expulsions, quoting Left Wing documents and the portions of the party constitution it had invoked. The convention's reaction to the further explanation was to pass a resolution stating that some kind of discipline had been needed, but that the NEC had not done enough "to acquaint the membership of the suspended and expelled organizations with the facts and endeavored to have them repudiate their officials." The resolution was no confirmation of the NEC's actions. Furthermore, the convention amended the party constitution to create a Board of Appeals to hear any charges that might lead to suspension or expulsion, should such a situation ever arise again. The convention elected a special committee to weigh the evidence on the alleged election frauds. The committee reported that in its opinion the election had indeed been fraudulent and that the NEC had been justified in nullifying it. The convention accepted this committee's report unanimously, but it agreed informally that few, if any, members of the old National Executive Committee should be elected to the new one, and to assure that decision it amended the constitution so that the convention would henceforth elect the NEC, rather than the entire party membership through a referendum. Oneal was the only member reelected.[4]

The convention did not change fundamentally any of the party's historic positions, but it did emphasize the need for increased militancy. It added a preamble to the constitution that declared the party's purpose. In this preamble the reformist demands were declared "subordinate and accessory to . . . [the party's] fundamental aim," which was "to bring about the social ownership and democratic control of all the necessary means of production—to eliminate profit, rent and interest, and make it impossible for any to share the product without sharing the burden of labor." The convention also issued a manifesto—in itself a departure from tradition—which promised "constant, clear-cut and aggressive opposition to all parties of the possessing classes," and which urged organized labor to organize along industrial rather than along craft lines, showing a disregard for the opinion of the AFL leadership which had seldom before been so blunt in official statements.

The party's membership, as well as its representatives in the 1919 convention, was swinging to the left. The convention's Committee on International Relations submitted a majority and a minority report. The majority report repudiated the Berne Conference and called for the creation of a new International to which "must be invited the Communist parties of Russia and Germany and those Socialist parties in all countries which subscribe to the principle of the class struggle." John Louis Engdahl and a fellow Illinois comrade, William Kruse, wrote the minority report. They called upon the party to join the new Third or Moscow International, "not so much because it [the Socialist Party] supports the 'Moscow' programs and methods, but because: (*a*) 'Moscow' is doing something which is really challenging world imperialism. (*b*) 'Moscow' is threatened by the combined capitalist forces of the world simply because it is proletarian. (*c*) Under these circumstances, whatever we may have to say to 'Moscow' afterwards, it is the duty of Socialists to stand by it now." The 1919 convention put the two reports to a referendum, which was not completed until January, 1920. The Socialist Party's membership voted 3,475 to 1,444 to adopt the minority report, to join the Third International.[5] In March the National Secretary applied to the Executive Committee of the Third International for the party's admission. The letter was never officially answered.

The history of the Socialists' attempts to affiliate internationally during the early 1920's is a long and tortuous one. At the May, 1920, convention of the party in New York City the Committee on International Relations again was split. The majority report called the Third International "virile and aggressive, inspired . . . by the militant idealism of the Russian revolution." But, it held, the Third International was "at this time only a nucleus of a Socialist International, and its progress is largely impeded by the attitude of its present governing committee, which seems inclined to impose upon all affiliated bodies the formula of the Russian revolution, 'The dictatorship of the proletariat in the form of soviet power.'" The majority report ended by recommending affiliation with the Third International if Moscow should relax its attitude toward dictatorship of the proletariat and urging the formation of an international embracing all "true Socialist forces." Engdahl and Kruse, together with Benjamin Glassberg, submitted a report calling upon the party to affiliate with the Moscow organization without any reservations. Victor Berger submitted still a third report. He was against playing any further at all with Moscow. When the majority and Engdahl reports were put to a referendum, the membership voted 1,339 to 1,301 to adopt the majority report, indicating that leftist strength in the party had waned since the referendum of the previous year.

Soon after the 1920 convention Engdahl organized a Committee for the Third International within the party. At the 1921 convention at Detroit the National Executive Secretary, Otto Branstetter, moved the expulsion from the party of all who favored the party's affiliation with the Third International. The resolution was overwhelmingly defeated, but not because the convention favored such affiliation. In fact, the convention defeated 35 to 4 a resolution to affiliate with Moscow without reservations, defeated 26 to 13 a resolution to affiliate with reservations, and defeated 35 to 4 a motion to affiliate with the Vienna group, one of the remnants of the old Second International. The party decided its primary task was to rebuild the party. International affiliation could be postponed until the party was stronger.[6]

But by the time of this convention in June, 1921, there was little else the party could have done. The Third International at its second congress in 1920 had written its famous twenty-one points as conditions for affiliation. In order to join the Third International a party had to renounce all its social democratic ideals and become a communist party of the Bolshevik mold. Had the American Socialists joined they would have had to work for the dictatorship of the proletariat, conduct revolutionary activities in the army, change their party's name, organize an illegal revolutionary underground, and agree to accept all decisions of the International's executive committee, including those having to do with purely domestic questions. Point seven of the twenty-one specifically condemned Hillquit as a "notorious opportunist." It is clear that the Third International wanted no connection with the Socialists. Gregory Zinoviev, president of the International, was reported to have said that the leaders at the second congress had taxed their minds to think of even more demanding conditions for affiliation, but that their "inventive faculties could do no more."[7]

The Socialist Party at its 1922 convention at Cleveland voted to join the Vienna group. The Vienna group merged with the London International, another remnant of the Second International, and became the Labor and Socialist International, sometimes called the Two-and-a-half International. At this organization's meeting at Hamburg in 1923, Hillquit and Berger were elected to the International's Executive Committee.[8]

During this period when the American Socialists were working out their relationships with European leftist parties, Eugene Debs ran one of his most successful races for the Presidency, doing all his campaigning from within the walls of Atlanta Penitentiary. Socialists began to talk of nominating Debs again, although he was imprisoned, almost from the time that he began to serve his sentence.[9] Debs's nomination, despite the handicap of not being able to stump the country, had certain advantages. He was well known in all parts of the nation, his wartime record was attractive to non-Socialist pacifists, and the novelty of a candidate's running from prison might attract free publicity. Besides, there was no one else in the party, in jail or out, who would make as good a candidate. Benson, the only other man the Socialists had ever nominated for President, had done miserably in 1916. Morris Hillquit and Victor Berger were the only Socialists besides Debs with a national reputation, and they were ineligible for the White House because of their foreign birth.

When the Socialists met in convention at the Finnish Socialist Hall in Harlem, New York City, in May, 1920, they were still a far from harmonious organization. A Left Wing still remained within the party. It wanted unconditional affiliation with the Third International and hoped to mold America along Bolshevik lines. The two groups fought over the writing of the platform. The Left Wingers fought for a plank calling for a soviet form of representation, representation by occupations instead of by geographical districts. They finally compromised on a plank calling for representation from occupational groups "as well as geographical groups," a compromise that would have been most confusing to implement if ever the Socialists wrote a new national constitution. But the Left and Right wings could join in enthusiastically supporting Debs for the nomination. After William H. Henry of Indiana nominated Debs in a speech in which he called him the "Lincoln of the Wabash" and Hillquit seconded the nomination, the enthusiastic delegates put on a spontaneous demonstration that lasted for twenty-five minutes. No other

Socialist's name was mentioned for the nomination. The Left Wing wanted to nominate Kate Richards O'Hare, who was also in prison, as Debs's running mate, but the convention defeated the proposal 106 to 26 in favor of Seymour Stedman, a Chicago lawyer, on the grounds that at least one of the candidates should be free to campaign. And, as Oscar Ameringer facetiously suggested: "A lawyer is the only man whom the Socialist Party can nominate at this time. He knows just what to say and say it well and keep out of jail at the same time." [10]

During the campaign the Socialists rode the issue of amnesty for the wartime "political prisoners" very hard. One plank in the platform called for the repeal of the Espionage Act and its amendments, the cessation of further prosecutions under the act, and the release of all prisoners convicted under it. Immediately after adjourning, the entire convention went to Washington to do what it could to persuade the administration to release Debs and the others in prison. A committee headed by Stedman, who had defended Debs in the Cleveland trial, called upon Attorney General A. Mitchell Palmer and received a respectful hearing. Then the whole convention, nearly two hundred people, called at the White House. They were unable to see President Wilson, and his secretary Joseph Tumulty gave them no more satisfaction than that the President would give their plea "conscientious consideration." Socialists were more successful in finding sympathizers in their campaign for amnesty in Congress. In the Senate Joseph I. France of Maryland and Robert L. Owen of Oklahoma introduced resolutions urging amnesty to Espionage Act prisoners, and their resolutions were vigorously supported by Senator Asle J. Gronna of North Dakota. Representative Edward Voigt of Sheboygan, Wisconsin, introduced a similar resolution in the House. All the resolutions remained lost in the respective committees on the judiciary. [11]

During the campaign other minor left-of-center political groups came out for Debs's release. The Montana Non-Partisan League not only urged his release; it endorsed his actions during the war. Parley P. Christensen, the presidential candidate of the new Farmer-Labor

Party, which was making its first bid for national office, wired to the major-party presidential candidates suggesting the three of them unite in asking Wilson to release Debs. Christensen argued that the rightness or wrongness of Debs's opposition to the war was of no matter now that the war was over. Apparently a great many people agreed with Christensen. Newsreels of Debs, dressed in prison uniform, accepting the Socialist nomination, brought applause in New York theaters, much to the annoyance of a *New York Times* editorial writer.

Running a campaign from a prison cell proved to have serious disadvantages. Debs had no systematic way of getting his views to the public. Not until September was he allowed to release press statements regularly, and then the Department of Justice restricted him to five hundred words a week.[12] Debs had always been considerably more effective on the public platform than he was in print, where his florid prose, seen with a cold eye, sometimes seemed a trifle ridiculous, and of course public speeches were impossible during the campaign.

One incident in the campaign deserves mention as a note on political foolishness. Late in the campaign Mrs. Charles Edward Russell, wife of the muckraking former Socialist journalist and herself a prominent woman suffragist, perhaps elated beyond reason by the recent ratification of the nineteenth amendment, declared she had received a visit from the spirit of Susan B. Anthony. The ghost of Miss Anthony, it appears, dropped in at the headquarters of the National Woman's Party in Washington and urged her fellow militant suffragists to cast their first presidential ballots for Eugene V. Debs.[13]

It is doubtful if this ethereal exhortation had much to do with it, but Debs polled 915,302 votes, the largest vote he ever received. This large vote, however, was only about 3.5 per cent of the total vote cast, considerably below the nearly 6 per cent Debs had received in 1912. The total vote in 1920 was unprecedentedly large because it was the first time women had been allowed to vote in all states. Still, it was an impressive vote for a federal prisoner to receive, particularly so since the party's membership had dwindled to only 26,766 and less than $50,000 was spent in the campaign. The large Debs vote was a reflection of Debs's personal popularity and a reaction against the repressionary actions of the Wilson administration rather than an endorsement of the Socialist program. In many states the third-party vote was not far behind the Democratic vote, indicating there was considerable dissatisfaction with the Wilson administration. Debs would probably have done much better if he had had behind him the kind of organization the Socialists had before the war. His guess was probably too high, but Theodore Debs, Gene's devoted brother and secretary, estimated after election day that with the organization the party had in 1912 the 1920 vote would have been three million.[14]

In the congressional elections the Socialists again returned one of their members to Washington. Berger lost in his Milwaukee district—the one that had elected him twice for the previous term only to have him denied his seat by a hysterical Congress—but Meyer London regained the seat from Manhattan he had lost in 1916 to Fiorello La Guardia. If the Socialists had cooperated with the Farmer-Labor Party they could have had another seat in Congress from New York. In the New York 18th Congressional District the Democratic incumbent, John F. Carew, won by only about two thousand votes. The Farmer-Labor candidate in that district, Jeremiah O'Leary, ran a very good race, almost equaling the Republican vote. If the Socialist candidate in the district had not diverted more than five thousand protest votes, O'Leary would have won handily. Incidentally, the New York newspapers did not report the vote cast for O'Leary.[15]

There was considerable sympathy for the Socialists in their struggle against the prosecutions and persecutions of the Wilson administration. The 1920 vote, at a time when the party's membership rolls were shrinking, is evidence of that sympathy, but better evidence of popular displeasure with the administration's attitude toward the Socialists is to be seen in the strong popular response to the party's campaign for the release of "political prisoners." The Socialist organization was weaker than it had ever been since its earliest days, but it was successful in getting thousands and thousands of people to petition the administration to release Debs and others convicted under the Espionage Act. The Pardon Attorney in the Department of Justice filled twenty-two large file boxes with correspondence urging Debs's release. The *Appeal* sent in four huge petitions, signed by thousands. Early in the Harding administration the Socialists organized an Amnesty Day in Washington. They presented two long petitions for Debs's release to President Harding, rolled up on cable reels, that had been signed by over three hundred thousand people. They also presented endorsements of amnesty made by seven hundred organizations claiming a total membership of three million.[16]

Organized labor, although generally as opposed to the Socialists' plans for society as ever, tried to use its influence in Washington to effect amnesty. During the election campaign of 1920 a delegation of labor leaders, including Samuel Gompers for the American Federation of Labor and Meyer London for the United Hebrew Trades of New York City, called upon Attorney General Palmer and urged him to pardon those imprisoned under the Espionage Act. The next month officers of many of the AFL's constituent unions informed the White House they hoped the administration would be magnanimous and release the "political prisoners." Among the labor leaders sending these messages were William H. Johnston, president of the machinists, and Daniel J. Tobin, president of the teamsters. Gompers was not backward about lending his prestige to the movement to release Debs. The Executive Council of the AFL reported to the convention at Montreal in 1920 that, while it did not approve the conduct of Debs and others during the war, it did believe that justice had already been served and that "It is not democratic to inflict continued punishment for the mere sake of punishing." Gompers wrote to President Wilson that no good purpose was served by keeping Debs in prison two years after the Armistice, and in September, 1921, the AFL chief went to the Atlanta Penitentiary to visit Debs.[17]

Many liberal intellectuals did what they could to persuade the administration to release Debs. Clarence Darrow wrote to Wilson that "to keep in prison one who felt it his duty to disagree, after the war had passed, would not be self-defense but a punishment undeserved." Norman Hapgood, formerly Wilson's minister to Denmark, reported to the President that the Debs case was alienating the Democrats from some of that party's most influential progressive friends and that he felt compelled to arouse public opinion in Debs's behalf. Soon after the Armistice John P. Gavit, an editor of the New York *Evening Post* and of Harper and Brothers, suggested to Wilson that he could "uplift and electrify the liberal forces in this and other countries" by granting an "immediate and unconditional amnesty for all those persons who have been convicted for expression of opinion." In the closing days of the Wilson administration the feminist Harriot Stanton Blatch urged Wilson to release Debs before he left the White House.[18]

It appears that it was the obstinacy of President Wilson himself that held up Debs's commutation of sentence. Several members of the Cabinet were for Debs's release. By the spring of 1920 Secretary of the Interior John Barton Payne was urging that Wilson release Debs. At a Cabinet meeting in August, 1920, the Debs case came up for consideration. At this meeting Payne, Secretary of the Navy Josephus Daniels, Secretary of War Newton D. Baker, and even Attorney General Palmer advocated Debs's release. Only Postmaster General Burleson was completely opposed to clemency for Debs; Secretary of State Bainbridge Colby was dubious. But Wilson put an end to the Cabinet's discussion of the case. As Daniels recorded the incident in his diary, "In N.J., said the Prdt the Governor is a member of the Board of Pardons. He can not pardon by himself, but his vote is necessary to secure pardon. He said this with finality and that ended hope for Debs and the others."[19]

During the campaign that fall Attorney General Palmer again brought the case before Wilson. Palmer began by asking the judge in the Debs case, D. C. Westenhaver, for his recommendation. When Westenhaver replied he thought clemency was in order, Palmer drew up a formal commutation of sentence for Debs and submitted it to

Wilson. Wilson's only answer was to take a pencil and write "Denied" on the face of the document and tell his secretary he would never release Debs because "while the flower of American youth was pouring out its blood to vindicate the cause of civilization, . . . Debs [had] stood behind the lines, sniping, attacking, and denouncing them." [20]

That Palmer, one of the reactionaries of his day, should recommend clemency for Debs and that Wilson, a President recorded in written history as one of the great liberals, should deny it is one of the ironies of American history. And the irony is compounded by the fact that Debs was finally released from Atlanta Penitentiary by Warren G. Harding. There is, in fact, nothing in Wilson's actions in the Debs case to increase his reputation for human warmth and understanding. When Debs heard the news in his cell that Wilson had denied his release, he bitterly remarked of Wilson: "It is he, not I, who needs a pardon. . . . No man in public life in American history ever retired so thoroughly discredited, so scathingly rebuked, so overwhelmingly impeached and repudiated as Woodrow Wilson." For this remark Wilson's Chief of the Division of Prisons rescinded Debs's mail and visiting privileges. There is no reason to believe that Wilson ordered the withdrawal of these privileges. But he must have been aware of his subordinate's action, for the story was carried in the daily press. Yet the privileges were not restored until the conservative Harding occupied the White House. [21]

The contrast between Wilson and Harding in the Debs case is an interesting one. One of Harding's first acts in office was to order his Attorney General, Harry M. Daugherty, to review the Debs case. Only a few days later he startled the nation, and probably Debs as well, by arranging to have Debs come to the White House without guard and in civilian clothes for a three-hour conference. [22] And over the protest of such groups as the American Legion, on Christmas Day, 1921, President Harding allowed the aged Socialist leader to walk out of Atlanta Penitentiary a free man.

But if parts of the American public supported the Socialist

amnesty campaign, they did not approve of the tack to the left the party began in 1919. Quite the reverse: as the Socialists experimented with manifestoes and applications for membership in the Third International its membership steadily declined. In the years immediately following the war and the Russian Revolution, ultraradicals logically and in good conscience could support the American communist parties and the Bolsheviks. The day of disillusion with the Soviets had not yet come—indeed, for many it was not to come until the pact with the Nazis in 1939—and it was natural, if unrealistic, for American revolutionaries to try to transplant the methods of the Bolsheviks to the American scene. So the left wing of American radicalism was not attracted by the Socialist venture into ultraradicalism. Why not, ultraradicals asked, go all the way and support the Communists?

Nor was the Socialist swing to the left to attract the more conservative elements of American dissenters. The agrarian and essentially progressive, rather than radical, wings of the party had deteriorated badly during the war years, and they were not to return after the war so long as the Socialists took steps, however tentative, in the direction of proletarian revolution. The former Western agrarian Socialists went into a myriad of farmer political movements. In the northern Great Plains farmers who before the war might have supported the Socialist Party now gave their support to the Non-Partisan League. In fact, many of the leaders of the League were former Socialists. The founder of the League, A. C. Townley, was formerly a Socialist organizer; Walter Thomas Mills, formerly a very popular Socialist orator in the rural West, became an organizer for the League; Charles Edward Russell, who had left the Socialists because he supported the war, was the editor of the League's newspaper. In the Far Northwest the story was similar. Former Socialists turned to farmer-labor movements. In Montana, where before the war the Socialist Party had been fairly strong, the Socialists were so weak that in 1920 and 1922 they were unable to put state and congressional tickets in the field. In Washington, according to one loyal Washington Socialist, the Farmer-Labor Party "completely absorbed the membership and sympathizers of the Socialist Party." Urban progressives were attracted to the new Conference for Progressive Political Action.

The Socialists also suffered from the undeniably conservative mood of the nation in the postwar years. Such a thing as the mood of a people or a climate of opinion is admittedly subjective and perhaps impossible to document, but it seems true nevertheless that the tide of popular opinion was against progressivism and radicalism. It was politicians and businessmen who pushed through the Transportation Act of 1920, who nominated conservative mediocrities like Cox and Harding, and who led a campaign against unionism under the euphemistic slogan of "the American plan," but it was the common people who elected Harding, who formed mobs to beat Wobblies, and who joined the Ku Klux Klan. And it was not only the readers of the *Saturday Evening Post*, the Hearst and McCormick press, and the like who were the conservatives. A disgruntled Californian who thought, "This is a white man's country, and must be run by white men," canceled his subscription to the *Nation* because it was too "pro-Nigger." [23]

The desertion of the extreme Left and the agrarians and the repressionary actions of conservatives depleted the party's national membership badly and in some states nearly made the party extinct. When the East European immigrants rushed into the party during the central and eastern European revolutions of 1918–1919, they swelled the party to 108,504 members, but these recent card holders, and others, bolted with the Communist splits and there were only 26,766 dues-paying Socialists in 1920. And things were to get worse for the Socialists. In 1921 the membership fell to 13,484, and the next year to 11,277. Membership declined slightly each year thereafter until the Great Depression. Some strong state organizations were wiped out. Oklahoma, which had polled more Socialist votes in 1914 than any other state in the Union, had only 72 paid-up Socialists in 1922, and these hardy few dwindled to 14 by 1924. By 1922 only New York, Wisconsin, Massachusetts, and Pennsylvania had as many as one thousand members.[24]

Socialist efforts to revive the organization were discouraging. In 1921 the New Yorker Gus Claessens made a speaking tour to the west coast and back to try to reorganize the party. His long journey was a failure. What few Socialists there were left in the country could not organize a meeting properly, attendance was poor, and interest was low. After Debs was released from prison he did what he could to revive the organization. He went on long speaking tours despite his broken health, and his messianic personality brought a temporary rebirth of the movement wherever he went. In 1923 Debs undertook an extensive speaking and organizing campaign over the country. In fifty-three meetings, through the unique Socialist practice of charging admission to political rallies, he raised nearly $6,000 for the national organization and nearly $20,000 for the state and local organizations. He also sold a great many subscriptions to the few Socialist newspapers still in existence. But Debs could not revive the party singlehandedly. He became ill, and the last eleven meetings had to be canceled; and, more important, there were no efficient state and local organizations to capitalize on the enthusiasm that Debs evoked. As one anonymous California Socialist wrote to National Executive Secretary Otto Branstetter, ". . . everyone recognizes that Debs can galvanize a corpse. If we do not follow up they will all say that the corpse is ready for the grave again." [25]

But there was no one to follow up, there was little enthusiasm in the movement, and the corpse was ready for the grave again. The war, a hostile administration in Washington with little regard for civil liberties, and a popular hysteria had all but killed the Socialist movement. The relative prosperity of the 1920's hindered the development of new converts. Furthermore, the movement had lost much of its zeal to the Communists, who now attracted young rebels. In fact, the Socialists were unable to keep their own youths. When William Kruse, national secretary of the Young People's Socialist League (Yipsels), had to resign soon after the war to serve a sentence for violation of the war-time Espionage Act, the national secretary elected to succeed him secretly joined the Communists. When his disaffection was discovered, the YPSL executive committee voted to expel him, but on his own authority he called a convention at which a majority of the delegates voted to deliver the League to the Communists.[26]

The party's lack of strength in the 1920's made it ineffective, but another factor in the Socialist failure to make an impact on American society was its dissipation of what little strength it had in the war with the Communists. After the split of the Communists from their Socialist mother, the two went at each other's throats with a bitter vigor which advanced the cause of neither against capitalism. In the 1920's, when both the Socialists and the Communists were weak and capitalism was strong, neither party did much more than conduct a guerrilla warfare against the other. This was especially true in New York City, where the power of both organizations was concentrated. In other parts of the country the Socialist-Communist fight was less intense only because seldom were both parties present. Incidents in this civil war of the Left abound. In 1923 W. J. Ghent, who had left the Socialist Party because of its St. Louis Proclamation against the war but who still regarded himself as a social democrat, published a little book called *The Reds Bring Reaction* in which he maintained that Communists by their extremism incite reactionary repression against all progressives, liberals, and social democrats. He wrote many essays on the same theme: the "fanatical outbursts of Bolshevik disciples in America" cause even those who have no love for industrial capitalism as it is to "support . . . the *old* order as something infinitely preferable to the thing offered by the professed harbingers of the new day." Communists replied with the epithet of "social fascist." In the New York City needle trade unions the battle between Socialist and Communist became violent, with blood being spilled by both sides. Norman Thomas recalls that being an editor of a radical labor paper was no pleasant task because both sides used pressure to get the paper slanted the way they wanted it. "The last thing that anybody wanted was an objective statement of the news." [27]

This intramural conflict seemed confusing to the typical follower of the major parties and disgusting to the neophyte in radical politics; the Republican or Democrat to whom communism was just "socialism in a hurry" made no sense of the conflict, and the new-comer to leftist politics, still hot from a recent disenchantment with industrial capitalism, could not understand why Socialists and Communists did not patch up their differences and make common cause against conservatism. Sophisticated intellectuals were fascinated by the battle. Some of them, with an air of intellectual superiority, thought the explanation of the phenomenon was very simple: it was born of the same impulse which causes religious sects to fight one another over obscure points of theology; the Socialist-Communist animosity was analogous, say, to Christian disputes over sprinkling or total immersion.[28] There is some validity to this point of view, but it neglects one important aspect of the controversy: it was perfectly logical and, in the long run, sensible for each party, given their basic principles and aims, to strike away at the other. Disputes over the interpretation of Marx may be analogous to disputes over the interpretation of scripture, but it is not enough merely to point out an analogy.

A debate between the social democrat James Oneal and the Communist Robert Minor in New York City early in the 1920's illustrated the divergent points of view of the Socialists and the Communists and the heat with which they fought each other. The most famous debate over Socialism before the war had been between Morris Hillquit and Father John A. Ryan, an enlightened Roman Catholic priest, and the debate was a good one that argued the merits of capitalism and Socialism. The Oneal-Minor debate struck no telling blows at capitalism although both principals were anti-capitalist, and their efforts did not bring the demise of capitalism one day closer. Yet to dismiss their debate and the whole Socialist-Communist struggle as an unwise family quarrel is short-sighted since their debate revealed basic and important differences which were as important as the cleavage between either of them and any major-party politician. Democracy was the issue which split Oneal and Minor, democracy in the sense of universal political participation and civil liberty, the meaning of the term that has been generally understood in western Europe and America, not in the sense of the "people's democracy" of the Soviet Union. Minor was for the dictatorship of the proletariat as it was practiced in the Soviet Union. He took comfort in his belief that historical laws necessitated such a political arrangement. "The dictatorship of the proletariat is not drawn from the brain of a theologian nor from anyone's likes. It is drawn from the hard bed-rock of history, and whether our friend Oneal wants it or does not want it, he shall see it." Oneal was diametrically opposed. "I favor all power to the working class, not all power to a handful of dictators, which is something entirely different —all power to the working class, not all power to a clique that assumes to have super-human knowledge, that it is infallible, that it cannot possibly err." They held utterly opposing views on the important question of freedom of speech. Oneal ridiculed the Communists for favoring free speech for themselves in the United States but opposing it as a "petty bourgeois idea" elsewhere. Minor readily admitted the charge. ". . . a modern materialist revolutionary . . . will do the things not that are metaphysically moral, but the things that work, and he will take a position for free speech when it is the bourgeois dictatorship that is on top, and he will take a position against free speech for the bourgeoisie, when it is the workers that are on top." It is only to be expected that groups differing on such basic issues as these should clash bitterly. And since they believed firmly in their opposite principles it was only proper that the clash was bitter. So Oneal referred to the Communists as "descendants of Bakunin," blindly and unintelligently following the "ukases . . . laid down by a central committee in Moscow," and Minor replied that capitalists had learned "that when you want to rule workingmen in slavery nowadays you cannot rule directly—you must get a yellow Socialist." According to the Communist editors of the published debate, Minor's invective against the Socialists evoked "Deafening and prolonged applause." [29] The analogy of the Socialist-Communist fight to disputes over fine points of theology is less apt than the analogy, if one must be drawn, to the struggles between radicals and conservatives in the American Revolution who agreed in their desire for independence but disagreed upon the question of what sort of state should be erected in the place formerly held by the British Empire.

After the Socialist swing to the left occasioned by the Russian Revolution had spent itself, the party moved to the right and tried to effect an alliance with non-Marxian progressives. Until the early 1920's the official stand of the Socialist Party had been uncompromising: Socialism or nothing. Efforts of individuals or groups within the party to bring the Socialists into a coalition with liberal non-Socialists to gain some progressive goal had been consistently opposed and defeated. But after the war there were several new conditions which caused the Socialist Party to reexamine its position. Hopes for Socialist success within the reasonably distant future were dimmer than they had ever been. Socialist votes and membership had grown steadily from the formation of the party until World War I. In 1912 it was not altogether foolish to believe that within a generation or so the Socialist Party would be, if not the dominant political party of the country, at least a major political group as strong as the British and Continental social democrats. But by 1921 only faith, not observation, could have led a Socialist to such a conclusion. Furthermore, the United States in the early 1920's appeared headed for a period of reaction which many Socialists felt could be headed off only by cooperation with the non-Marxian Left. This had not been true before during the party's history. At the Socialist convention in 1921 the party took its first hesitant and tentative step in the direction of progressive fusion, a step which was in time to bring the already weakened party almost to the point of extinction.

In June, 1921, at the Socialist Party convention in Detroit, Morris Hillquit introduced a resolution instructing the National Executive Committee to make a survey of all radical and labor organizations in the nation to ascertain the strength of these groups and their possible readiness to cooperate politically with the Socialists upon a platform "not inconsistent with that of the party, and on a plan which will preserve the integrity and autonomy" of the Socialist organization. The NEC was to report the results of this survey at the next annual convention. There was much opposition to Hillquit's resolution, but it carried. In the fall of 1921 the NEC began its exploration of the progressive forces of the country and accepted an invitation from the railroad labor brotherhoods to meet at Chicago in February, 1922, "to discuss and adopt a fundamental economic program designed to restore to the people the sovereignty that is rightly theirs, to make effective the purpose for which our Government is established, to secure to all men the enjoyment of the gain which their industry produces." [30]

The Socialist delegates to this meeting—Morris Hillquit, Daniel Hoan, Victor Berger, James Oneal, Otto Branstetter, and Bertha Hale White—were the left wing of a very heterogeneous assemblage. There were representatives of the railroad brotherhoods and other labor organizations, groups which traditionally had rewarded its friends and punished its enemies within the major political parties. There were representatives from the Farmer-Labor Party and the Non-Partisan League. There were representatives from the Committee of Forty-eight, originally Roosevelt Republicans who had followed their leader out of the GOP in 1912 but who refused to follow him back into the Republican camp in 1916. Church groups like the Methodist Federation of Social Service, the Church League for Industrial Democracy, and the National Catholic Welfare Council had sent delegates. And there was a group of social-gospel ministers, single-taxers, and agrarians who showed up at the Chicago meeting who represented no one but themselves and their consciences. That such a diverse group was able to accomplish anything is testimony to its good will and its fear of an American black reaction.

The meeting did not accomplish much. It formed itself into a permanent organization, taking the name Conference for Progressive Political Action, usually called the CPPA. It named an executive committee, called the Committee of Fifteen, headed by William H. Johnston, president of the International Association of Machinists, which included Hillquit as the only Socialist member. And it issued an "Address to the American People," a 1922 version of Populism and prewar progressivism that came out *against* many reactionary things but was *for* only government of, by, and for the people. The meeting did not produce a new political party; it did not even officially form a pressure group to be used within the major parties, although there was general agreement to campaign actively for liberals in the 1922 congressional and state elections.

The Socialists were disappointed, but they were patient. They continued to participate in the CPPA. The party convention at Cleveland in 1922 and again at New York in 1923 endorsed the decision of the Socialist delegates to the CPPA to stick with the progressives and to try to form a third party something like that of the British Labor Party, with the Socialists being to this party as the Independent Labor Party was to its larger organization.

At the second conference of the CPPA in December, 1922, at Cleveland, after the CPPA had helped to defeat a few very conservative congressmen in the elections of that year, the Socialists were disappointed again. At that meeting they were among those who voted for the immediate formation of a political party, but the conference was against such an action 64 to 52. Labor was too cautious and conservative to declare itself for a third party as yet— indeed, it never supported the idea of a new political party at any time during the election of 1924—and many of the farmers in the CPPA were committed to the Non-Partisan League tactic of capturing the major parties through the primaries. The large minority that was for the establishment of a new party in 1922 was composed of Socialists and progressive intellectuals. About the only hopeful feature of the second CPPA meeting from the Socialist point of view was that the efforts of the Communists to get into the CPPA were firmly foiled.[31] The Communists then moved on the Farmer-Labor Party in 1923 and successfully captured and wrecked that organization.

The prospects for a third party were to be even dimmer during the next several months. The first CPPA conference had urged the organization of state CPPA groups, and in 1923 the railroad brotherhoods in New York State invited other groups, including the Socialists, to meet at Albany on July 29th to form a New York CPPA. When the Socialists went to Albany they were surprised to find the railroad labor leaders debating whether or not the Socialists, whom they had already invited to the conference, should be admitted. The brotherhoods finally decided the Socialists should be allowed to participate in the conference, but the atmosphere after such a poor start was hardly conducive to cooperation and harmony. It was obvious that the railroad brotherhood leaders were close to major party politicians and wanted to avoid any kind of move toward a third party. When the brotherhood delegates suspected that the Socialists were moving the conference in the direction of independent political action, the railroaders quickly carried a motion to adjourn the conference. The chairman of the conference, Thomas E. Ryan of the Brotherhood of Locomotive Firemen and Enginemen, used his gavel to quell any hint of Socialist influence in the state CPPA. It is ironic that his union was largely the creation of Eugene V. Debs, who had been one of its most important officials in his youth.

The affair at Albany turned out to be the low point in relations between Socialists and labor leaders in the CPPA. Thereafter relations between the two groups improved even if there never developed any real harmony. The delegates to the third conference of the CPPA, at St. Louis in February, 1924, tried to assuage the discontent of the Socialists. This third conference was thinking of the conduct of the railroad union leaders at Albany when it provided for the expulsion of state organizations which violated the rules and policies of the national CPPA. It also adopted a resolution welcoming the recent success of the British Labor Party, an action that reassured the Socialists and distressed such unionists as Ryan.[32]

But most encouraging to the Socialists was the decision of the St. Louis conference to run a slate of candidates in the 1924 elections. The conference went on record with an official statement saying that the CPPA had been "created for the purpose of securing the nomination and election of Presidents and Vice Presidents of the United States, United States Senators, Representatives to Congress, members of State Legislatures and other state and local public officers who are pledged to the interests of the producing classes and to the principles of genuine democracy in agriculture, industry and government."

And the conference indicated that it meant what it said by issuing a call for a nominating convention to be held at Cleveland beginning July 4, 1924.

The decision to nominate CPPA candidates had been more than the Socialists had expected. The Socialist Party NEC met in St. Louis two days before the CPPA meeting opened to conduct its regular business and to caucus for the meeting with the labor and progressive forces. At that meeting the national committee called for the next national convention of the Socialist Party to be held in New York City on May 17th. The national convention was to nominate Socialist candidates as usual but would inform the CPPA that its nominations would be subject to change if CPPA action made such change desirable. The CPPA's setting a date for a nominating convention put a new light on the situation, and the NEC subsequently rescinded its call for a national party convention at New York in May and called for a convention in Cleveland immediately following the CPPA meeting.[33]

The delegates to the 1924 CPPA convention in the Cleveland municipal auditorium were a refreshing contrast to the staid business types who had been delegates to the Republican convention in the same auditorium three weeks before and to the professional politicians in the Democratic convention then in progress at Madison Square Garden in New York. They were an enthusiastic crowd, representing nearly all possible groups that could be behind a progressive political crusade. There was a surprising number of college undergraduates in the auditorium, either on the convention floor as delegates or in the gallery. The political clubs of some colleges had been accredited as members of the CPPA. There were farmers, there were progressive church people, there were old-time Populists and lost Bull Moosers. And there were crackpots, sincere but unbalanced cranks that appear at nearly all left-of-center political meetings, sometimes at the expense of a major party politician who hopes to discredit a movement. Among the lunatic fringe at the Cleveland convention was a Bostonian called Old Sock Joe, who proposed a law requiring Klansmen to wear their regalia twenty-four hours a day and a national referendum on the question of whether prohibition should be suspended ten days of each year. This alcoholic hiatus, he remarked, "would give the Drys plenty of fresh arguments for abstinence every year and the Wets a chance to express their true sentiments." Another eccentric in attendance was John J. Streeter, from an old soldiers' home in Milwaukee, whose truly magnificent beard had been growing since he took a vow in the 1890's never to shave again until the Populists won. "General" Jacob S. Coxey of the famous "Petition in Boots" was at the convention, vainly hoping to get the CPPA to support his proposal that all interest be abolished. But men such as these had no influence in the CPPA. A better measure of the ability and direction of the convention is seen in the men who spoke before the meeting, men such as Fiorello La Guardia, then a Republican congressman from Manhattan; Edwin Markham, the poet of the common man; and Peter Witt, a Cleveland municipal reformer who had been closely associated with Tom Johnson.

But it was the labor delegates who controlled the convention, and it was a foregone conclusion that the convention, led by the labor delegates, would nominate Senator Robert Marion La Follette for President. The railroad labor leaders earlier had been inclined to William Gibbs McAdoo, who had administered the nation's railroads for the federal government during the war. But McAdoo had been tainted in the Teapot Dome oil scandals, and labor support swung to the progressive senator from Wisconsin. La Follette was a natural choice for the CPPA. His long progressive reform record was a good one. He had a large following among the agrarians, his voting record on labor issues in the Senate was favorable to labor, and his opposition to the war endeared him to the Socialists. Most of all, La Follette was tremendously popular among just the people the CPPA hoped to attract. In 1922 he had won reelection to the Senate by a thumping vote; in March, 1924, he received 40,000 write-in votes in the North Dakota presidential primary.

Even before the convention opened, the National Committee of the CPPA, of which Hillquit was a member, unanimously invited

La Follette to be their presidential candidate. This unusual preconvention invitation was a device of the labor members of the CPPA to prevent the formation of a third party. In their opinion, a formal nomination from the floor of the convention would smack of a party organization, and they wanted to take no action that could be interpreted as the development of a new party. Senator La Follette accepted the nomination in a message read to the convention by his older son, Robert, Jr., on the afternoon of the first day of the convention. He made it clear that he accepted the CPPA invitation as an independent, not as the candidate of a new political party. He predicted, however, that a new party would be formed after the election, when the people would "register their will and united purpose by a vote of such magnitude that a new political party" would be imperative. Immediately after La Follette's acceptance, the head of the Brotherhood of Locomotive Engineers moved that the convention endorse La Follette's candidacy. Hillquit, hoping the nomination would be delayed for a while to give an opportunity to form a regular political party, objected that the endorsement was not in order since the convention was not yet permanently organized. The credentials committee had not reported—it was slow because it was being very careful to keep out any Communists—and any action the as yet unaccredited delegates might take would not be binding. The presiding officer, William H. Johnston, ruled the motion for endorsement out of order.

The next afternoon, after the committee on credentials had reported and the convention was technically organized, the delegates nominated La Follette and accepted the platform of the committee on resolutions by acclamation. The convention lasted just one more hour, during which the delegates passed various relatively unimportant resolutions omitted from the platform, and the Socialists and others who wanted to commit the CPPA to the formation of a third party had no chance to accomplish their purpose. The Socialists made no special effort at the convention to persuade the delegates to form a third party; they submitted no motions to that effect. They decided not to press the issue out of a desire to keep the alliance between the various CPPA factions, such as it was, harmonious. Had they pressed at the convention for the immediate organization of a third party along the lines they wanted, it is problematical whether the proposal would have passed. La Follette himself was clearly against such action before the election, and the powerful labor organizations were adamantly opposed. Nevertheless, some Socialists were critical of their delegates' failure to bring the issue to a vote at the Cleveland convention.[34]

The Socialist Party met in national convention at Cleveland the day after the CPPA meeting closed to endorse La Follette's candidacy. The delegates insisted they still "firmly adher[ed] to the principles of Socialism as set forth in the Platforms and Declarations of the . . . Party," but they endorsed the La Follette platform, which was certainly not a Socialist document. With the possible exception of the CPPA platform plank on monopolies, there was nothing in the document with which Socialists could disagree. They too were for the abolition of child labor, for cooperatives, a government guarantee of the right of collective bargaining, and a federal tax law more in harmony with the economic facts of life; and they certainly could give wholehearted support to the statement "opposing equally the dictatorship of the plutocracy and the dictatorship of the proletariat." But the CPPA platform was a reform document; it did not call for the public ownership and democratic control of any industries but hydroelectric power and railroads, and it did not look forward to the demise of capitalism. The party's endorsement of the platform is evidence the Socialists sincerely tried to cooperate in bringing a new alignment in American politics.

Further evidence of this sincerity is seen in the Socialist convention's action in granting the NEC discretion to endorse the CPPA's Vice Presidential candidate when nominated. The CPPA convention had adjourned without nominating a Vice President and had empowered its National Committee to select a candidate. There were rumors that the nomination would go to Justice Louis Brandeis, a nomination the Socialists would probably have warmly approved. It was not until nearly two weeks after the adjournment at Cleveland that the National Committee of the CPPA acted. It then nominated Senator Burton K. Wheeler, Democrat of Montana, who had declared he could not support the Democratic candidate John W. Davis, a Wall Street lawyer. The Socialist NEC subsequently concurred in the Wheeler nomination.[35]

Socialist hopes soared in August, 1924, when the American Federation of Labor abandoned its traditional nonpartisan policy to endorse La Follette and Wheeler. It was clear, however, that the AFL's endorsement was an act of desperation, and it developed later that the endorsement was no more than lukewarm at best. The AFL's report went to great pains to point out it had no sympathy for some of the groups supporting La Follette—meaning, of course, the Socialists—and it made clear that its endorsement implied no support of any political group. No sooner had the AFL made its painfully timid endorsement of La Follette than it began to back out. A reader of Samuel Gompers's article in the September, 1924, *American Federationist* might have wondered if the AFL was really supporting La Follette after all. Leaders of important AFL unions supported major-party candidates: George Berry of the Pressmen supported Davis, and John L. Lewis of the Miners and William Hutcheson of the Carpenters supported Coolidge. In October William English Walling, former Socialist and himself a candidate for the Senate from Connecticut on the La Follette ticket, wrote of the campaign, and his point of view was significant because he was very close to Gompers. Walling made it clear that the AFL's endorsement was only a temporary aberration, that the AFL would oppose any effort to form a new party, and that it would not be grievously disappointed by La Follette's failure. Nor did the AFL give La Follette significant financial support. It contributed only $25,000 to his campaign fund, less than was donated by William T. Rawleigh, a Freeport, Illinois, manufacturer of patent medicines.

Despite the fact that there was no coalition of progressives and Socialists on the state and local level—in some states La Follette's name appeared in the Socialist column and in some states he appeared both in the independent and in the Socialist columns—the Socialists worked very hard for La Follette's candidacy. Looking back over several years Socialists concluded they worked so much for La Follette they allowed their own organization to go to seed. In the Socialist emphasis on the Presidency they let their state and local campaigns suffer.[36]

The major parties united in smearing La Follette during the campaign. The Republican Vice Presidential candidate, Charles G. Dawes, he of the unique pipe and the explosive language, implied that Soviet money was behind the La Follette campaign, a charge that lesser Republicans made explicit. The publisher Cyrus Curtis, whose many magazines were all-out for Coolidge, ran an article in his *Saturday Evening Post* which implied that La Follette was in league with the Communist William Z. Foster. One anti-La Follette *Country Gentleman* editorial was reproduced on the back of Pennsylvania Railroad dining-car menus, where it probably was read by fewer potential La Follette voters than it would have been if printed on the wrapping of the arid sandwiches sold in the day coaches.

The professed fear of the Republicans that a large La Follette vote would throw the election into the House of Representatives probably hurt the La Follette cause considerably. Their argument was tenuous, but the Republicans claimed that if there were not a majority in the electoral vote the House might make the Democratic Vice Presidential candidate, Charles W. Bryan, governor of Nebraska and a brother of the Great Commoner, the new President. They assumed that such an unlikely development was a fate much to be avoided. Regardless of the irrationality of the argument, the slogan "Coolidge or Chaos" hurt the independents' chances.[37]

The Republican charges of Communist influence in the La Follette camp were more than usually ridiculous in view of the bitter fighting that there was in that campaign between La Follette and his supporters and the Communists. La Follette made much of his opposition to the Communists. The *La Follette–Wheeler Campaign Text-Book* reprinted a letter from La Follette to Herman L. Ekern, attorney general of Wisconsin, which referred to the Communists as "the mortal enemies of the Progressive movement and democratic ideals," and declared all progressives should refuse "to make common cause with any Communist organization." The fight with the Communists became most bitter when William Z. Foster and Debs traded insults. Foster in a letter to Debs rebuked him for his "complete capitulation to this petty-bourgeois reformer" La Follette. "The petty bourgeois united front is now complete from Hearst to Debs." Debs was caustic in his reply. "You may be right in your criticism of my position and I may be wrong, as I have often been before. Having no Vatican in Moscow to guide me I must follow the light I have, and this I have done in the present instance."

Ex-Socialists tried to embarrass the Socialist campaign for La Follette. David Karsner, the Debs biographer, in firing the parting blast that had become customary for intellectuals leaving the Socialist Party, deprecated the value of the Socialists to the new political line-up. There was hardly enough left of the Socialist Party, he wrote, "to salvage and weld with another group. It has neither goodwill nor bad to bequeath to another organization. It is a political ghost stalking in the graveyard of current events seeking respectable burial." John Spargo tried to use whatever influence he might have left among the Socialists to support President Coolidge. This brought Hillquit's caustic comment: "John Spargo has been graciously received in audience by the President and immediately thereafter he proclaimed to the world that the true interests of international socialism as expounded by the late Karl Marx would be best promoted by the election of Mr. Coolidge. It would seem that a little red support would not hurt any candidate for office." 38

Red support or not, Coolidge won in a landslide. La Follette carried his own state of Wisconsin to be the only progressive third-party candidate since 1912 to score in the electoral college—he received 4,826,471 popular votes, about 17 per cent of the total. In the three-cornered race, President Coolidge got an easy popular majority, but La Follette ran a strong third, receiving 59 per cent as many popular votes as did the Democrat John W. Davis. Besides carrying Wisconsin, La Follette ran second in Iowa, Minnesota, North and South Dakota, Montana, Wyoming, Idaho, Nevada, Washington, Oregon, and California. In several of these states, Davis did not carry a single county, although La Follette carried many. It is impossible to determine accurately how many votes the Socialists gave La Follette. There were 858,264 votes cast for La Follette on the Socialist ticket, but this does not indicate very much since in some states, California, for example, the only way to vote for La Follette was to vote Socialist. The historian of the 1924 election, Kenneth MacKay, estimates the Socialists produced about one million votes for La Follette, or roughly one-fifth of his total, but the estimate seems high.[39]

In New York State La Follette was on the ballot both in the Progressive and in the Socialist rows, and he received more votes under the Socialist designation than under the Progressive banner. But the Socialist candidates for state office did very poorly, perhaps giving weight to their claim they campaigned harder for La Follette than for themselves. Norman Thomas, running against Al Smith for governor, received slightly less than 100,000 votes. Charles Solomon, Socialist candidate in New York for lieutenant governor, was the high man on his ticket with 126,679 votes. La Follette ran so far ahead of the rest of the Socialist ticket that it is likely that he carried the Socialists along a little rather than the reverse. In no state did the vote for state Socialist candidates approach the La Follette vote. Even in Wisconsin the Socialist gubernatorial candidate polled a measly 45,268 votes, less than the combined totals of Socialist congressional candidates. Victor Berger's congressional district returned him to Washington by a 500-vote margin over his Republican opponent, but Leo Krzycki lost in the other Milwaukee district.[40]

The Socialists were at first heartened by the election results, but their enthusiasm for a new and permanent third party was soon dampened by the AFL's announcement that the election results proved the inefficacy of a third party. According to the AFL, the 1924 campaign had shown that "the launching of third party movements has been proved wasted effort and injurious to the desire to elect candidates with favorable [labor] records." "To be successful politically," the AFL leaders went on to say, labor "must continue in

the future . . . to follow its non-partisan policy." Socialists were
not surprised by the AFL's action, but they were disappointed. As
Eric F. Goldman so well put it, Socialists and others who were disappointed with the AFL's failure to help create a new party were
discouraged because the AFL acted like the AFL.[41]

As determined before the campaign, the National Committee of
the CPPA met in November after the election and issued a call for
a convention to be held in Chicago in February, 1925, to consider
the formation of a new political party. Socialists hoped the CPPA
would transform itself into an American version of the British Labor
Party, but they had no faith that it would. As Debs pointed out, a
labor party obviously could get nowhere without the unions and
the union leaders were "almost to a man opposed to a labor party."
Debs thought that any hope for a labor party lay with the union rank
and file and concluded that if the CPPA could not form a bona fide
labor party it would be better not to form one at all.

In the words of Morris Hillquit, the delegates to the 1925 CPPA
meeting at Chicago "had come to bury Caesar, not to praise him."
Most of the labor delegates to Chicago were opposed to the idea
of a new party, and even of those who favored a new party none was
empowered to speak for his union. On the afternoon of the first
day of the convention the CPPA adjourned, allowing those who favored a new party to meet that evening. Most of the labor men then
went home, leaving the field to the Socialists and the farmers. The
farm delegates wanted any party they might form to be on a basis
of individual membership; the Socialists insisted they could enter
no organization the Socialist Party could not belong to as a party.
The Socialists wanted to retain their identity as a caucus or wing
within a national progressive party, as they had within the CPPA.
There was no agreement, and Hillquit moved the conference adjourn
sine die. Two days later the Socialists met in convention and severed
all connection with the CPPA. They did not, however, completely
give up the idea of a new party. Any state Socialist organization
would be permitted, with the approval of the NEC, to join any state
labor party which would allow the Socialists to join as a unit. But no

state labor parties appeared, and the Socialist experiment in cooperating with nonsocialist progressives was at an end.[42]

What were the results of the CPPA venture for the Socialists? Nothing, or less than nothing. In a sharp decline even before 1924, the Socialists came out of the La Follette campaign weaker than ever. Victor Berger was back in Congress again, but that did not mean much. When Berger was first elected to Congress in 1910, Socialists thought it would not be long before he would soon have Socialist colleagues there; in 1924 Socialists knew very well they were lucky to have one congressman and that Berger was in Washington because he had a municipal political machine behind him and because he oozed *gemütlichkeit* with an Austrian accent that endeared him to Milwaukee's beer-drinking population. No longer were Socialists confident of the success of social democracy. They certainly had no reason for confidence. Labor indicated it would have no more to do with independent political action, intellectuals withdrew politically to amuse themselves with H. L. Mencken's superior wisecracks about the "booboisie," and the "booboisie" was keeping cool with Coolidge. It was, up until that time, the nadir of American socialism.

VIII

ENTER NORMAN THOMAS

IN the late 1930's James Thurber published a cartoon in which one of his formless but expressive women, looking up from her newspaper, asked her husband, "What ever happened to the Socialist Party?" In that depression decade her husband might have been able to answer the question, but in the mid-1920's he probably was as uninformed as his wife. For from the election of 1924 until the crash in 1929 the Socialist Party did very little to attract the attention of the general public. Outside of a few islands of Socialist strength, Lower Manhattan Island, Milwaukee, and Reading, Pennsylvania, about all the party could do was fight a few civil liberties cases, keep the idea of social democracy alive among a few intellectuals (here it had the help of its sister organization, the nonpolitical League for Industrial Democracy), and hold together a remnant of organization while waiting for a more favorable economic and social psychological climate than Coolidge prosperity offered. The organization was all but completely dormant.

Part of the party's weakness during the mid-1920's was due to a lack of vigorous leadership. Debs died in 1926, and for five years before his death he had not been strong enough to lead the party with his customary force. His prison- and campaign-racked body was not equal to the task his fighting heart assigned it. Victor Berger continued his able leadership in Milwaukee until his accidental death when hit by a streetcar in the summer of 1929—Meyer London, popular among the New York garment workers, was killed in a street accident the same year—but Berger's main interest had been his congressional constituency and his local political machine and he had never been a popular national figure in the party. Morris Hillquit did what he could during this period, but he was forced to give most of his time to his law practice in an effort to improve the personal financial pinch which his bout with tuberculosis had caused. And in this effort one aspect of Hillquit's law practice embarrassed the party.

When Hillquit returned from Saranac he accepted the case of a Russian refugee inventor against the National City Bank of New York. Before the United States entered World War I the inventor came to America and sold to an American firm for $50,000 the right to use a shell fuse he had devised. The money was deposited in the National City Bank and made payable in that bank's St. Petersburg branch. By the time the inventor returned home to collect his money, the Bolsheviks had come to power and confiscated the account. The Russian then returned to the United States and demanded payment from the bank. When payment was denied, he retained Hillquit, a logical choice since Hillquit had both a mastery of the law and a knowledge of the Russian language. Hillquit won the case on the grounds that the United States had not recognized the Soviet government and that, therefore, an American firm could not recognize that government's confiscation decrees. It was a case worthy of *Alice in Wonderland*. Here was the national chairman of the Socialist Party defending a munitions man from nationalization and the counsel of the National City Bank, of all institutions, arguing the right of government confiscation of private property.

Hillquit's success in this case brought him several suits, which were both very profitable to him and embarrassing to his Socialist comrades. In 1931 Hillquit took the case of some Russian refugees whose oil lands had been confiscated by the Soviets. Standard Oil subsequently leased these oil lands from the Russian government, and the refugees sued the company for a share of the profits from this Russian oil. To Norman Thomas, James Maurer, and a considerable section of the party this was the last straw; there were plans for deposing Hillquit as national chairman. Finally, Judge Jacob Panken, an old friend of Hillquit's, persuaded him to withdraw from the case. It is to Hillquit's credit, however, that he did not permit his personal interest to dictate his attitude toward American recognition of the Soviet government. Although as a social democrat he damned the Bolsheviks' totalitarianism, he publicly argued for American recognition of the *de facto* Russian government.[1]

The top leadership of the party was weak, but it was the next lower level of party officials that was most damagingly inept. When the capable Otto Branstetter resigned as national executive secretary in February, 1924, the NEC appointed Bertha Hale White to fill the office temporarily. From a Midwestern farm background, she had been a teacher and a journalist. From 1913 until her appointment in 1924 she had served the party as assistant national secretary. The NEC replaced Mrs. White with George R. Kirkpatrick, another former teacher, after the campaign. He served only a brief term and was succeeded in the national office by William H. Henry of Indiana.[2] Henry's appointment was an indication of how far the party had declined; the appointment of such a national secretary would have been inconceivable ten years earlier.

Henry was originally from Terre Haute, Indiana, Debs's home town, and he had been in the party since its earliest days. A typical hard-working, devoted "Jimmie Higgins," he slowly became a leader in the Indiana organization. He had the support of Debs, and he had a brother, an Indianapolis insurance man, who paid the rent for the state office. Henry and his wife, Emma, devoted their lives to the party, and he in time became Indiana state secretary. As a party organizer and even as a state secretary Henry gave the cause good service, but as national executive secretary he was in beyond his depth. In a party which took pride in its intellectuality, Henry's lack of education was embarrassingly clear. A letter he wrote to his old friend William Williams, a faithful Socialist coal miner of Dugger, Indiana, who religiously sent the national office a dollar of his hard-earned money each month, is typical:

DEAR WILLIE:
Got your letter with the dollar payment for Jan 1929. . . . Well William I guess You are digging coal as usual are You not? Looks as

if the Miners are the beggest asses on earth. Gee how they have been skinned and still they vote for their masters.

We are few Socialists but by the gods We are ahead of the old party Dubbs. We do know what's wrong and are showing the way out, so let's keep right on and some of these days they will say We were right for a long time.

Yours for the cause,

Faithful, coal-digging Willie was only slightly less literate. He wrote a note with his February, 1929, dollar contribution: "Dear comrade Willie I hear in close $1.00 for to help the Dumbell army to get their mental eyes open to se what monkeys they are making of them selves." The two old cronies, dutifully paying and receiving the hard-earned contributions, painfully writing deprecations of the "old party Dubbs," may present a striking picture of simple party loyalty, but it hardly amounted to effective party organization and management. Yet Henry served as national executive secretary for about four years, and when he was finally removed in 1929 it was because of a personal scandal rather than incompetence.[3]

The party was at ebb tide in 1926 and 1927; in 1928, although there were only 7,793 members, over 3,400 of whom were in foreign-language affiliated organizations, there was a considerable revival generated by the presidential campaign and the new national leadership of Norman Thomas. Such was the condition of the party and the inefficiency of the national office that the entire file of official records for 1926 consists of one thin folder. At the 1926 national convention only 33 delegates answered the roll call. State organizations of the party disappeared one by one, forcing the party to organize regional offices to maintain itself in those districts. Massachusetts went under, and the party organized a New England District; where once there had been vigorous organizations in all the Western mountain states there was now nothing but a paper organization, the Rocky Mountain District.

Curiously enough, the party and the entire social democratic movement outside the party were kept alive partly by capitalistic enterprise and the great bull market. The immensely successful *Jewish Daily Forward* of New York, the largest Yiddish newspaper

in the world, subsidized the party. Although the *Forward*'s publisher, Abraham Cahan, and its columns were becoming steadily less
socialistic, the newspaper contributed $500 to the national office each
month. Without this help it is doubtful that the office could have
remained open. This subsidy continued until the spring of 1929,
and by then the party was beginning to get back on its feet.[4]

The great stock market speculations of the latter part of the
decade made it possible for the so-called Garland fund to subsidize
a great many left-wing activities. In 1922, Charles Garland, a young
liberal Harvard College graduate, inherited over a million dollars
from his father, a Wall Street broker. Young Garland, caring more
for progressive and radical causes than for personal wealth, set up a
foundation called the American Fund for Public Service and en-
dowed it with over $900,000. By the fall of 1926 the Garland Fund
had spent hundreds of thousands of dollars for radical causes, and
the newspapers reported with a tone of conservative satisfaction
that the funds had been completely spent. But the newspapers reckoned without the great bull market. The foundation's capital was
invested in common stock of the First National Bank of New York,
and by the spring of 1929 the supposedly depleted fund had grown
to nearly $2,000,000, more than twice what it had been before any
money had been spent. The furious activities on Wall Street were
creating money for the Garland Fund faster than the radicals could
spend it. The governing board of the fund was a diverse group,
representing many left-of-center groups. The president of the fund
was James Weldon Johnson, executive secretary of the National
Association for the Advancement of Colored People. Others on the
board were Roger Baldwin of the American Civil Liberties Union,
Elizabeth Gurley Flynn, Benjamin Gitlow, Scott Nearing, Norman
Thomas, and the liberals Morris L. Ernst and Freda Kirchwey. They
gave money to Brookwood Labor College and other labor colleges,
the *New Masses*, the Rand School Research Department, the *Labor
Age*, the antifascist *Il Nuovo Mundo*, the Vanguard Press, the
Brotherhood of Sleeping Car Porters, and the Sacco-Vanzetti Defense Committee, among others. More than one idealistic worker in

the unremunerative vineyard of reform was able to feed his family through the beneficence of young Charles Garland.⁵

Although the party was all but dead during these years between the La Follette campaign of 1924 and Thomas's first presidential campaign in 1928, Socialists fought and won two celebrated civil liberties cases. The first of these was in boss-ridden Kansas City. There J. G. Hodges of Kansas City and Esther Friedman of New York were arrested for conducting a Socialist street meeting. Their case went on for weeks before they were successful in getting a demurrer, which meant that the case was dropped unless the prosecution wanted to retry the case at the city's expense. The legal costs of the affair fell upon the handful of Kansas City Socialists because the national organization was able to pay only about a third of the expense.

A more important and better publicized case was one that grew out of the Passaic, New Jersey, textile strike of 1926. A former Socialist, then a Communist, named Albert Weisbord, had instigated the strike, but he stirred up more than he expected. The textile workers had real grievances, and the walkout soon became a bona fide strike. There were struck mills both in Passaic and on the other side of the Passaic River, in Bergen County. The vigorously anti-labor sheriff of Bergen County fought the strike by reading the riot law frequently throughout the strike area to prevent strikers' meetings. With the riot law continually in effect the situation was much the same as if there had been martial law, but martial law could have been declared legally only by the governor of the state. Norman Thomas, with the help of the American Civil Liberties Union, determined to right this situation. To make a test case, Thomas organized and spoke before a strike meeting in an open field in the strike area of Bergen County. The sheriff's deputies, carrying sawed-off shot guns, arrested him and took him to the Hackensack jail, where he was held for bail in the outrageous amount of $10,000. The Civil Liberties Union and the strikers were then successful in getting an injunction against the sheriff, and Thomas brought a suit against him for false arrest, which came to nothing because the sheriff died

before the case was tried. The Passaic struggle was no great event in
the history of civil liberties, but it did establish the principle that a
sheriff cannot declare what amounts to martial law.[6] A decade later,
however, a similar fight had to be made all over again, this time in
nearby Jersey City with its Mayor Frank Hague.

One bright spot in the gloomy Socialist picture during these
years of the heyday of American capitalism was the election in 1927
of a Socialist administration at Reading, Pennsylvania. Reading, a
city of light industry in the "Pennsylvania Dutch" region of the
state, had long been a center of Socialist strength. Since 1912 it had
given approximately 15 per cent of its vote to Socialist presidential
candidates, much higher than the national figure, and in 1924 over
one-fourth of the Reading voters had voted for La Follette. The
party's strength there was due to its close relationship with the AFL,
and this Socialist-labor harmony was due largely to the remarkable
personality of James Hudson Maurer, a salty veteran of both the
labor and Socialist movements. Conservative in his Socialism, traditional in his unionism, pleasant, steady, and good-natured, Maurer
was a figure popular in both labor and Socialist circles.

Neither major party had governed Reading conspicuously well,
and in 1927 the Socialists, who had a strong and efficient organization, surprised them with victory. The Socialist J. Henry Stump
was elected mayor, and Maurer and George W. Snyder took seats
on the city council. The Socialists also elected the city controller
and two school board members. Thereafter the Socialists were a
major factor in municipal politics. Like their comrades in Milwaukee, the Socialists gave Reading a relatively clean administration,
but it was certainly not a radical one. Aside from a more sympathetic attitude toward labor in industrial disputes than would be
likely in a typical small-city administration at that time, the Socialist
administration there was not far different from any other. The
Reading Socialists were of course restricted in what they could do
by the legal framework of their state and city, but they were re-
strained by political expediency and their own gradualist philosophies as well. Jim Maurer in a speech before a League for Indus-

trial Democracy conference during the late 1920's epitomized
Reading Socialism: "Capitalism is not now beyond mending as we
used to say twenty-five years ago, on the soap box. 'It can't stand
another patch!' You remember that talk. It used to go good. We
were going to have the cooperative commonwealth some twenty
years ago ushered in on a silver platter. We have found since then
that capitalism will stand a good bit of patching and more patching.
And don't misunderstand me, perhaps it is better so." [7]

The American people in general agreed that capitalism would
stand a great deal of patching, if indeed anything at all was wrong
with it. In such a climate of opinion no anticapitalist movement
could thrive, but in the late 1920's, under the new leadership of
Norman Mattoon Thomas, the Socialist Party ceased its decline and
began slowly to rebuild itself. Thanks to Thomas's vigor, the Socialist Party was in a fairly good position to exploit the advantage that
came to it in the economic crash of late 1929.

Norman Thomas was born in 1884 in Marion, Ohio, the oldest
of six children of a Presbyterian minister. His father's strict Calvin-
ist orthodoxy was tempered by a personal kindliness which prevented the family's being overly stiff-necked. To use Thomas's
language, his father "believed . . . very literally in Hell, but would
not be willing to say anybody was going there." Young Thomas
had an uneventful and typical Midwestern small-town boyhood. He
attended the public schools and helped support himself through high
school by delivering the *Marion Star*, owned and published by Warren G. Harding, then only a local Republican politician. The summer after he graduated from high school his father accepted a
pastorate at Lewisburg, Pennsylvania, thereby enabling the young
man to attend Bucknell University. He was not happy in his fresh-
man year at Bucknell; he wanted to go away to college. The next
year a wealthy uncle by marriage gave Thomas $400 so that he could
go to Princeton. At Princeton, working to provide about half his
expenses, he was a happy and conventional undergraduate. He graduated from Princeton in 1905, and after some settlement-house work
and a trip around the world he attended Union Theological Semi-

nary. In 1911 he graduated from Union and was ordained a minister in the Presbyterian Church.

As the minister of the East Harlem Presbyterian Church, located in a slum neighborhood with a large immigrant population, Thomas began to have his first serious doubts about the desirability of capitalism. His duties there involved "social work" to a considerable extent, and he began to doubt that the welfare of his flock could be any more than temporarily ameliorated if the economic *status quo* were perpetuated. But he became no flaming radical overnight. In 1912 he was an enrolled Progressive. In 1916 he voted for Woodrow Wilson, with whom he had taken a course when he was a student at Princeton. His conversion to socialism was slow; there was nothing in Thomas's experience like Debs's supposed conversion to socialism in his cell in the Woodstock, Illinois, jail. Thomas read the Christian Socialist Walter Rauschenbusch, but he still clung to the ideas he'd learned at Princeton in a course which, whatever its real title, was in Thomas's words a course in "Why Socialism Ain't So." Then he read the famous debate on socialism between Father John Ryan and Morris Hillquit and thought Hillquit had the better argument. But he did not rush out to join the Socialist Party.

It was opposition to the World War, based on Christian ideals of pacifism, that drew Norman Thomas to the Socialists. When Morris Hillquit made his campaign for mayor of New York in 1917 on an antiwar position, Thomas wrote to him expressing his good wishes. Quite to his surprise, Hillquit asked him to work for the Socialist ticket in the campaign. With Judah L. Magnes, Amos Pinchot, Dudley Field Malone, and Allan McCurdy, Thomas was active as an independent for Hillquit. Thomas was particularly attracted to Hillquit's municipal program, which among other things called for public housing projects, housing that was needed very badly in Thomas's parish. But if working for Hillquit might in the long run improve the conditions of Thomas's congregation, his association with the Socialists was hurting the congregation in the short run. Financial support to the church began to decline; Thomas thought this support was being withheld because of his political activities, and he resigned his pastorate. Soon thereafter he joined the Socialist Party.

Although he did not now have a church and was a regular card-carrying Socialist Party member, Thomas's orientation was still more Christian than Marxist. Indeed, Thomas never became a very conventional Marxist. Before the war Thomas had been the secretary for the Fellowship of Reconciliation, then an unpaid job. The Fellowship of Reconciliation was and is yet a Christian pacifist organization. After leaving his church, Thomas devoted more and more time to the Fellowship, and when the organization started a magazine, the *World Tomorrow*, Thomas became its paid editor. Under the leadership of Thomas and Devere Allen, the *World Tomorrow* became a remarkable periodical, the leading journal of liberal Christianity and Christian-motivated political radicalism. Thomas also had a brief taste of the academic world. During the academic year 1918–1919, holding the rank of lecturer, Thomas taught a course at Teachers College, Columbia University, called "The Assimilation of the Immigrant as an Educational Problem." [8]

In 1928 the Socialist presidential nomination went to Thomas largely by default; there was no one else for the job. Debs was dead. The only Socialists of national reputation, Hillquit and Berger, were ineligible for the Presidency because of their foreign birth. Dan Hoan would have been a logical choice, but he was too busy as Socialist mayor of Milwaukee to make a campaign, and it would have been foolish to have resigned the mayoralty for certain presidential defeat. To Socialists outside New York Thomas was an unknown figure. He had run for office on the Socialist ticket four times—for governor of New York in 1924, for mayor of New York City in 1925 against Jimmie Walker, for state senator in 1926, and for alderman in 1927—and had not been very successful in attracting votes in any of them. In 1924 he had run behind his ticket. Unknown to the American public upon his nomination in 1928, this tall forty-four-year-old former minister with the gray hair, pale blue eyes, and rich voice was soon to become the very symbol of American Socialism. The party of Debs was to become the party of Thomas.

The difference between Eugene Debs and Norman Thomas was vast. Debs had come to Socialism from the labor movement, he had little formal education, and he directed his appeal to the workingman. Thomas came to Socialism from the ministry, he had two college degrees, and his strongest appeal was to intellectuals. The change in the party's leadership was a reflection of what was happening to the Socialist Party.

The composition of the NEC elected at the 1928 convention also reflected the degree to which intellectuals and relative conservatives controlled the Socialist Party. The national committee elected was composed of Maurer, Joseph Sharts of Dayton, Ohio, Hillquit, Hoan, George E. Roewer of Boston, Oneal, and Jasper McLevy of Bridgeport, Connecticut. The convention elected Victor Berger chairman of the NEC by acclamation.[9] Of these eight men, none had ever been associated with the radical wing of the Socialist Party. Only Maurer had a long record of activity directly in the labor movement. Hillquit, Sharts, Hoan, and Roewer were lawyers. Berger and Oneal had devoted their whole lives to the Socialist movement, serving mostly as journalists. There were no rural people on the NEC and there was none who was then working with his hands. The term "intellectual" is admittedly vague and a word that escapes exact definition, but in the common usage of the term only Maurer and McLevy were clearly not intellectuals.

Thomas and the NEC set to work to rebuild the Socialist Party, and they enjoyed a measure of success. One of the first tasks was to establish an efficient national office. When it developed that William H. Henry had too many friends in the party to allow his removal as national executive secretary, Thomas and Hillquit circumvented his inefficiency by setting up a duplicate national office in New York under the name of the Socialist Action Committee. It was composed exclusively of New Yorkers, and it did most of its work in the East. Hillquit was its chairman, Algernon Lee its treasurer, and G. August Gerber its secretary. Such duplication was hardly calculated to rebuild the national character of the party, but it did more in its area than William H. Henry could do there or anywhere else.

In an effort to get more women into the Socialist Party the convention authorized the creation of a Women's National Committee. The NEC named Mrs. Lilith Wilson of Sinking Springs, Pennsylvania, near Reading, to be chairman of the group. Mrs. Wilson was eager and able—she was later to serve several terms in the Pennsylvania State Assembly—but the Women's National Committee had little success. The organization was naturally most active only where there was already a going Socialist organization, especially New York and Reading, and it had little success in attracting new non-Socialist recruits.[10]

One of the difficulties in the campaign and in the rebuilding of the party was the lack of strong and efficient local organizations. The Socialists had been warned that they would never have much success without strong grass-roots organizations,[11] but with the party's poor finances and its lack of a firm footing in the labor movement in all but one or two states the party found it almost impossible to establish strong locals. Where the party could afford them, it sent organizers, sometimes surprisingly young men, to work at the local level. But the strategy was not to rebuild at the local level and thence up to the national level; it was the reverse. What local organizations there were were concentrated on the national campaign. This was due partly to the dominance of intellectuals in the party. Thomas, for example, was embarrassed by the incompetence of local Socialist candidates. He unconsciously cringed when, seated on the platforms of small-town auditoriums, he heard local Socialist candidates demonstrate their lack of intellectual grasp in ungrammatical language.[12] There can be little question that many of these local candidates and leaders were men of little distinction or ability. One has only to read some of their correspondence to see that. But then no American political party is distinguished by the quality of its local leaders—particularly the successful parties, whose organizations extend up from the ward and township level.

But if the speeches of local Socialist candidates did not reflect quality of thought, the speeches of their presidential candidate did. Thomas conducted a vigorous, high-level campaign that covered the country. In reading his campaign addresses it is evident that he was determined, in the words of the Democratic presidential candidate twenty-four years later, "to talk sense to the American people." Socialists have been accused of living in another world, of failing to keep their eyes on the political issues of the here and now.[13] Such a criticism of Norman Thomas in 1928 would be unfair. For example, the manner in which he discussed the tariff question was both direct and in line with the best economic thinking.

The Republicans in the campaign attributed part of the reason for American prosperity to the high protective tariff and argued that an even higher tariff would bring even more prosperity. The Democrats straddled on the tariff as best they could, trying to appeal to everyone. Thomas pointed out how the American high tariff strained international relations and aided business at the expense of farmers and consumers generally. And as for Herbert Hoover's argument, "attributing high American wages to our tariff is mostly bunk wholly unworthy of his reputation as an economist. How, for instance, does the tariff help our highly paid building trade workers whose wages he cites?" American prosperity was due in part, said Thomas, not to the protective tariff but, quite the reverse, to the fact that America enjoyed the "greatest internal free trade market between our states to be found in all the world." But the Socialists were not all-out free traders who believed free trade to be the cure for all economic ills. They were for lowering the economic barrier around the nation but not for razing it at one stroke because "having got so far along on the protectionist track the United States cannot jump to another, even if better, track without a wreck." Any possible labor dislocation brought by a tariff reduction should be alleviated by a comprehensive public works program.

Thomas and the Socialists were equally explicit on other issues. Noting that there were about four million unemployed even in that year of "prosperity," the Socialists urged the federal government to adopt a public works program and to lend money to the states and municipalities for public works in order to put the unemployed to work "at hours and wages fixed by bona-fide labor unions." They urged the adoption of a constitutional amendment prohibiting child labor and the shortening of the working day and week in accordance with the increased productivity of labor. They were also for federal old-age pensions and unemployment insurance, to be financed by increased corporation taxes, inheritance levies, and taxes on large individual incomes. The foreign relations part of the platform was internationalist and pacifist. The Socialists were for the cancellation of the Allied war debts and the reparation obligations of the Central Powers on the condition that these powers reduce their military expenditures to below prewar levels. The party denounced the war debt settlement the Republican Congress and administration had made with Italy on the grounds that it favored the fascists and helped to perpetuate the political enslavement of the Italian people. As for the League of Nations, the Socialists held that it should be strengthened and made more inclusive and democratic, and that the United States should join the League in order to help achieve these goals. The United States should do everything possible to effect international disarmament and should show its good faith by decreasing its own military and naval appropriations. While condemning Soviet "despotic and brutal" totalitarianism, the Socialists urged "the speedy recognition of Russia, not as an expression of approval of the Bolshevik regime, but as a contribution towards the establishment of international stability and good will." Finally, the United States, the Socialists argued, should grant the Filipinos their independence, give home rule to Puerto Rico and the Virgin Islands, and withdraw all troops from Nicaragua. Victor Berger read this platform into the *Congressional Record*, and under his frank—and also under the frank of Representative Fiorello La Guardia, who generously helped the Socialists—the Socialist program gained a considerable circulation.

Being a party of socialism, the Socialists of course had in their platform a demand for the socialization of the American economy. "We stand now as always, in America and in all lands, for the collective ownership of natural resources and basic industries and their democratic management for the use and benefit of all instead of the private profit of the privileged few." Possibly because, as with the tariff, the United States had gone so far down the track of capitalism that it could not without a wreck jump to the better track of socialism, Thomas subordinated the socialist feature of the platform to the reformist and progressive aspects of it. The nationalization demand was not deemphasized altogether out of sight, but during the campaign it became clearer than ever that the Socialist Party had become in large part a left-wing progressive party, as much in the tradition of Bryan, Roosevelt, Wilson, and La Follette as in the tradition of Karl Marx. To be sure, Socialists retained their social democratic criticism of capitalism and the social democratic philosophy remained as their guide. But so far as practical things to be done in the United States immediately were concerned, the emphasis of their program was not far different from that of a left-wing "patcher of capitalism." Yet there was a difference between Socialists and progressives, no matter how similar their immediate programs were. It was the same difference that there is between the New Deal and the British Labor Party, a difference in philosophies and ultimate goals. They would use roughly similar programs for different purposes, the one to save capitalism and make it work, the other purposefully to move the economy in the direction of democratic socialism. Just after the campaign, in urging a new political alignment, Thomas put it quite clearly: "A new party need not worry over much about Marxian orthodoxy; it should talk the American language; but it cannot get far without tackling this philosophy of cooperation in an age of machinery. . . . The appeal to a vague discontent or an ill-defined Liberalism has not, will not, and cannot get us far in this dangerous age, when our social thinking and social machinery lag so far behind our skill in mechanical production— and war time destruction." [14]

But in the campaign of 1928 an uninitiated observer, unfamiliar with the broad purposes and social democratic philosophy of the Socialists, might well have wondered how Thomas differed from any other thoroughgoing reformer. The Socialist standard-bearer urged that the power of the federal courts to issue labor injunctions be inhibited and that the Constitution be amended to eliminate "lame-duck" Congresses, and each of these demands was within a very few years effected under major-party auspices. He urged the direct and popular election of the President and Vice President, a reform not unknown among reformist Democrats and Republicans. And, like a good Northern liberal, he urged that Negroes be allowed to vote on the same basis as whites and that to ensure Negro voting congressional representation be reduced for those states that through one ruse or another denied the suffrage to a large group of citizens.

With such a program and emphasis and with his obvious university background, Thomas attracted a considerable number of intellectuals during the campaign. In August the debunking historian and novelist W. E. Woodward announced his support of Thomas and his running mate James H. Maurer. He sent a letter to seven hundred writers and artists urging them to vote for Thomas because a vote for the Socialists "will help lay the foundation for a powerful party of progress and social justice." He said nothing, significantly, about a working-class party or a party of mercy. By election day several university professors had publicly announced their intention of voting for Thomas. Among them were such learned men as the geographer J. Russell Smith of Columbia University, Robert Morss Lovett of the University of Chicago, and the theologian Reinhold Niebuhr of Union Theological Seminary.[15] If the Thomas voters were not to be numerous, they were at least to be select.

Alfred E. Smith, the Democratic presidential candidate, was a Roman Catholic, the only major-party candidate of that faith ever to run for the Presidency, and the campaign came to have overtones of a very ugly nativism. Only three years before, the anti-Catholic Ku Klux Klan had still been a potent force in many states. The party had opposed the Klan, and now Norman Thomas lashed out against this nativism in no uncertain terms. "Religious prejudice is being dragged into the campaign, openly and secretly, on both sides, in a degree that is most profoundly hurtful to our democracy," he charged in an open letter to the Protestant churches of America. In the campaign Smith was a "Wet" and Hoover was a "Dry," and Thomas charged that Protestant leaders were using the prohibition issue as a "mask for religious partisanship." If they sincerely thought the prohibition issue a moral one, and were sincerely concerned with the nation's morals, why did not ministers and other religious leaders "take more pains than they have done to rebuke the unblushing hypocrisy and corruption of many of their political bedfellows?" And if church leaders give quasiofficial support to Hoover, thus involving themselves in politics, why do they keep silent on such important political questions as imperialism, the armament question, "the coal tragedy, the power lobby and civil liberty?" Thomas wrote to his former colleagues in the ministry, "The Bible, if memory serves me, contains no explicit Volstead act, but it is fairly explicit on matters of the exploitation of the poor." [16]

But the American voters that November demonstrated they were more concerned with prohibition, Protestantism, and prosperity than with exploitation of the poor. In the Hoover landslide Norman Thomas received only 267,420 votes. Debs had polled over a hundred thousand more in 1904, and in percentages the vote was even worse than the first time the Socialists had run a presidential candidate in 1900. Furthermore, over one-third of the Thomas vote came from New York State alone. If the Socialists had had only the election returns with which to judge their strength, they might as well have quit as a political party.

But the Socialists, ever optimistic about their pessimistic view of a capitalist society, saw other things in the campaign that heartened them. There was no denying that the party was stronger after the election than it had been before. Had the election been held in 1926, the Socialist record probably would have been infinitely worse. One sign of strength was the new local organizations that had taken root here and there. Another was the success the Socialists had had in getting signatures on petitions to get on the ballot. At the start of the campaign the Socialists were on the ballot automatically in only four states; through special petitions they got a place on the ballot in all but eleven states.[17] But most of all, the Socialists had found a new leader in Norman Thomas who could command attention in non-Socialist circles. Thomas brought to the Socialist movement no large personal following such as Debs had brought with him from the ranks of labor. What personal following Thomas had was among intellectuals rather than among laboring men, and he did not have the charismatic qualities of Debs. But he was, nevertheless, an attractive personality. He spoke and thought in an American idiom at a time when many people were extremely distrustful of anything alien. Of Midwestern origin, a minister's son, a Princeton graduate, and himself a Presbyterian minister, what could be more respectable in American eyes? The campaign of 1928 showed the Socialists that in Thomas they had a figure who would receive the country's respect—even if he would not receive its votes.

There were indications here and there that Thomas's campaign really had begun to revive the party. Former organizers who had grown tired and left the party wrote to national headquarters asking what they could do to help. One such volunteer, who had twice been a Socialist candidate for Congress before the war, asked to be allowed to organize in the South. "I can furnish my car and pay my expense for $5.00 and I believe I can make good, and would like to hear from you. I am fixed for camping out in most kind of weather and keeping expences [sic] down to the minimum." A more efficient and better financed national office might have made some progress with these volunteers. But the party's financial resources were slim and the national secretary was still the inept William H. Henry. After waiting over two weeks to answer one such offer, Henry could do nothing for the man but suggest that perhaps the Socialist newspapers might give him a commission for new subscriptions.[18]

A vigorous and decently financed party headquarters probably could have had at least a modest success in rebuilding the organization. When in February, 1929, Henry mustered enough imagination, force, and funds to send out a thousand letters to former Oklahoma party members, the results were gratifying. Oklahoma, which once had the highest percentage of Socialist votes in the nation, had not had a state organization for years. Within a month after the thousand letters were mailed, enough applications for party membership had come in to begin plans for a state convention and reorganization. But the success of the technique in Oklahoma did not move anyone to try it in other states, in some of which there is good reason to believe it would have brought the party large returns. In the summer of 1929 in the Minnesota municipal elections Socialist candidates received a total of over 18,000 votes without anywhere making a strong campaign. Only then, after these votes had been cast with almost no asking for them, did the party begin to be active in Minnesota.[19]

The inefficiency and inaction of the national office was not the only condition which hindered the party's exploiting the anticapitalist sentiment that Thomas's campaign had evoked; there were cases of outright unethical practices that caused friction within the party, thereby putting a brake on Socialist action. During the campaign in 1928 the Socialist Action Committee had been able to raise nearly $75,000, and it felt it could afford to hire some paid organizers. Among the organizers hired was J. W. Brown of Maine, who was to receive for his work six dollars a day and expenses. According to Brown's claim later, he worked for several weeks and received no money at all. Brown borrowed the money necessary to go to New York to see G. August Gerber, who served in the dual capacity of secretary of the Socialist Action Committee and national campaign chairman. Brown presented Gerber with a statement. Gerber accepted it as correct and made a partial payment of it. Weeks later Brown wrote to Gerber that the party still owed him $158. Gerber sent him a check for fifty dollars, on the back of which was the statement, "This payment is accepted in full for work done for the Socialist Party National Campaign Committee." Brown was understandably angry and started a campaign against Gerber within the party that did the cause no good.[20]

In Virginia in 1928 there was a situation that caused the party considerable hurt. So weak was the party in that conservative state that no one but an eighteen-year-old youth, David G. George, could be found to serve as state secretary, and so poor was the state organization that it had no funds to carry on the national campaign. The young state secretary started a bitter feud among the Virginia comrades when he made a deal with the Democrats to enrich the party's treasury. George arranged with the Democratic State Chairman that for $1,250 the name of the Socialist candidate for United States Senator, John G. Bowman of Winchester, would be withdrawn from the contest. The Democrat paid George $500, George withdrew Bowman, and then the Democrat defaulted on the rest of the amount. George used the money he received entirely for party purposes. The national organization, knowing nothing of this arrangement and impressed with the young man's energetic organizing activities, a few months later made him secretary of the newly formed Southern District. But Bowman and other Virginia Socialists were not so impressed with George. Bowman, displeased with being so summarily removed from the race, broadcast the story among his comrades in the state but did not bring formal charges against George to the state committee, constitutionally the only agency which could discipline George. When George tried to hush up the whole matter and appeared to have the support of the national organization, his opponents in the state became more bitter against him. Finally, after four years of feuding, the matter was referred to the National Executive Committee, which found George guilty as charged and censured him; but the committee was powerless constitutionally to expel him.[21]

Fortunately for the Socialists these breaches of ethics did not become generally known outside the party. It is amusing to contemplate what a vigorous Republican editor could have done with the George affair. Nor were these matters of common knowledge even within the party. But to the extent that these affairs were known within the party they shamed and divided an already weak organization.

In the spring of 1929 William H. Henry became involved in personal difficulties and resigned as national executive secretary. The exact story is obscure, but Henry's wife, Emma, then state secretary in Indiana, brought suit for divorce. Henry left the national

office and became an organizer in Wisconsin, a job better suited to
his talents.[22] Here was a break the more vigorous members of the
national leadership had been looking for. The NEC made Mabel H.
Barnes, Henry's assistant and the wife of J. Mahlon Barnes, acting
national secretary and set about finding a capable man to take charge
of the national office. After considering such able people as Paul
Blanshard and Powers Hapgood, the NEC selected Clarence Senior,
then the young director of the Cleveland Labor College. The choice
proved to be a good one. He had not the experience in the Socialist
movement that Henry had—since he had been a party member for
not quite two years the NEC had to waive the constitutional re-
quirement that the national secretary be a member for at least three
years—but he had the vigor and executive ability that the party so
sorely needed to capitalize on the increased interest in Socialism that
Thomas's campaign had evoked. A graduate of the University of
Kansas, Senior had been associated with the League of Municipalities
before he went to Cleveland. Besides participating in the worker and
adult education movements there, he was instrumental in the reorganization and revitalization of the local party organization. Once a
center of Socialist strength, the party in Cleveland had dwindled
to almost nothing; but with Senior's leadership the Socialists there
were able in 1929 to run very strong races in the municipal election.[23]

The problems that faced the new twenty-nine-year-old national
secretary were knotty. Raising money was perhaps the greatest of
them. The party was in debt to its printer. The International's officers in Switzerland sent polite but firm notices that the American
party was nearly two years in arrears in its dues. The British Labor
Party, its finances crippled by the Trades Disputes Act of the Baldwin government, had appealed to the American Socialists for help.
Financial troubles were to continue, but at least now the national
secretary would go out and beat the bushes for money. Gone were
the days when the national secretary sat in the party's office on
Washington Boulevard in Chicago, moaning about the creditors'

bills and declaring that "God or Marx only knows how [they are] to be paid." [24]

And it was high time that the Socialists shake themselves and rebuild their organization, for in only a few months was to come the great crash on Wall Street and the greatest economic depression in the history of the United States, when the capitalism that the Socialists had been so long cursing and criticizing was to come a cropper as it never had before.

IX

THE SOCIALISTS AND
THE DEPRESSION
1929–1933

FOR three decades Socialists had preached from their soapboxes that capitalism was the root of most, if not all, social evil. The capitalistic system, if indeed it could be dignified by the term system, was an economic arrangement that was basically unworkable, that had inherent in it periods of boom and bust, and that was based upon exploitation even during the periods of prosperity. To end wild fluctuations of the business cycle, wars, economic exploitation, poverty, hunger, and misery the Socialists had told the American people they would have to abandon capitalism and reorder their economy to one in which the people collectively owned the means to produce and distribute the goods necessary for material well-being. But in three decades the Socialists had been able to reach only a relatively small proportion of the American people and had convinced even fewer that their argument was valid. Now in the autumn of 1929 American capitalism—wider than that, world capitalism—began a downward turn that brought doubts to many people about the desirability of capitalism. The course of events was to bring in a few years more dissatisfaction with America's economic arrangements than the Socialist Party had been able to evoke in nearly one-third of a century. It seemed to some that the Great Depression would swell the ranks of Socialism, perhaps even make the Socialists the dominant, or at least a major, political organization.

It is impossible in only a few paragraphs properly to describe the extent and intensity of the Great Depression and the suffering it caused. Economists, those experts in what was once known as the dismal science—and certainly during the depression decade they had a dismal subject matter—can tell us in their cold statistics something of the extent of the depression. Unemployment was one of the most serious aspects of the Great Depression. In 1929 there were 1,499,000 unemployed people, or 3.1 per cent of the civilian labor force. These numbers grew to 4,248,000 the next year, to 7,911,000 in 1931, to 11,901,000 in 1932, and to 12,634,000 in 1933, the worst year of unemployment. In that year 25.2 per cent of the civilian labor force was unemployed. These figures are only estimates; they perhaps should be higher. The numbers of those only partially unemployed or working at jobs that required significantly less skill than the workers had and paying significantly less than their skills would normally command will never be known. Nor will it ever be known how many people of the American working force were at one time or another out of work during the depression years. Even the shockingly high unemployment figures do not reflect the true worker displacement of those years.

Other impressive statistics indicate the serious extent of the economy's failure. In 1931, 2,298 banks, with total deposits of over $1,500,000,000, suspended business. In the year that Franklin Delano Roosevelt was elected President, 31,822 American businesses failed. The physical volume of American industrial production dropped nearly 50 per cent from 1929 to 1932. Net income from agriculture declined from $7,708,000,000 in 1929, which was not a good year for farmers, to $2,821,000,000 in 1932.[1]

These statistics of the economists are very useful, but they do not describe the suffering brought by the Great Depression. Literary artists can tell us something of that. Thomas Wolfe, in his prowling through the "great web and jungle" of New York City during the early depression, saw "a man whose life had subsided into a mass of shapeless and filthy rags, devoured by vermin; wretches huddled together for a little warmth in freezing cold squatting in doorless closets upon the foul seat of a public latrine within the very shadow, the cold shelter of palatial and stupendous monuments of wealth." [2] But no artist could report on more than an extremely small part of the American scene; no observer, no matter how sensitive, could see or appreciate the total impact of the Great Depression. The price of the depression, the failure of laissez-faire capitalism, either in terms of dollars and cents or of suffering, can never be fully and accurately measured.

To say that Socialists were gratified by the depression's confirmation of their diagnosis of capitalism's weaknesses is too strong a statement, but for the comrades there was undoubtedly some satisfaction in the economic calamity. For a number of reasons, but mainly because of the relatively good record of American capitalism in the 1920's, the Socialist Party had been in decline since the end of the war. But no longer would Socialists have to begin their proselytizing work by making their audiences dissatisfied with the economic *status quo*. Their task now was to convince the dissatisfied that their best hope of salvation lay in social democracy by way of the Socialist Party.

Within a matter of days after the Wall Street debacle Socialist candidates in municipal elections gave good accounts of themselves. The voters of Reading reelected a Socialist administration. In Cleveland, John G. Willert, a candidate for the city council, ran a close race and had the support of that city's Scripps-Howard newspaper. In New York City, Norman Thomas ran the best race any Socialist mayoralty candidate in that city ever had, polling just under 175,000 votes, more than Hillquit had received in his great campaign in 1917. The *World* and the *Telegram* supported Thomas editorially, and all the daily newspapers gave more space to Thomas's campaign than Socialists usually got in the daily press. Although the vote for all Socialist candidates in the city increased significantly—Charles Solomon, for example, received more votes for controller than Thomas had received for mayor in 1925—the Thomas vote was not a Socialist vote. His support came from independents, largely from intellectuals such as John Haynes Holmes, Harry Emerson Fosdick, and John Dewey, and the issues of the election had to do with municipal reform rather than with Socialism. Thomas received more votes in the city in 1929 than he had received in the whole state in his presidential race the year before, but the increase undoubtedly was due to his greater personal popularity, faith in his good sense and integrity, and disgust with the Jimmie Walker administration rather than any rejection of capitalism.[3]

Socialist leaders were gratified by their relative success in the 1929 municipal elections but they were not so foolish as to think that the depression was going to make the party strong without a great deal of work. For the next five years or so the principal activity of the Socialists was building the party, organizing, trying to mold America's inchoate discontent into a strong movement for democratic socialism.

When Clarence Senior became national secretary in the summer of 1929, he brought to the national office some long-needed vigor. The results were immediate. By the end of 1929 the Socialist Party had gained more members than it had in all the years since 1923. Through the United Socialist Drive it had raised more funds than it had in years, it had revived the flow of Socialist pamphlets which had all but dried up since the war, and it had boosted the circulation of Socialist newspapers. For 1930 the NEC set for itself the goal of signing up 30,000 new members and began its work eagerly by arranging a Western lecture tour for each of the NEC members.

Senior brought a great deal of imagination to his task. In the spring of 1930 he proposed an idea that would both "spread the Socialist message" and bring much needed money into the national office. He proposed that the party organize a lecture bureau, to be called the Social Problems Lecture Bureau, under whose auspices an impressive suggested list of labor leaders, intellectuals, Socialists, and liberals would speak and give to the bureau 25 per cent of their fees. If all the proposed lecturers had accepted the arrangement, the

Socialists would have had a most brilliant staff working for them. On the proposed list, besides the usual Socialist speakers, were such names as Roger Baldwin, Harriot Stanton Blatch, Paul F. Brissenden, Howard Brubaker, Stuart Chase, Paul H. Douglas, Floyd Dell, Morris Ernst, Walton Hamilton, John Haynes Holmes, John Ise, Paul U. Kellogg, Jacob Potofsky, A. Philip Randolph, and Mark Starr. Relatively few of the nonparty members proposed ever spoke under the bureau's auspices, but there was set up a better organization than previously existed to get Socialist speakers before non-Socialist groups.[4]

Senior tried as much as possible to enlist the aid of Socialist sympathizers who for one reason or another did not join the party. This was a fairly large group, probably larger than the party membership at this time. Senior in 1931 organized a big fund-raising campaign called the Socialism Forward Drive. He sent out 10,000 letters asking for financial contributions to the party and for cooperation in distributing Socialist literature, most of them to Socialist sympathizers rather than to party members. The party also solicited funds from hundreds of cooperatives, unions, and workingmen's fraternal organizations. This attempt to broaden the party's financial support beyond the membership was consistent with the desire of Norman Thomas and his personal followers to bring about a realignment of American political parties. Late in 1928 Thomas and Paul Blanshard, then a party member and Thomas's associate in seeking to reform New York City's politics, formed the League for Independent Political Action with such nonsocialist liberals as John Dewey, Paul H. Douglas, Oswald Garrison Villard, and W. E. B. Du Bois. The LIPA, in some ways similar to the Conference for Progressive Political Action of the early 1920's, hoped to serve as a liberal pressure group and as a basis upon which a new political party, embracing all of the Left between the Communists and the progressives in the major parties, could be founded.[5]

All these fund-raising activities enjoyed relative success. The Socialist Party never had enough money to do all it wanted to, but Senior's money-raising enabled it to do more than it had for over a decade. By 1932 the party could afford to have thirteen paid organizers at work in all parts of the country but the deep South. Here and there were signs of possible revival to prewar virility. In Oklahoma the party had been dead since the war, but now the LIPA was active there and things looked promising for a resumption of Sooner Socialism. A few old Socialist leaders who had not been active for years volunteered to work for the cause again. Walter Thomas Mills, then seventy-five years old, spoke at Socialist meetings in California. Fred Warren had such success in the Socialism Forward Drive on the Great Plains that he planned to revive the *Appeal to Reason*, although he never did.[6]

The growing strength of the party was reflected also in mildly successful elections in 1930. The Socialists of Milwaukee increased their representation in the lower house of the state legislature from three to nine and added a second state senator. But the seat in Congress held by Berger before his death the previous summer was lost by a narrow margin to the Republican candidate. William J. Quick, Socialist candidate for Congress in a district adjacent to Berger's, ran a surprisingly good race. The Socialists of Reading succeeded in electing two of their members, Darlington Hoopes and Lilith Wilson, to the state legislature. The following year, however, Reading Socialists in a municipal campaign marked by charges of Socialist hostility to religion, the home, and the flag, lost to a fusion ticket. Except for a few small-town administrations, these were the only Socialists holding public office.[7]

Elsewhere, Socialist candidates increased their votes over previous years but came nowhere close to electoral victory. Upton Sinclair polled over 50,000 votes for governor of California on the Socialist ticket, and Louis Waldman, running against Franklin D. Roosevelt for governor of New York, received over 120,000 votes. The columnist Heywood Broun attracted considerable publicity but few votes in his campaign for Congress in a New York City "silk stocking" district. In Maryland, Elisabeth Gilman, daughter of Daniel Coit Gilman, former president of Johns Hopkins University, was a distinguished but quite unsuccessful gubernatorial candidate.[8]

By the beginning of the presidential election year of 1932, the beginning of the third year of the Great Depression, the Socialist Party had rebuilt itself to a condition roughly comparable to its strength about 1908. But its character in 1932 was little like that of 1908. The change in the party is symbolized by the contrast between Debs and Thomas. Debs's main appeal was in the working class; Thomas's appeal was strongest among well educated, middle-class people who had a strong sense of idealism. Liberal Protestant ministers and rabbis frequently supported Thomas, and there were several college professors in the Socialist Party in the 1930's. At the meetings of the American Economic Association in 1932 four Socialists were on the program: Harold Underwood Faulkner, who had run for the Massachusetts senate on the Socialist ticket that fall; Broadus Mitchell of Johns Hopkins University; Maynard Krueger of the University of Chicago; and Harry W. Laidler of the League for Industrial Democracy. The nomination of Mrs. Laetitia Moon Conard for governor of Iowa in 1932, while not a typical nomination perhaps, epitomized the middle-class intellectual aspect of the Socialist Party; Mrs. Conard was a mother of three children and a professor of sociology at Grinnell College.[9] Intellectuals in the Socialist Party were nothing new by any means, nor were representatives of labor altogether missing in the Socialist rolls. At this time the leadership and the older members of the International Ladies Garment Workers' Union and the Amalgamated Clothing Workers were still predominantly Socialist, and there was some Socialist support among the Detroit auto workers and a few state AFL organizations. But the labor support of the party in 1932 was undeniably weaker than it had been before the war. Of farmer-Socialists, who once had been numerous in some states, there now was almost none.

But if the party's character had changed, it nevertheless had been resuscitated. It must not be forgotten that in Mr. Coolidge's America the Socialist Party had been all but dead. By 1932 new blood in the party's leadership had revived the organization considerably. There was less optimism about the party's future than there had been in the prewar years, but the organization's growth had caused it to be not without hope.

As the party grew in the early years of the depression it developed within it new factional alignments, divisions within the party that were both geographical and ideological. There were three main groups. First there was the Old Guard, composed largely, but not exclusively, of members of middle or old age who had been in the party since its early days. Devoted social democrats they were, having stayed with the party during its thin days in the 1920's when less dedicated members strayed from the movement, but devotion and loyalty were about all that some of the Old Guard were able to give the party. The Old Guard occupied most of the organization's leadership positions by virtue of their seniority. Such Old Guard leaders as Hillquit, Algernon Lee, and James Oneal were men of great ability, but many of the Old Guard leaders at lower echelons in the party occupied positions of importance for which only their length of party service qualified them. Geographically, the Old Guard was strongest in Pennsylvania, New York, and Connecticut, but it controlled most of the state committees and offices.

A distinction can and should be made within the opposition to the Old Guard between the radical doctrinaire Marxists known as the Militants and the radical non-Marxists, whom we shall call the Progressives. Fundamentally these two groups had little in common except opposition to Old Guard party leadership and, usually, rather recent membership in the party. There was a generation between the Old Guard and its opponents. In 1932 Hillquit was 62 years old, Lee was 59, Oneal was 57, and Maurer was 68; many of their opponents were not yet 30, and significant numbers of them were still college undergraduates. The Old Guard leaders could have been the grandfathers of some of their opponents. But even when an actual generation did not separate the groups, a party generation did. The Old Guard's opponents had come into the party during the depression, and since the Socialists had made very few converts in the 1920's a Socialist in the 1930's had either been in the party a very long or a very short time.

The Militants were numerically a small group, but they were an extremely vocal one. Philosophically the Militants were Marxists, as were their Old Guard opposition. But the Militants leaned much further toward Marxism as developed by Lenin than did the Old Guard, whose favorite theoreticians were Karl Kautsky and Hill-quit. Yet the Militants were not Communists. They were opposed to the rigid discipline of the Third International, and they were critical of the Soviet Union's denial of civil liberties, just as were Old Guard Socialists. In many respects the ideological differences between the Old Guard and the Militants were differences of emphasis. In one of their first open conflicts, at the convention of New York City Socialists late in 1930, the Old Guard and the Militants presented the convention with different resolutions on the Soviet Union. Both demanded United States recognition of the Soviet Union. Both condemned foreign interference with Russian internal affairs. Both stated disapproval of Russian extermination of minority opinion. But the Militants advocated "a definitely friendly attitude towards Soviet Russia" and dealt only briefly with Soviet totalitarianism, while the Old Guard asked only for "normal diplomatic and trade relations" with Russia and spoke at length of Russian "denial of elementary civil rights . . . governmental terrorism, and . . . ruthless suppression of all dissenting opinion." There were ideological differences between the Militants and the Old Guard, but both sides magnified them. The Militants, for example, saw more of a conservative bogey in the Old Guard than there actually was, although certainly these old Socialists were hardly fire-breathing reds. The Militants equated the American Old Guard leadership with the conservative leadership of the British Labor Party and the German Social Democracy, fellow parties with the American Socialists in the Labor and Socialist International. To write a Marxian criticism of Ramsay MacDonald was a simple matter; to criticize Hillquit, for example, assuming he was an American MacDonald, was also easy. But it was not valid. Similarly, it was easy—and invalid—for the Old Guard from a social democratic position to criticize the Militants as Communists and even, strangely enough, as fascists.[10]

One important difference between the Militants and their Old Guard opponents was their viewpoints on democracy. The Old Guard was composed of convinced democrats who held that socialism would advance democracy and could come to America only by democratic means. The Militants' view toward democracy was in some respects similar to that of the Communists. Democracy was to them a bourgeois quality, a device adopted by the bourgeoisie to defeat the aristocracy that was now being abandoned by capitalists as their conflict with the proletariat became more intense. Wrote one Militant, "Capitalist democracy can be viewed as a game between capital and labor in which the capitalist is at liberty to make the rules, count the points, or suspend the rules entirely." Socialists, then, should not make a "fetish" of democracy.[11]

The Militants were noisy, but the Progressive opponents of the Old Guard were more numerous. The Progressives were no caucus within the party such as the Old Guard and the Militants. They were a vague group of recent members, representing many shades of opinion, who were greatly dissatisfied with the slowness, the lack of activity, of the Old Guard. They were not doctrinaire Marxists; indeed, many were not Marxian at all. Their goal was a realignment of American politics whereby there would be a party to represent labor and dirt farmers, based upon principles rather than upon thirst for office and political opportunism. This party once in office would extend democracy and civil liberties, socialize basic industries, and move rapidly in the direction of what is nowadays called the welfare state. If the American electorate should support the Socialist Party and make it such an organization, well and good; if such a party should have to be a new organization, a national farmer-labor party, then the Socialists should go into the new organization.

Most of these Progressives were attracted to the Socialist Party by the failure of American laissez-faire capitalism and their conviction that Norman Thomas was the only political leader in the country presenting a concrete program for economic reform and recovery. For most of them this was their first experience with any left political organization. John Dos Passos wrote in 1932 that joining the Socialist Party would have "just about the same effect on anybody as drinking a bottle of near-beer," [12] but to these new party members Socialism was a very heady wine. Coming as they usually did from middle-class backgrounds, frequently from Midwestern communities where a Socialist was a most suspect individual, and quite often from conservative campuses, these new Progressives plunged into Socialism with the zeal of new converts. They demanded the party move along more quickly, display a more vigorous attitude, and redouble its efforts to convert the American laborer and farmer. Perhaps the most important difference between the Progressives and the Old Guard was one of tempo. The Progressives wanted no more of the funereal, dragging step that had characterized the party since the end of the war; they demanded a quick march rhythm.

As Socialists prepared to meet in Milwaukee for their 1932 national convention, they anticipated a conflict between the Old Guard and the new blood in the party, whether Militant or Progressive. Hillquit, fearful of what might happen at the convention, hurried to get his views before the membership before they met at Milwaukee. There were "younger members," he wrote, "with the natural impetuosity of recent converts [who] have undertaken to re-examine all articles of the Socialist faith and all principles of Socialist policy, a very healthy and commendable procedure, which, however, offers no guaranty against false or doubtful conclusions." It was obvious that Hillquit regarded their conclusions as false or doubtful. Hillquit had good reason for being fearful. The Progressives and Militants were out for his head, to depose him as national chairman of the party.

Hillquit was a logical target for the insurgents. In the first place, he was the very symbol of the predepression Socialist Party. The Socialist Party was the party of Hillquit after it had been the party of Debs and before it was to be the party of Thomas. In the second place, Hillquit's relations with avowed enemies of the Soviet Union made him vulnerable in many eyes. Only the year before he had withdrawn as counsel for the Standard Oil and Vacuum Oil companies in their efforts to recover losses in Russian oil properties. In the third place, Midwestern Socialists, whether Old Guard or new blood, resented control of the party by New Yorkers. They had defeated a proposal to move the party's national office to Washington from Chicago, where it had always been except for a brief period in Omaha in the party's earliest days.[13] Midwestern Socialists wanted their party to be an American party, advocating a socialism fitted to American traditions and not an imitation of European socialist parties. They thought, in a manner that can be understood only by Midwesterners, that somehow the Mississippi River was more American than the East River. Therefore, Socialist Party headquarters should be in the Midwest and its national chairman should be from that region.

The delegates to the convention were not long at their business before the first show of strength between the Old Guard and its opponents developed. The issue was the party's attitude toward the Soviet Union. Six separate resolutions were presented to the convention, but the fight narrowed down to two. The resolution supported by the Old Guard was a long declaration of the differences between Communism and Socialism. The Militants and Progressives supported a resolution introduced by Paul Blanshard, Oscar Ameringer, and Newman Jeffery and amended by Thomas to make clear that Socialist approval of Russia was limited to the Russian economy. The Blanshard resolution carried easily, 117 delegates voting for it and 64 against, representing a membership vote of 9,114 to 4,073. The resolution reflected the qualified approval of the Soviet Union typical of the Socialists in the early 1930's.

Whereas, the Socialist party recognizes that the Soviet experiment is being watched closely and with intense interest by the workers; that its success in the economic field will give an immense impetus to the acceptance of Socialism by the workers, while its failure will discredit an economy based on planned production and the abolition of Capitalism,

Be it resolved, that the Socialist party, while not endorsing all policies of the Soviet government, and while emphatically urging the release of political prisoners and the restoration of civil liberties, endorses the efforts being made in Russia to create the economic foundations of a Socialist society, and calls on the workers to guard against capitalist

attacks on Soviet Russia. We believe that economic and political conditions in each country should determine the revolutionary tactics
adopted in that country, and that the Russian experiment is a natural
outgrowth of the conditions peculiar to that country.

The opposition to the Old Guard was confident after this vote
that the convention was theirs, but the next issue on which there
was an important division, the resolution on trade unionism, illustrated that in 1932 the lines between the factions were not yet hard
and fast. The agenda committee, composed of Oneal, Hillquit, and
Harry W. Laidler, presented a trade union resolution that incorporated Oneal's idea that the party should accommodate itself to
trade union sentiment and not attempt to force its point of view on
trade unionists nor interfere in their internal business. Arthur
McDowell for the Militants asked that the party, "through the agency
of labor organizers, employed by the party, stimulate and press the
organizing of workers, especially in the basic industries, along industrial union lines. . . ." McDowell's resolution was defeated 95
to 62.[14]

There was no fight over the presidential nomination. The Old
Guard, while certainly feeling no great fondness for Norman
Thomas, had no member eligible for the Presidency who would
have made as good a candidate. Waldman, an Old Guardsman, nomi-
nated Thomas, and there were no other nominations. A possible fight
over the vice presidential nomination was averted when Meta Berger,
Victor Berger's widow, declined to run for the nomination against
James H. Maurer.[15]

Then came the election of the party's national chairman and
the convention's hottest fight. The opponents of Hillquit first tried
to head off his election by a motion which would have had the
National Executive Committee elect its own chairman. This was
defeated 111 to 48. Then Maurer nominated Hillquit, and William F.
Quick of Milwaukee arose to nominate his mayor, Daniel W. Hoan.
Quick's speech was an unfortunate one, and Heywood Broun's remarks in support of Hoan were equally so. Quick and Broun argued
that the national chairman of the party should not be a New Yorker,

that he should be someone unmistakably recognized as "American." When Thomas, hoping for Hillquit's defeat, heard these speeches his heart sank. The Jewish delegates interpreted the Quick and Broun statements as anti-Semitic, although that was probably not the intention of the speakers. Hillquit, ever the clever attorney, made the most of the opportunity. He told the convention there were three groups opposing his election: the Militants, "well-meaning, immature, effervescent people, who will settle down in time but who for the moment are wild, untamed, and dangerous"; "college men and white collar elements"; and the "practical" Socialists of Milwaukee "who believe in building modern sewers and showing results right away." Then came his dramatic ending, "I apologize for being born abroad, for being a Jew, and living in New York." Socialists, of all people, could not afford being labeled anti-Semites. Hillquit won the election 108 to 81, a represented membership vote of 7,528 to 6,984.[16]

The rest of the National Executive Committee elected was about evenly divided between the Old Guard and its opposition. Those elected were Albert Sprague Coolidge of Massachusetts, James D. Graham of the Montana State Federation of Labor, Daniel W. Hoan, Powers Hapgood of Indianapolis, Darlington Hoopes of Reading, Leo Krzycki of Milwaukee and the Amalgamated Clothing Workers, Jasper McLevy of Bridgeport, Connecticut, John C. Packard of California, Norman Thomas, and Lilith Wilson of Reading.[17]

It is significant that of all the conflict at the Milwaukee convention, of all the arguments over matters very important to any radical party, the only issue referred to the membership for a referendum decision was concerned with repeal of the 18th Amendment to the United States Constitution. The majority report of the platform committee recommended a party referendum on the subject of repeal. Heywood Broun, whose physique belied total abstinence; Daniel Hoan, mayor of a city famous for beer; and Oscar Ameringer, who later in his autobiography wrote one of the most thirst-provoking paeans to beer in American literature, fought for a repeal plank from the convention floor, and their proposal passed 80 to 77.

The dry forces, however, insisted on a referendum, and led by George H. Goebel of New Jersey, the drys got the required number of signatures to a petition to force one. In the hot, dry summer of 1932 the Socialists voted two to one in favor of a platform plank calling for repeal, government ownership and operation of the liquor industry, and the right of states to maintain prohibition.[18]

Whatever bitterness developed at the Milwaukee convention was suppressed before the sessions adjourned in the determination to conduct a strong campaign. The Socialists realized that, whatever the differences among them, they had to work harmoniously and hard during the campaign, for theirs was a case of now or never. They did work harmoniously. Hillquit ran for mayor of New York City to complete Walker's unexpired term, and Hoan went to New York to work for Hillquit's election as he had worked for Hillquit's defeat in May. Broun, Thomas, and Devere Allen from the party's new blood and Hillquit, Lee, and Jacob Panken of the Old Guard spoke together from the same platform at Madison Square Garden. John Dos Passos from his seat in the audience thought he "could detect a faint cloud cross Mr. Hillquit's face at [Thomas's] mention of a capital levy," but the possible faint cloud never grew to a storm. And the Socialists did work hard. The campaign had good organization and direction from the campaign committee, Hoan, Meta Berger, Krzycki, William A. Cunnea, and Hapgood, and the candidates conducted a long and vigorous campaign that hit mid-campaign intensity in July.[19]

The Socialists made the depression their main campaign theme. They asserted that such breakdowns of capitalism as the United States was then suffering from were inherent in the nature of that economic arrangement. Only through democratic socialism, they told the public, "will it be possible to organize our industrial life on a basis of planned and steady operation without periodic breakdowns and disastrous crises." There was in the party's uniquely Socialist demands a retreat from its prewar position. In their platform the Socialists demanded the socialization of only "the principal industries," and, as usual, the platform avoided altogether the question of how the nation was to acquire the ownership of these industries. In a campaign leaflet Thomas touched the question of compensation versus confiscation, but he straddled it. In some industries, Thomas told his readers, Socialists advocated a mixed economy, social enterprise competing with private enterprise. But "In most cases it will probably require condemnation and compensation by the substitution of bonds of a social corporation for private securities, which bonds must be amortized in 30 years and income from them, like all wealth, be subject to drastic income and inheritance taxes." He did not, however, deny "the right to confiscate if and when social conditions and the resistance of a small owning class make it necessary," but such an assertion of the right did not necessarily imply a promise to confiscate.[20]

But it was not their uniquely Socialist demands that Socialists emphasized most in the campaign of 1932. They put their primary emphasis on those parts of the platform—which, incidentally, were the major part of that document—that called for measures of economic reform, relief, and recovery which could be effected without necessarily abandoning an essentially capitalistic arrangement. In other words, they emphasized the reformist features of their program. The Socialists had a constructive program of reform, and the next eight years were to see the New Deal enact a good many planks of it.

The Socialists had in their domestic program planks calling for the socialization of banking and, for agriculture, a federal marketing agency for the purchasing and marketing of agricultural products, but their main attention was directed toward unemployment and labor legislation. The Socialists had been concerned about unemployment even before the crash on Wall Street. In May, 1929, the NEC had urged the establishment of unemployed councils in every city to agitate for public works programs and better public relief systems. As unemployment became more serious each month, the NEC decided to concentrate its agitation on unemployment insurance, old-age pensions, and a child-labor law. Socialists of New York State urged on Governor Roosevelt a state program of public works, including housing, and a state law requiring a five-day work week and a six-hour day. Now in 1932 the Socialists pressed such measures as these and a federal appropriation of $5,000,000,000 to supplement state and local unemployment relief funds and another federal expenditure of the same amount for a public works program. They also urged "Legislation providing for the acquisition of land, buildings and equipment necessary to put the unemployed to work producing food, fuel and clothing and for the erection of homes for their own use." [21]

In the campaign Thomas attacked his rival candidates more than was typical of Socialist presidential candidates. He frequently jibed Herbert Hoover, "perhaps rather cruelly," he thought years later. Thomas told his listeners that "it was nonsense to blame the whole depression on Hoover because he wasn't a big enough man to make such a big depression." But it was Roosevelt who drew the most shots from Thomas and other Socialists. After all, to shoot at such a sitting duck as Hoover was in 1932 was no test of marksmanship. There were two articles in the Socialist campaign book devoted exclusively to criticism of Roosevelt, and in a book Thomas wrote with Paul Blanshard, *What's the Matter with New York*, published during the campaign, the authors were hard on the Democratic candidate. Thomas and Blanshard charged that Roosevelt, whom they described as "a nice person who once graduated from Harvard, has a good radio voice, and is as sincere as old party politics will permit," had pussyfooted shamefully in the investigations of Tammany corruption in New York City, had postponed doing anything until his presidential nomination was secured, and had been one of the luckiest politicians in American history in emerging from the mess as the "White Knight" in the fairy tale called "How Roosevelt Slew the Tammany Dragon." [22]

The Socialists in 1932 made more than their usual effort to enlist the support of labor organizations, and their success, while very far from complete, was greater than they had had since before the war. The party was not content with its usual support from the rank and file of the New York garment workers. In 1932 the Socialists organized the Labor League for Thomas and Maurer, and the League secured the endorsements of a handful of labor union officials. Emil Rieve, president of the Full Fashioned Hosiery Workers, was chairman of the League, and Leo Krzycki, of the party's NEC and the Amalgamated Clothing Workers, was its secretary. Among the more important union men in the League were James D. Graham, president of the Montana State Federation of Labor; H. H. Freedheim, vice president of the Idaho State Federation of Labor; Henry Linville, president of the Teachers Union of New York City; and J. J. Handley, secretary of the Wisconsin State Federation of Labor. The American Federation of Labor itself declined to support any presidential candidate. The Socialists pointed out that of the eighteen important labor planks which the AFL's executive council had submitted for the consideration of the major-party conventions, only the Socialists had in their platform endorsement of all the AFL proposals. The Republican platform ignored eight of these planks, endorsed eight of them, and hedged on two. The Democratic platform was silent on thirteen of the AFL demands, endorsed two, and was vague on three. Yet the AFL refused endorsement of the Socialists, and probably most AFL members voted for the Democrats, whose platform least supported AFL demands. The Socialist exhortation to the union man, "Don't Scab at the Ballot Box," was ignored by all labor organizations except the Full Fashioned Hosiery Workers and the Vermont State Federation of Labor. Each of these organizations' conventions endorsed the Socialist ticket, but neither of them was a very numerous body.[23]

The Socialists gained some votes—how many it is impossible to determine—from the few scattered state labor parties. Within the Socialist Party there was no unanimity as to how far the party should yield its historic positions should an opportunity to found a national labor party present itself. In general, the Old Guard was for yielding little, and the new blood in the party was more enthusiastic. Here and there, in Illinois, Minnesota, and West Virginia, farmer-labor parties of varying degrees of importance were organized, and the Socialists of those states established contact with these parties. In Minnesota the Socialists agreed to back Farmer-Labor Party candidates for state office if the Farmer-Labor Party did not endorse the candidates for national office of either of the major parties. There were efforts at the Farmer-Labor Party convention in 1932 officially to endorse Roosevelt's candidacy, but the efforts failed and the Minnesota Socialists continued their support. In general, the Socialists in 1932 had more organized labor support than they had had for several years, but the labor support was still quite meager.[24]

Intellectuals gave more support to Thomas in 1932 than did labor. Independent backers of Thomas, most of them intellectuals, formed the Thomas and Maurer Committee of Ten Thousand, an organization that had such good support that its leaders raised their sights a thousand per cent and renamed the organization the Thomas and Maurer Committee of One Hundred Thousand. Its chairman was Paul H. Douglas, then a professor of economics at the University of Chicago, and among its other officers were Morris R. Cohen, John Dewey, Francis J. McConnell, Oswald Garrison Villard, and Reinhold Niebuhr. The list of those who announced their affiliation with the committee was quite impressive. Among the Thomas supporters were Elmer Davis, Henry Hazlitt, Lewis Gannett, Stuart Chase, Joseph Wood Krutch, W. E. Woodward, Stephen Vincent Benét, Robert Morss Lovett, Van Wyck Brooks, Lorado Taft, Ordway Tead, W. E. B. Du Bois, Ben Huebsch, Kirby Page, Franklin P. Adams, Alexander Woollcott, Deems Taylor, George Gershwin, Eva Le Gallienne, Edna St. Vincent Millay, and Irwin Edman. Some editors supported Thomas. Paul U. Kellogg, editor of the *Survey Graphic*, announced that, while he was supporting the Democratic candidates for governor and senator of New York, he was for Hillquit for mayor and Thomas for President. The *New Republic* gave its editorial support to Thomas. Several ministers urged the election of the Socialist ticket. John Haynes Holmes in a speech at Chicago urged liberals to vote for Thomas. The Republicans, he asserted, had amply demonstrated their inadequacy, and the Democrats were "a hopeless combination . . . of Southern Negrophobes and Northern gangsters." The Social Action Conference, an organization of Methodist ministers and laymen, endorsed the Socialist Party, as did

Rabbi Stephen S. Wise. Thomas was popular on the college campuses of the nation. By the summer academic vacation of 1932, 44 campus Thomas for President clubs had been organized, and by the month before election there were 123 such organizations. If the direction of thought of society's intellectuals indeed presaged the direction of the entire society's social thinking, the prospect looked good for the Socialist Party.[25]

By diligent circulation of petitions and a few hard-fought court cases, the Socialists succeeded in getting Thomas and Maurer on the ballot in all but five states, Nevada, Idaho, Louisiana, Florida, and Oklahoma. In some of these states a write-in vote was possible. Socialists, of course, never expected to win the election, but some of them optimistically predicted a vote of as much as 3,000,000. Thomas himself did not anticipate such a good showing—at least in public. On election day he announced he would consider a vote of 1,500,000 as an encouraging Socialist victory.[26] But the actual Thomas vote was less than two-thirds of Thomas's fond hopes. On election day 884,781 voters marked their ballots for Thomas. This was more than three times the vote Thomas had polled in 1928, but it was a long way from frightening the major parties. There are two factors impossible of measurement in the Socialist vote of 1932. One is the accuracy of the count of the Socialist vote. In election districts without voting machines it was not uncommon to give the candidates who had no chance of victory a most hurried and probably inaccurate ballot count. Another immeasurable factor is the number of voters who wanted to see Thomas poll a good vote, who were for his candidacy, but who at the last minute voted for Roosevelt in the fear that a vote for Thomas might reelect Hoover. In the weeks after the election Thomas received hundreds of letters from such cautious voters, now contrite after finding that Roosevelt's margin over Hoover was more than 7,000,000 votes. But even if all Thomas's supporters had voted their convictions, and if all election districts had made accurate ballot counts, the election results probably would not have been significantly different. The cold fact was that the Socialist Party had relatively little popular following.

It is the custom of Socialists and other minor party members to say after an election defeat, or even before an expected defeat, that victory or a big vote was not expected, that the party was using the election campaign solely as a vehicle for educating the electorate to its point of view. In 1932 the Socialists had more justification for taking refuge in such consolation than they usually did, for the campaign had done more to rebuild the party than had the total efforts of the preceding twelve years. In 1930, Senior's first full year as national secretary and the first full year of vigorous administration for the party since Branstetter resigned in the early 1920's, the party organized 32 new locals. In 1931 it organized 96 new local organizations. On January 1, 1932, there were just under a thousand locals in the party, and by November, 1932, there were nearly 1,600. During the late weeks of the campaign new locals were joining the party at the rate of 30 to 40 each week.[27]

The radio was a most useful medium to the party. Throughout the campaign, and well on into 1933, the national office received hundreds of letters from people who had heard Thomas or other Socialist speakers on the radio. These people volunteered to help organize in their communities, requested the address of the nearest local of the party so that they could join, and asked for Socialist literature to distribute among neighbors. Many of them were old Debsites who had strayed from the movement during the 1920's. The following letter from a West Virginia farmer was typical:

I was a member of the socialist party in Moline Ill. from 1914 to 1918, when I was drafted into the army. Since coming out of the army I have been unemployed a lot of the time and have shifted around and finally come back to my birthplace in the hills of West Virginia and have long neglected to get in touch with the socialist movement, as there is no organized movement here on the farms.

I heard Norman Thomas speak over the Radio and heard him announce the party's Chicago address. I heard him speak the night of Nov. 7 in which he said this was not the closing of the socialist campaign but the beginning of another four years battle, and I want to be in that battle, and I want the National office to send me all information necessary (such as address of W. Va. state headquarters etc.) to start me into the work of carrying the socialist message to the farmers and workers of Mason County W. Va.

These volunteers did not agree with Clarence Darrow, who had said in 1931 that he "couldn't join the Socialist Party because I'd be too lonely." [28]

Several of the old-timers now seeking to rejoin the party confessed they had left the organization because of employer pressure, or at least because of the fear of employer disapproval. They now wanted to make amends for their years of political idleness. Now that they were unemployed or involuntarily retired they could resume their Socialist activities without fear of economic reprisal. It is questionable, however, that the numbers of those who regained their political freedom through unemployment balanced the numbers of the still employed whose anxieties about employer pressure were heightened by the buyers' market in man power.[29]

Although the party had grown encouragingly during the campaign, although many of the people who mold public opinion in the United States had stated their approval of the party's candidates, although there were many indications of further growth, still for the Socialists there was the unpleasant and inescapable truth that the reaction of the American people to the depression had not been revolt against capitalism. Again, for the *n*th time in American history, radicals and reactionaries were mistaken in their predictions as to how the American common people would react to adversity. The Socialists in 1931 hopefully thought they saw "Seething discontent that may burst into blind fury next winter. . . . Evidences of growing radical sentiment in labor union weeklies indicate that more and more organized workers will turn to political action." Conservatives fearfully made the same sort of prediction. The officers of the 33rd Division, Illinois National Guard, studied "Plans for the suppression of radical disorders" that included such police tips as "Never fire over the heads of rioters" and "The picking off of a few rioters [in the rear of a mob] will generally cause others to flee." [30] But, compared to what was expected, relatively little "blind fury" was manifested, and there were, fortunately, few opportunities for national guardsmen to exercise the brutality of their technical manuals.

By and large, the revolt of the American people consisted of bolting the Grand Old Party to vote for Governor Roosevelt, a Hudson Valley country gentleman who in his first presidential campaign offered the electorate hope and sympathy but little that was concrete. But once in the White House that country squire was to champion a program of social reform that cut the ground out from under the Socialist Party. Such as it was, the election of 1932 was the high tide of the party of Norman Thomas.

X

THE SOCIALISTS AND THE
NEW DEAL

DURING the four long months between Roosevelt's election in November and his inauguration in March, while the nation's economy floundered worse each week, the Socialists continued their efforts to direct the discontent brought by the Great Depression into social-democratic channels. The Socialists concentrated that dreadful winter upon making a success of their Continental Congress for Economic Reconstruction, a demonstration of social protest with an advertising man's gimmick.

Seeking public identification with the traditions of the American Revolution, the Socialists organized many local Committees of Correspondence preparatory to the meeting of the Continental Congress to be held at Washington early in May, 1933. The committees did their work of organization well. In the spring about 4,000 victims of the depression straggled into Washington, as had the veterans in the Bonus Army the year before and the soldiers of Coxey's army forty years earlier. Most of the delegates to the Congress were unemployed urban workers, but there were representatives from the depression-pinched and angry farmers from the upper Mississippi Valley. A. C. Townley, colorful former leader of the Non-Partisan League and now a delegate sent by the Des Moines convention of the Farm Holiday Association, and James Simpson, president of the Farmers Union, addressed the Congress. The Socialist officers of the Congress, Emil Rieve as chairman and Daniel Hoan as vice chairman, were gratified by the apparent solidarity between farm and labor groups. The delegates, employing the War for Independence theme, wrote a new Declaration of Independence. This twentieth century declaration declared independence from "the profit system of business, industry and finance," which had "enthroned economic and financial kings . . . more powerful, more irresponsible and more dangerous to human rights than the political kings whom the fathers overthrew." These economic kings, stated the declaration's bill of grievances, had "taken the products of our labor, and not paid us enough to buy back the goods we have produced." The delegates hammered out a series of resolutions that very much resembled the Socialist platform and agreed to make their organization permanent—under the name Continental Congress of Workers and Farmers—and to "explore the best methods of economic and independent political action by the producing classes for the achievement of a cooperative commonwealth." [1] The Socialist Party was enthusiastic about its revolutionary brain child. The Continental Congress was not strictly a Socialist organization. It contained representatives from farm, labor, and unemployed groups that had no direct connection with the party, but its officers were Socialists, as were many or most of its members, and the party had official representation on the Congress's executive committee.

Socialists still look back fondly upon the Continental Congress, but Socialist hopes for the gimmick were soon to wane. For even by the time the Continental Congress met in May, the very groups to which it addressed its appeal were beginning to look in another direction for their salvation. Poverty-stricken farmers, organized labor, and the unemployed were already looking with interest toward Franklin D. Roosevelt and his New Deal. By the end of Roosevelt's famous first "hundred days" there were still large sectors of the Left and the potential Left who shunned him. But by the end of his first term in office the New Deal had taken a tack toward the left, probably dictated by political expediency, that made the victims of the depression almost solid for Roosevelt. To say that Roosevelt "stole the thunder" of the Socialists is to give too much satisfaction to those enemies of both Socialism and Roosevelt's state capitalism who see the New Deal as "creeping socialism." Surely, by the time the Democrats left the White House American capitalism, although considerably changed from what it had been twenty years before, still lived—and in the best health it had had for years. But if Roosevelt did not creep toward Socialism, if he did not steal the Socialists' thunder, he did undercut most of their actual and potential support. The story of the decline of the Socialist Party since 1933 is, for the most part, the story of the political success of the New Deal.

While Roosevelt enlisted support with his rhetoric and charm, he also led Congress to enact in rapid succession a series of acts intended to reform some of the more inefficient or unjust features of capitalism, to restore that economic system to health, and to relieve the suffering caused by its breakdown. New "alphabet agencies" were born at a dizzying pace. There were NRA, AAA, CWA, CCC, FDIC, SEC, and many others. Socialists, seeing their audience enlisting under the emblem of the Blue Eagle rather than under that of the red flag, were sharply critical of the Roosevelt program.

The Socialists concentrated their fire on two of the most important New Deal measures, the National Industrial Recovery Act and the Agricultural Adjustment Act, although there was hardly any feature of the Democratic program that did not come in for a share of criticism. The NIRA, said the party's NEC in an official statement, was "an official admission that capitalism can make no recovery without governmental supervision. It marks a new stage in the struggle of workers against exploitation for profits, but falls far short of giving them their freedom." The party saw hope in Section 7(*a*) of the act. Here was an opportunity for labor to organize on an unprecedented scale, but if labor should not fully organize the results would be disastrous. "The gravest danger of all is that the new industrial set-up may easily become the framework of a Fascist state. If labor fails to rise to its opportunity Fascism will be the next step." Socialists did not assert the NRA was fascist, but, pointing out the similarity to the European cartel system and the Italian corporate state, declared "it can easily be made into Fascism." [2]

Socialists were particularly critical of the New Deal farm pro-gram. Their criticisms of the New Deal's agricultural measures were perhaps better taken than their objections to the NIRA, but they came with less grace because the Socialists had not presented the farmers a very concrete program of their own. There were few farmers in the Socialist Party of the Great Depression, and the party could not see agricultural problems from the same vantage point that dirt farmers saw them. The farm planks of the 1932 platform had not been very strong. The Socialists had declared themselves in favor of easier credit for the farmers, "social insurance" against crop fail-ures, and farmer cooperatives; but they had nothing to say about the farmer's greatest problem of the moment: low prices for his products. A small group of Socialist farmers from Michigan, western Ohio, and Indiana expressed their dissatisfaction with the Socialist agricultural proposals and after the election met at the farm of one of their num-bers to develop a Socialist agricultural platform that would have more appeal. But nothing came of these grass-roots efforts. In Feb-ruary, 1933, just a few days before Roosevelt's inauguration, the best the party's national headquarters could do to help its organizers and speakers on farm questions was to send them a copy of Oscar Ameringer's old speech "Little Bugs and Big Bugs"—the farmers had more to fear from the big two-legged parasitic bugs called middle-men than they did from the small multilegged varieties that crawled in their fields—and to recommend the distribution of "The Parable of the Water Tank" from Edward Bellamy's *Equality*.[3]

But not having a well developed farm program of their own did not prevent Socialists from heatedly criticizing the New Deal's pro-grams. Many of these criticisms, several economic historians agree, were ones the Congress and the Department of Agriculture might well have heeded. The crop destruction and restriction program of the AAA was a pretty target for the Socialists. Socialists made the bitter comment that the killing of little pigs and brood sows and the plowing under of cotton represented an effort to solve the paradox of poverty in the midst of plenty by eliminating the plenty. They also charged the New Deal had made no fundamental attack on the problem of absentee landlordship and had not been sufficiently bold in reducing the enormous farm debt. If reduction of the farm debt were to be effected by further inflation, the Socialists pointed out, it would be at the expense of city labor.[4]

One particularly unfortunate aspect of the AAA's crop restriction program drew fire from Socialists. The New Deal failed to work out an effective way for AAA benefit payments—payments to farmers for not growing crops—to be shared between landlords and tenants. The plight of the cotton-growing sharecroppers was particularly acute. Landlords with share tenants and croppers on their land received the checks from the government and were supposed to pass on a share of the benefit to their tenants, but it was easy for them not to do so. Under the law hired farm laborers were to get nothing from the benefit payments, and it was a simple matter for landlords to make their tenants hired laborers. In many cases landlords bought tractors and other farm machinery with their benefit checks and thereby eliminated many tenants and hired hands entirely. Surely the AAA had as much to do with putting John Steinbeck's Oakies into their jalopies as had the droughts and the dust storms. The Oakies knew their straits were due to man-made as well as natural causes, and the grapes of their wrath were exceedingly bitter.[5]

Norman Thomas made a hard fight for the tenant farmers who suffered from this provision of the AAA. He urged Secretary of Agriculture Henry Wallace to take corrective measures. Wallace refused to see Thomas about this matter, and Thomas had to do his persuading by correspondence. He asked Wallace:

What about the sharecroppers driven from the land under any system of limitations? Will the Bankhead bill or any other legislation see that the rewards of *not* planting cotton are passed on to the men who have been forced to stop planting cotton? . . . I do not comment on the irony of compelling a reduction in the cotton crop when the children of cotton growers run naked or clothed in rags or sugar sacking.

Wallace's reaction, Thomas later charged, was to deny that the problem was serious. Roosevelt, who granted Thomas an interview on this matter, admitted the existence of the problem but took a

"Well, what can be done?" attitude. When Thomas could get no place seeing people in high places in the administration, he took to agitation. He used the radio to spread his views on the AAA and the sharecropper and helped H. L. Mitchell of Tyronza, Arkansas, to found the Southern Tenant Farmers' Union, later called the National Farm Labor Union.[6]

About other features of the New Deal the Socialists had less to say, but they said it no less bitingly. Thomas, in a speech during his 1936 campaign, criticized Roosevelt's record on civil liberties. He blamed the President and Democratic chief for not preventing "the epidemic of loyalty oaths, the ride of the vigilantes in California, military law in Indiana, flogging and murder in Florida." Thomas might have added that he himself had broken the martial law decreed by Democratic Governor Paul V. McNutt for Sullivan County and Terre Haute, Indiana. As for Negro rights, Thomas asked, "Did he [Roosevelt] ever put an antilynching bill on his *must* list?" [7]

The party's National Executive Committee pointed out the adverse effects of the New Deal's inflationary monetary policies upon foreign trade. The effect of the New Deal dollar devaluation "has been to make the rates in the Smoot-Hawley bill about 60 per cent higher than when the act was passed. This is simply one part of the dangerous trend toward economic nationalism which is leading us ever nearer to another capitalist war." As for the New Deal's banking legislation, Thomas claimed "a new government-controlled banking system could have been established with the money that has already been sunk in banks to keep the money changers in the temple." The Securities and Exchange Act was just "a private matter between our big and little capitalists." [8]

Socialists approved of the direction of such measures to relieve unemployment and promote security as the public works programs and the Social Security Act of 1935, but they felt that these measures and programs were either not sufficiently bold or badly administered. Thomas held that the Civil Works Administration program of the early New Deal, with its make-work performed with hand tools, was "degrading . . . at a time when there is such dire need of clothing and shelter among [the unemployed]. Either the government should pay them the direct cash subsidies to which they are entitled if the system cannot give them decent jobs, or the government should take over idle factories and give them work producing the things they need for a decent standard of living." Socialists joined Republicans in criticizing the Democratic administration for cutting WPA rolls after the balloting in 1936. Socialists also agreed with Republicans in their concern over the growth of the federal debt, incurred to finance economic "pump priming." Thomas characterized the debt as a "crushing burden." But Thomas's plan for reducing the debt certainly found no favor in the GOP. He proposed "a carefully worked out capital levy; that is a tax not on the income of the capitalists, but a levy of a certain per cent of the capital itself." The NEC thought the Social Security Act a pitifully short step in the right direction. It wanted domestic and agricultural workers included in the act, a scheme of health insurance, the elimination of the payroll tax and compensation for this loss of revenue through an excess profits tax and higher income and inheritance taxes, the reduction of the retirement age from 65 to 60, higher unemployment benefits to be graduated according to the number of the unemployed worker's dependents, and benefits to be paid throughout the entire period of unemployment. The NEC pointed out that for an unemployed worker to receive unemployment compensation he had first to get a job and then lose it.[9]

In sum, the Socialists were critical of the New Deal for not being socialist, for building a state capitalism which they held contained dangerous tendencies toward fascism, and for being considerably less than thorough in relieving the suffering of the Great Depression. But the Socialist criticisms did not impress very many Americans. The Roosevelt program attracted to it the very people whom the Socialists would have to attract if the Socialists were to be a significant political force. In the 1934 congressional elections the Democrats returned greater majorities to both houses of Congress than they had in 1932, and the Socialists enjoyed no spectacular electoral success. The swing was plainly to Roosevelt. The dismal economic conditions of the nation that possibly could have made the Socialists important or could have created a new national party of workers and farmers only strengthened the New Deal wing of the Democratic Party.

The Roosevelt Democrats and other nonsocialist liberal political groups here and there attracted able Socialist leaders the party could ill afford to lose. As early as the summer of 1931, even before the Socialists had reached the peak of their depression-stimulated growth, the process of defection to liberalism began. In July, 1931, Thomas M. Duncan, a Socialist senator in the Wisconsin state legislature and a former private secretary to Mayor Hoan, resigned from the party to accept a position as Governor Philip La Follette's executive secretary. After Roosevelt's inauguration the number of defections increased. In 1933 and 1934 the California Socialist movement broke up over Upton Sinclair's EPIC plan. In the fall of 1933 Sinclair joined the Democratic Party and wrote two pamphlets, *I, Governor of California*, and *How I Ended Poverty in California*, which proved to be immensely popular. The following spring Sinclair announced he would seek the Democratic nomination for governor, and the Socialist organization, both state and national, denounced him. The California state committee of the party announced, "Those Socialists who feel they can better serve their convictions by supporting Sinclair are urged to leave the party." Thomas criticized Sinclair's EPIC plan (End Poverty in California) as a superficial and dangerous compromise with capitalism. He wrote to Sinclair, "The one matter of vital importance is the organization of workers with hand and brain for the capture of power, and that you . . . can't do by achieving a snap victory in the old Democratic party—even assuming that you achieve the victory." Sinclair won the Democratic nomination, defeating George Creel, Wilson's propaganda chief during the war, but in an extraordinarily dirty campaign lost to the Republican candidate in the fall. Another California Socialist, Jerry Voorhis, left the party for the Democrats and later was a Democratic congressman. In the fall of 1933 Paul Blanshard, one of the ablest journalists and lecturers in the Socialist movement, left the party to support Fiorello La Guardia's campaign for mayor of New York City. His grounds were discouragement over the lack of Socialist practical results rather than a loss of faith. After four years of depression the Socialist Party was still impotent, and Blanshard felt his energies would be better directed outside the party. Others felt the same. Only two years after Andrew J. Biemiller, the chairman of the party's education committee, wrote, "The forgotten man has been only partially remembered by the New Deal," he was a representative of the New Deal party in the Wisconsin state legislature. Later he served on the War Production Board and for two terms in Congress.[10]

Years later Norman Thomas put his finger upon what happened to his party. The early years of the depression, he wrote, were "the Indian Summer for the Socialist Party." From about 1931 to about 1934 "it looked as if we were going to go places. . . . What cut the ground out pretty completely from under us was this. It was Roosevelt in a word. You don't need anything more." [11]

Certainly Roosevelt was all that was necessary to cripple the Socialist Party, but there was more: there was a bitter factional struggle within the party that ended in a split. Without the political bonds of patronage, without even the hope of patronage, there were only principles to hold the party together. The principles held by Socialists became increasingly diverse, and the party split. Soon after the war the party had been all but killed by a combination of a strong external force, the antiradicalism of the era of A. Mitchell Palmer, and internal division. The party had revived to a degree in the early years of the Great Depression only to become a casualty again of a strong external force, the popularity of the New Deal, and internal factionalism.

The previous chapter described the three factions of the Socialist Party in the early 1930's, the Old Guard, the Progressives, and the Militants. No sooner had the campaign of 1932 ended, during which factional struggles were submerged in the effort to make a good showing, than the bitterness that had shown itself at the Milwaukee convention reappeared. Thomas, a Progressive who was tolerant of the Militants although he disagreed with them, complained that some of the activities of the Old Guard in New York

City embarrassed him when he tried to agitate for Socialism in other parts of the nation. In the fur industry of New York City there were two rival unions, one led by Old Guard Socialists and one led by Communists. According to Thomas, who made a personal investigation, "the larger part of the workers" in the industry supported the Communist union. The Old Guard union went to the courts and obtained a labor injunction against the Communist-dominated rival organization. Thomas charged the Old Guard "went into collusion with the employers to use police and other powers to establish a union which they had been unable to build by other methods." Such Old Guard activities as these, Thomas charged, nullified his efforts to build the party:

> I cannot possibly be expected to go all over the United States arguing for Socialism with such a weight around my neck without dissociating myself from any such position as this. . . . I admit the difficulty of the whole situation. No Socialist more than I dislikes to see the growth of Communist organizations as long as they use the tactics which they do use. At the same time the Socialist Party is coming close to suicide when it is so much quicker to see the sins of Communism than the sins of capitalism or of the embryonic Fascism in America.

This situation among the furriers and the Old Guard's general tendency "to tie up blindly to the A.F. of L. leadership no matter what happens," Thomas later asserted, was playing into the hands of the Communists. "It is my sober judgement . . . that now practically for the first time since the original split our Communist friends, or enemies, are definitely making headway in New York City. A large part of it is our own fault." [12]

The Old Guard's opposition first demonstrated its growing strength in the summer of 1933 when the NEC ordered the *New Leader* to cease advertising itself as the official organ of the Socialist Party. This action started a bitter fight. James Oneal, Old Guardsman editor of the *New Leader*, argued that the NEC had not advised him that it contemplated dropping its endorsement of his paper, that it had been unfair in not granting him a hearing at the meeting, and that the party's constitution did not grant the NEC the power to withdraw its endorsement. National Secretary Senior, replying for the NEC, countered that the NEC would have advised Oneal what it was going to do if the members had known before their meeting that the issue was going to arise. But, wrote Senior, the complaint against the *New Leader,* from the Washington Heights branch of the New York City local, had not arrived until the NEC had already begun its sessions. As for the NEC's constitutional power to withdraw endorsement, Senior replied that it had been the NEC which originally had designated the *New Leader* as the party's official organ, and if it had been constitutional to grant endorsement it was constitutional to withdraw it.[13]

The Old Guard was now determined to get rid of Senior, whose appointment was at the pleasure of the NEC, in which the Old Guard had not quite half the votes. Hillquit wanted to replace Senior with Marx Lewis, who had created some dissatisfaction among Midwestern comrades over the way he had raised funds for the party. Hillquit proposed the next meeting of the NEC be held at a time when Thomas would have been unable to attend, thereby giving the Old Guard a majority of those present. But Hillquit's strategy was detected,[14] and Senior remained as national executive secretary.

In October, 1933, Hillquit died, and the Old Guard's position was weakened. The Old Guard not only lost the chairmanship of the NEC,[15] but it lost its most able and best known leader. There was no man his equal in the Old Guard faction. The leadership of that group fell upon three men, James Oneal, Algernon Lee, and Louis Waldman, each of whom had handicaps preventing vigorous leadership. Oneal was in poor health, Lee was a quite ineffective public speaker, and Waldman was unpopular with many members of his party. None of them was well known outside the party. Had Hillquit lived, the developments within the Socialist Party for the next few years might have been quite different. It is unlikely that even Hillquit could have headed off the opposition to the Old Guard, but that champion of compromise and political in-fighting might have been able to salvage more for the Old Guard than did Oneal, Lee, and Waldman.

Waldman and Thomas had a battle almost immediately. In January, 1934, on Mayor La Guardia's first day in office, David Lasser, a young Militant, led a demonstration at city hall by the League for Industrial Democracy organization for the unemployed. Waldman issued in the name of Julius Gerber, executive secretary of Local New York, a statement to the *New York Times* that disavowed any connection between the party and the Lasser demonstration and that criticized Lasser for "nagging" La Guardia on his first day in office. When Thomas took Waldman to task for his statement, charging that the newspaper account did neither the unemployed nor the party any good, Waldman adopted an anti-Communist attitude. Lasser's tactics, he wrote to Thomas, had been "typically Communist," and he had publicly disavowed Lasser because the Socialist Party should in no way be associated in the public mind with the Communists. Thomas replied that he too did not want the public to confuse the Socialists and the Communists, but that he hated "to see the Party so much more sensitive to fear of identification, even partial and mistaken identification, with Communism or near Communism than with some other much more dangerous institutions and practices." [16]

Waldman's anxiety that the public might identify his party with Communism was undoubtedly heightened by the influx into the party of significant numbers of young and erratic radicals. Waldman was alarmed at the increasing number of young men who appeared at Socialist meetings wearing blue work shirts and red ties and giving the Communist clenched-fist salute. In retrospect, these young Militants—Reinhold Niebuhr called them "romantic leftists"—are more amusing than alarming. Many of them were college undergraduates and more than a few were of middle-class backgrounds, earnestly playing at being proletarian and vociferously criticizing men such as Waldman, a product of the immigrants' steerage, the lower East Side, the early strikes of the garment workers, and night school. Thomas, for one, and a great many other Socialists, were not deeply disturbed by the romantic leftists. Thomas had provocation enough to be irritated with them, but as he said later, "I was willing to take a lot of chances with the young folks being too radical for a while if we could only hold them in the party. I was right. Most of them settled down, to my delight—some of them swung too far to the left." The Old Guard, however, had little sympathy for these zealous youngsters. Old Guardsmen tried to silence them or expel them from the party. Niebuhr acutely reported the situation when he wrote that the Old Guard "meets the genuine disillusionment of young and vigorous elements in the party merely by repression and mouths the old platitudes about democracy." Niebuhr also had a pointed question for the young Militants. "If constitutional rights are nothing but a façade for capitalism," as many of the Militants claimed, "ought the labor movement not welcome fascism as being more honest than democracy . . . ?" [17]

At the special party convention held at Detroit early in June, 1934, when the party adopted what came to be known as the Detroit Declaration of Principles, it was demonstrated that the Old Guard had lost its hold on the party. The Progressives and Militants at Detroit hammered out a statement of Socialist creed which they held every Socialist should believe and advocate. Part of the disagreement at the convention about the Declaration was of the kind that puzzles the uninitiated leftist unable to see the subtle differences in points of view that generate radical heat. But some of the disagreement about this creed was clear and fundamental. Two sections in the Declaration particularly exercised the Old Guard. One had to do with Socialist action in the event of capitalist war.

. . . recognizing the suicidal nature of modern combat and the incalculable train of wars' consequences which rest most heavily upon the working class, they [Socialists] will refuse collectively to sanction or support any international war; they will, on the contrary, by agitation and opposition do their best not to be broken up by the war, but to break up the war. They will meet war and the detailed plans for war . . . by massed war resistance, organized so far as practicable in a general strike of labor unions and professional groups in a united effort to make the waging of war a practical impossibility and to convert the capitalist war crisis into a victory for Socialism.

The other section had to do with the Socialist view of democracy.

Capitalism is doomed. If it can be superseded by majority vote, the Socialist Party will rejoice. If the crisis comes through the denial of majority rights after the electorate has given us a mandate we shall not hesitate to crush by our labor solidarity the reckless forces of reaction and to consolidate the Socialist state. If the capitalist system should collapse in a general chaos and confusion, which cannot permit of orderly procedure, the Socialist Party, whether or not in such a case it is a majority, will not shrink from the responsibility of organizing and maintaining a government under the workers' rules. True democracy is a worthy means to progress; but true democracy must be created by the workers of the world.[18]

It is true that the Socialists, with their relative handful of members and their limited labor support, were more than a little quixotic in their confident reference to "massed war resistance" and "our labor solidarity," but the point for the moment is not the Socialist disregard for reality but their internal fighting. It was not the unrealistic aspects of the Declaration that aroused the Old Guard but what the Socialist right wing regarded as communistic. The Old Guard would have opposed the Declaration had the party actually had the strength it dreamed of.

But by 1934 the Old Guard's strength was not sufficient to prevent the Progressives and Militants from making party policy. When Waldman called the Declaration "anarchistic, illegal, and communist," he convinced no one. The convention's delegates voted 99 to 47 (a weighted vote of 10,822 to 6,512) to adopt the Declaration.[19] The party membership subsequently endorsed the Declaration in a party referendum, 5,993 to 4,872. A breakdown of this vote by states indicates the areas of strength of the factions. Of the major states in the party, the Old Guard carried Jasper McLevy's Connecticut 189 to 164, Massachusetts 450 to 257, New York 1,537 to 1,189, and Pennsylvania 771 to 546. Their opponents carried Wisconsin 1,032 to 169, Illinois 454 to 181, and most of the smaller state organizations. The Old Guard also suffered a defeat in the election of new NEC members. Of the eleven members of the new committee elected in 1934 only two were clearly identified with the Old Guard.[20]

After the Detroit convention the conflict between the Old Guard on the one hand and the Progressives and Militants on the other became increasingly sharp, especially in New York, where approximately one-sixth of the Socialist membership was concentrated. There continued to be a steady movement into the party there of young radicals, many of them only recently disillusioned with the major parties. One of the features of the entire Left during the Great Depression was the phenomenon of recently converted leftists wandering through many of the revolutionary sects in search of political salvation—more than one young man belonged at various times to the Communist Party, the Socialist Labor Party, and the Socialist Party—and through many of the factions within each. And there was an extraordinary number of these sects in the 1930's.[21] When these wanderers in the forest of revolutionary politics applied for admission to the Socialist Party, there was usually a fight between the Old Guard and its opponents. The only recruits the Old Guard wanted, of course, were steady and safe social democrats, but few of these presented themselves. The Progressives and Militants, while not quite for indiscriminate admission, were much more catholic in their taste. And once the new converts were in the party, the Progressives and Militants were willing to tolerate a lot of what they considered nonsense or worse until the youngsters settled down. To keep a close rein on them, in the opinion of such Socialist leaders as Thomas and Paul Porter, would be to drive them into the hands of the Communists. Parts of the New York party even briefly embraced the champion political wanderer, Benjamin Gitlow, who was then on one leg of his journey from Lenin to Senator Robert A. Taft.[22]

These new Socialist members swarmed to the party's Left Wing, where they caused consternation in the Old Guard, as well they might, considering the Old Guard's political orientation. Some of them organized a caucus in the New York organization called the Revolutionary Policy Committee that took an extreme left position. The RPC caucus members had little more use for the Progressives than they had for the Old Guard. They denounced as "pompous and fantastic" the contention that the adoption of the Detroit Declaration of Principles and the election of a Progressive-dominated NEC was a turn to the left. The NEC, they claimed, was guilty of "red-baiting." They tried to convert the New York local of the Young Peoples Socialist League—usually called the YPSL or the Yipsels—into an organization very close to the Communist position. Some New York Yipsels now declared themselves for dictatorship of the proletariat, and urged the party to become a "vanguard party" shunning reformism and "gaining power thru a parliamentary majority . . . [or] using the parliamentary institutions of capitalist democracy as the organs or means of seizing power." [23]

Members with such views were, however, only a small if noisy part of the New York organization. When the Progressives and their further-left comrades worked together, as they did in the formation of the *Socialist Call*, a new newspaper started in opposition to the Old Guardist *New Leader*, their declarations were somewhat more moderate. For example, the *Socialist Call* sponsored institutes in the fall of 1935, one held at Bound Brook, New Jersey, the other at Chicago, that drafted a Left Wing program for the Socialist Party. This program was somewhat doctrinaire in its language—"The class struggle will grow more intense; there will be a constant thrusting forward of the more advanced sections of the working class, who, becoming aware . . . of the limitation of reformism will play an increasingly important role"—but there was no arguing for a dictatorship of the proletariat nor a rejection of parliamentary action. There was a vast difference between Norman Thomas or Paul Porter and the rabid revolutionists in the New York Yipsels, although the Old Guard refused to admit it. Waldman persisted in saying in public print that Thomas was "the conscious or unconscious tool of the Communist Party." [24]

Throughout 1935 the Socialists of New York did little but fight one another. Finally, in January, 1936, the Progressive-dominated NEC suspended the charter of the New York State organization until such time as it was clear which faction was dominant. The NEC had considered such drastic action for nearly a year. In March, 1935, it had called before it the New York State Executive Committee "to show cause why the charter of New York should not be revoked."

The principal charge against New York was that the Old Guard had violated the party's rule of requiring admission to membership of all qualified applicants at the age of eighteen. The Old Guard had tried to prevent the moving up to full membership of radical Yipsels when they came of party age. Nothing came of this threat. The NEC appointed a special subcommittee to consider the New York situation. This subcommittee recommended a compromise which satisfied no one, but the NEC adopted the recommendation by a vote of seven to four. Now the NEC suspended the New York organization "until such time as all registered members democratically elect a new State Committee" on the grounds that the New York organization was "split in two nearly equal groups" and that "the regular state and local machinery has proven itself unable to preserve and build a united vigorous party." [25]

New York's Socialists elected their new state committee in the regular party primaries in the spring of 1936. The Old Guard suffered a bad defeat. Despite the fact that Old Guard candidates were unopposed in 25 upstate districts, there were only 48 Old Guard candidates elected, as against 82 for the combined Militant-Progressive opposition. The Old Guard also did badly in the election of delegates to the 1936 party convention.[26] But the Old Guard did not give up the fight. It continued to act as if it were the official state organization until the national convention at Cleveland in May.

Two delegations from New York appeared at the Cleveland convention. The convention's credentials committee recommended the seating of the Progressive-Militant delegation. Although he was not yet an officially seated delegate—nor was he ever to be—James Oneal was allowed to present a dissent from the credentials committee's ruling. Oneal proposed that the Old Guard delegation be seated, that the party unequivocally record itself against any kind of united action with the Communists, that it not accept to membership any ex-Communists who do not expressly repudiate Communist principles, and that the party declare a lack of confidence in the present NEC. The debate was on. For a day and a night the Socialists displayed their bitterness and an unusual capacity to tie themselves in knots of parliamentary procedure. There were two attempts to compromise the issue. The compromise offered by Darlington Hoopes would have seated half of each delegation; the one offered by Mayor Hoan would have seated only a few Old Guardists. The convention rejected both compromising suggestions. Then came the roll-call vote on the recommendation of the credentials committee that the Progressive-Militant delegation be seated. Before the announcement of the official count of the vote, it was apparent that the Old Guard had been badly defeated. There was much cheering and applauding over the result of the vote while, for some strange reason, an emissary of the Mexican Confederation of Workers was allowed to address the convention. At the conclusion of his brief speech the convention broke out with the "Internationale," without which no Socialist crisis would be complete. Louis Waldman and Algernon Lee refused to stand and sing, and when David Lasser was granted the floor to call attention to Waldman's and Lee's lack of action these Old Guardsmen were roundly booed. Then Chairman Krzycki announced the official vote. "For the adoption of the committee's report, 9,449; against the adoption, 4,809." The roll call revealed the usual geographic centers of factional strength. The Old Guard carried all of the votes of Connecticut and Maryland and most of the votes of Massachusetts and Pennsylvania. It picked up very few votes elsewhere.

The Old Guard's defeat on the issue of the seating of the New York delegation did not start a bolt from the convention. Old Guard delegates from Massachusetts, Pennsylvania, and elsewhere stayed on at the convention and did not object to the nomination of Thomas for President by acclamation. They did threaten to bolt when, in the closing minutes of the convention, the question of a policy toward a united front with the Communists was under consideration. But Thomas smoothed over the growing tension by pointing out that no one advocated a united front in the sense of a common presidential ticket or of any kind of organic unity, and that the only question was what the party policy should be toward the Communists when specific problems arose, such as the case of the Scottsboro boys. He succeeded in getting the convention to postpone consideration of the question of working with the Communists until after the election.[27]

But there was a bolt from the party before the campaign was over. The New York Old Guard, the Connecticut organization, most of the Socialists of Reading and Pittsburgh, and the Maryland organization formed the Social Democratic Federation, which was not a political party, but which did not support the Socialist candidates. The Social Democratic Federation in New York joined the new American Labor Party, which supported Roosevelt, Garner, and Lehman. Ironically, the Old Guard, which had thought the majority Socialists too close to communism, now had avowed Communist comrades in their new American Labor Party.

The split of the Social Democratic Federation was a serious loss for the party. The actual numbers of those who left were not great, but they took with them a significant part of the little financial support the party had. Abe Cahan's *Jewish Daily Forward*, which had been growing steadily more conservative since the World War, went over to the federation, and the party had always been able to count upon the *Forward* for a little financial assistance when the party's creditors became insistent. Leaders of the strong and closely knit Jewish Socialist Verband aided the formation of the Social Democratic Federation, and the party had no recourse but to revoke the Verband's party charter.[28] Two of the three important municipal political machines in the party, Reading and Bridgeport, Connecticut, where Jasper McLevy was elected mayor in 1933, left with the rest of the Old Guard.

These losses, however, were not so great as the loss attributable to Franklin D. Roosevelt. With the passage of the Wagner Act in 1935 some of the trade unions that had been traditionally Socialist began to swing their support to the New Deal. Needle trades leaders like David Dubinsky, president of the International Ladies Garment Workers, and Sidney Hillman, president of the Amalgamated Clothing Workers, wanted to support Roosevelt and the New Deal but did not want to support the Southern white supremacists and big-city machine politicians that would have to be included in a blanket endorsement of the Democratic Party. The American Labor Party was the way out of this dilemma. The ALP could nominate those Democrats considered worthy of labor's vote, and then after the election, when the labor Democrats compromised with the Southern Bourbons and the city boodlers, the ALP could claim it had not been a party to the deal. In 1936 Dubinsky resigned from the Socialist Party and gave the support of the ILGWU's rich treasury to Roosevelt through the American Labor Party, even if he did it with some misgivings. Hillman had no misgivings. His support of Roosevelt was enthusiastic, and he used his influence in the union to make Amalgamated officials who were inclined to stay with the Socialists go along with him. Leo Krzycki, an Amalgamated vice president, explained to Thomas that his connection with Hillman required that he resign from the Socialist Party and support Roosevelt even though he still personally wished the Socialists success.[29]

The defection of the needle trades to Roosevelt left the Socialists almost without labor support. The Labor League for Thomas and Nelson in 1936—George Nelson of the Farmers Union was Thomas's running mate—was a pitifully weak organization. It represented no big unions and no rich ones. The chairman of the Labor League was A. Philip Randolph, president of the Brotherhood of Sleeping Car Porters. The attraction of Randolph to the Socialist cause back in the 1920's was a result of the Socialist abandonment of its old position that the only way for the Negro to escape his second-class citizenship was through Socialism. Other officers were Jerome Davis of the hardly numerous American Federation of Teachers and George Baldanzi of the Dyers, Finishers, Printers, and Bleachers.[30]

Between 1932 and 1936 the Socialists also lost to Roosevelt a considerable number of their intellectual supporters. There were a few important names still around to adorn a letterhead, such as John Dewey, Reinhold Niebuhr, Robert Morss Lovett, John Haynes Holmes, and Freda Kirchwey, who had all announced support of Thomas before, and there were a few recruits from the intellectuals —Franz Boas, James T. Farrell, Louis Hacker, and Goodwin Watson.

But there was nothing like the support for Thomas among independent intellectuals there had been in 1932. A *New Republic* poll published during the weeks immediately before the election revealed the degree of the swing to Roosevelt among independent progressives.[31]

Thomas and Nelson conducted a fighting campaign, but they aroused no response like the one in 1932. Few old-time radicals wrote to the national office wanting to get back into the Socialist movement as they had in the previous campaign. In his speeches Thomas showed considerable alarm over the growth of the Union Party, a new national party composed of supporters of Huey Long, Father Coughlin, and Dr. Francis Townsend which ran William Lemke of North Dakota for President. While Long was still living—he was assassinated in the fall of 1935—Thomas had vigorously expressed his opposition to Long's demagoguery. During the campaign of 1936 Thomas addressed the Townsend convention and amidst the boos of the old people condemned Father Coughlin and described the Townsend plan as treating tuberculosis with cough drops.[32] Thomas's efforts against the Union Party were not very effective; Lemke in November polled well over four times the popular vote for Thomas.

Socialists examining the election returns of 1936 could find nothing encouraging. The results were disastrous. Thomas and Nelson received 187,342 votes, as against 884,781 in 1932. Not since 1900 had a Socialist presidential candidate received so few votes, and Debs in that year had polled a better percentage of the popular vote. The vote in all the states was down. The Socialist vote in California dropped from 63,299 in 1932 to 11,331 in 1936, in Colorado from 13,565 to 1,594, in Illinois from 67,258 to 7,530, in Iowa from 20,472 to 1,373, in New York from 177,397 to 86,897, in Pennsylvania from 91,199 to 14,375, and in Wisconsin from 53,379 to 10,626. In Reading the vote for Thomas was only one-third of the number of voters registered Socialist. In New York apparently large numbers of former Socialist voters swung to the new American Labor Party. Roosevelt in that state polled 274,924 votes on the ALP line, more than three times the Socialist vote.[33]

After the election of 1936 only the most stubbornly optimistic among the Socialists could look at their party and conclude that it had much of a future as an electoral instrument. The party's Indian summer was clearly over. Winter descended upon the Socialist Party, and there are not yet any signs of spring. Nor are there likely to be. To Norman Thomas the reason for the Socialist failure was clear: "It was Roosevelt in a word." [34]

XI

LAST RITES AND POST MORTEM

A FEW days after Roosevelt's reelection in 1936 the National Executive Committee of the Socialist Party met to survey the damage, and found it so great that it called a special convention of the party to consider what should be done.[1] The special convention at Chicago in March, 1937, indicated just how weak the party had become and the kinds of problems that were to plague it for the next few years.

The convention was a miserable affair, mismanaged and confusing. At the convention's close the new executive secretary, Roy Burt, who succeeded Senior late in 1936, apologized to the delegates for the general lack of smoothness which characterized the sessions. Burt's report on the state of the party was most discouraging. The campaign of 1936 had demonstrated the party's weakness. The party had been able to spend less than $25,000 on the entire campaign, less than half it had spent in 1932. Mail response to Socialist radio speeches had been one-tenth what it had been in 1932. Socialist locals in the campaign had not been efficient enough to arrange meetings for all the speakers national headquarters could provide.

Burt had to report that membership had dropped precipitously. In February, 1937, the month before the convention, only 6,488 members had bought their dues stamps. In February, 1936, the number had been 15,648. So far as the national office knew there were only about 1,300 trade union members in the Socialist Party. The decline in membership was due largely, but not entirely, to the split of the Old Guard and the formation of the Social Democratic Federation. The following table of party membership, based on the monthly average number of dues-payers, shows that the decline started before the Old Guard left the party:

1929— 9,560	1933—18,548
1930— 9,736	1934—20,951
1931—10,389	1935—19,121
1932—16,863	1936—11,922

The 1936 split was all but the *coup de grâce* to an already declining party. The decline in membership attributable to the split can be seen in a comparison of the state membership figures in February, 1936, before the split, with those for February, 1937. Old Guard Connecticut dropped from 1,160 to 300, Massachusetts from 1,710 to 249, New York from 3,153 to 1,856, and Pennsylvania from 2,235 to 116. Only Georgia, Indiana, Minnesota, New Mexico, Utah, and Vermont gained membership in that twelve-month period, and the numbers in each of those states were insignificant.[2]

A membership of only about 6,500 was a new all-time low. The party had had more members than that when it was founded in 1901. In the worst days of Socialist doldrums in the mid-1920's, when William H. Henry blundered around in national headquarters, the membership had never fallen below 7,000. As any kind of political force at all the Socialist Party was dead. Its subsequent history is the story of the tortured gyrations of a political sect. It is ironic that the party of Debs, which had predicted the collapse of American capitalism, itself collapsed during the worst crisis American capitalism ever had.

Years later, looking back with several years' hindsight at the spectacle of Socialist failure during the Great Depression, some Socialists have seen the party's insistence upon continuing to contest elections as a tragic mistake. Their argument is that Socialist influence in the new CIO unions would have been maintained and extended if the party had worked out a way by which Socialist unionists could have remained loyal to the party while supporting Roosevelt and other New Deal candidates, something in the manner of the present-day Americans for Democratic Action or the New York Liberal

Party. But such speculating has been Monday-morning quarter-backing. This was not the road taken.

Even as a sect rather than a political party, as a small group of propagandists trying to point the way for American laborers and farmers, the Socialists were conspicuously ineffectual. The departure of the Old Guard had not rid the Socialists of factionalism. If anything, factionalism became more intense after 1936. During the early 1930's the party's internal battles had been between the Old Guard and a coalition of Progressives and Militants. In the absence of an Old Guard the Progressives and Militants now divided. The left wing of the party was now known as the Clarity caucus, the name coming from its periodical *Socialist Clarity*. Led by Herbert Zam, Gus Tyler, and Max and Robert Delson, two young New York lawyers, the Clarity caucus took a revolutionary position, calling upon the Socialists to be a "vanguard" party. Those that had been the Progressives—at the time frequently called Militants because they had allied themselves with the party's extreme Left in the fight with the Old Guard—were now the right wing of the party. And there was now a new faction, far more obstreperous than any in the party ever before, for in the spring of 1936 the Trotskyites, or the Appeal group, dissolved the Workers Party and joined the Socialists. The Trotskyites published a periodical, the *Socialist Appeal*, from which they took their name. The Trotskyites had a checkered history of movement among almost all parties of the Left. For about a year in 1936 and 1937 the Trotskyites, led by James P. Cannon and Vincent R. Dunne of the Minneapolis Teamsters, were a faction within the Socialist Party.

The differences among these factions as to the proper position of the Socialist Party were constantly apparent at the 1937 convention. The convention had been called to consider specific questions: the party's organization and constitution, its relationship with labor unions and other political groups, and ways to strengthen its position and program against war and fascism. There was conflict among the factions as each of these questions was considered.

On the question of how the party could best help to prevent war, for example, there was a sharp division. Gus Tyler of the Clarity group presented a highly abstract and doctrinaire resolution declaring the party would support no war whatsoever except a war for socialism. The distinction between democratic-capitalist nations and fascist countries, Tyler said, would be meaningless should such nations go to war because the very act of war would make democratic nations reactionary dictatorships. Tyler argued that the only course for the Socialist Party was "to make a realistic valuation of the forces produced by war in order to organize them and smash the capitalist system." In reply David Lasser ridiculed the suggestion of turning "the guns of our 6,000 Socialists against the capitalist governments." The only way the Socialists could prevent a war or smash it once it came, argued Lasser, was to create a mass movement. There was nothing in the Tyler resolution to attract the American labor movement, Lasser continued, and the acceptance of such a resolution "would further isolate the Socialist Party and we would find at the time of our next convention that we might have 3,000 members instead of 6,000 members to turn an imperialist war into civil war." Meta Berger of Milwaukee, Victor Berger's widow, wanted the party to urge the United States government to support collective security of all democratic nations against the fascist powers. Tyler had already condemned agitation for collective security as "merely asking the working class to sign a blanket check even before a war, endorsing support in the event of war." [3]

The differing concepts of the role of the party and the obligations of members in it were nowhere more clearly revealed than in the debate on the question of affiliation with the American League Against War and Fascism. There was fairly general agreement that the party should not join the league as an organization. The resolution under consideration stated that the party "will not put upon individual members a complete and binding prohibition . . . that individuals who do enter the League activities must do so subject to the direction of their local and state committees." Lasser and Mrs. Berger interpreted this as lax party discipline, holding that any member who wished to join the League could get permission from his comrades. The Clarity and Appeal groups interpreted the resolution quite differently. They believed a Socialist should join the League only when sent by his comrades, there to act as an agent of his party. In other words, they supported the idea of a highly disciplined organization. Tyler revealed his position clearly: "Individuals who act merely as individuals are worthless to the Socialist Party; individuals acting as an arm of the Socialist Party are valuable in any sort of an organization." Trotskyites Dunne, Albert Goldman, and Carl Pemble agreed with the Clarity group in this matter. To Mrs. Berger the individual party member was more important than the party; to the Clarity group and the Trotskyites the individual member was only a pawn of the party.

A political party may be able to contain within it people and groups with such divergent points of view; a political sect cannot, for a sect by its very nature demands doctrinal unity and purity. The convention of 1937 made an effort to put an end to the factional fighting, but in the very discussion of party factions the passions of factionalism became hotter. After long argument the convention voted to suppress factionalism by demanding the discontinuance of all factional publications—except for six weeks before each convention when all factions could propagandize for their points of view—and the establishment of an official party publication to be governed by a board representing all points of view in the party.[4]

The Trotskyites, the most zealous seekers of doctrinal purity of any revolutionary group, would not obey the injunction of the convention. Believing, like the Puritan hierarchy of seventeenth century New England, that they and only they had a grip on truth, they held that to compromise their position would be to compromise with evil. The NEC, seeing the directions of the convention ignored, appointed a special subcommittee to investigate the Appeal group and to recommend action. The subcommittee, headed by Arthur G. McDowell of Illinois, recommended that the Trotskyites be expelled. The NEC unanimously voted their expulsion. Thus ended the history of one faction in the party. The Trotskyites subsequently founded the Socialist Workers Party.

The whole Trotskyite affair hurt the Socialist Party rather

badly. The Trotskyites had captured the whole California organization. To expel them there the NEC had to revoke the California charter and reorganize the state. The Appeal group was so large in New York City that expelling them presented serious administrative problems, and probably no one fully understood the complicated method the NEC adopted to rid the New York organization of the Trotskyites.[5] But the Socialist Party was dying before its invasion by the followers of Trotsky. Their invasion was like a slight cerebral stroke for one already dying of malnutrition.

In the late 1930's and the 1940's the Socialist Party went on down, down, down. Outside Milwaukee it had practically no successes. Norman Thomas did help to restore civil liberties in Mayor Frank Hague's Jersey City, but the victory was a gain for liberty instead of for Socialism. Elsewhere there was little to encourage Socialists. Everywhere was defeat. In November, 1937, Thomas withdrew from the mayoralty race in New York City, so feeble was his party. In the elections of 1938 the Socialist vote in New York State was so small that the party lost its permanent place on the ballot. Subsequently the Socialists could get on the ballot only by special petition.[6] As the war approached, more and more Socialists abandoned the party.

The problem of war and peace and fascism was one the Socialist Party never satisfactorily met. Socialists were vigorous opponents of fascism. Indeed, during the 1920's when many Americans either ignored or looked with favor upon Italian fascism, the Socialist Party was one of the relatively few groups in the nation consistently to oppose Mussolini and his followers. The party's opposition to Hitler was even more intense. Socialists organized men and raised funds for a military contingent, the Debs Column, to fight with the Spanish Loyalists. The party was extremely critical of the Roosevelt administration's policy toward Spain. But while antifascist, the party was also vigorously antiwar, and it never resolved the dilemma of how to destroy fascism without resort to war. To go to war with the fascists, Socialists argued, would be only to destroy democracy in the United States. And after the outbreak of war in Europe in September, 1939, the Socialists argued that, even as evil as the Nazis were, their Allied opponents were little better. A declaration on war adopted by the party's convention in 1940 well summarized its position:

> The cause for which Hitler has thrown the German masses into war is damnably unholy. But the war of Chamberlain and Reynaud is not thereby rendered holy. The fact that Hitler is the opponent does not make the Allied war a fight for democracy. . . . The Allied governments have no idealism in the conflict, no war aims worthy of the sacrifice of the democracy and life of their peoples, no purpose of overthrowing fascism except to replace it by a more desperate and brutal government, if need be, that would crush the economic demands of the German workers, and leave England and France free to pursue their star of profit.

The party went on to demand absolute neutrality, to urge a constitutional amendment granting the entire electorate a chance to vote on the question of war participation, to advocate the defeat of bills for a larger military and naval establishment, and to oppose military training in colleges. To defeat the fascists the Socialists suggested only "The continuance of independent working class action through the medium of workers' boycott of German and Japanese goods." [7]

One could not say the American electorate was prowar in 1940, but the electorate certainly did not rally to the Socialists' antiwar program. Thomas's vote in 1940 was only 99,557, about half his miserable vote in 1936. In a handful of so-called "isolationist" states Thomas increased his vote, but in most states his vote fell precipitously. In New York the vote for Thomas declined from 86,897 in 1936 to 18,950 in 1940. Roosevelt polled 417,418 votes there on the American Labor Party ticket.[8]

After the election Thomas continued his antiwar activities. He opposed the policy of "all aid to the Allies short of war" on the grounds that such involvement in the conflict would inevitably lead to America's entrance into the war as a full-fledged belligerent. Much to the distress of several Socialists Thomas testified before congressional committees to oppose such measures as Lend-Lease and the extension of the draft. More than one party member was disturbed in

May, 1941, when Thomas spoke at an America First rally in New York City and when the next morning's *New York Times* carried a group photograph of the rally's speakers, Burton K. Wheeler, Charles A. Lindbergh, Kathleen Norris, and Norman Thomas.[9]

By Pearl Harbor so many Socialists had quietly dropped away there was nothing even approaching 6,000 Socialist guns to turn the war into a civil conflict to smash capitalism, as had so fondly been contemplated at the convention in 1937. Indeed, after the declaration of war few Socialists had any desire to obstruct it. Here and there were a few peace demonstrations, but the majority of Socialists agreed to give the war "critical support." The party never adopted a clear statement on the war. In Thomas's words, the party's position was one of "general condemnation of wickedness." There were very few around even to condemn wickedness. When Thomas ran for President in 1944, he polled only 78,229 votes, less than Morris Hillquit had received when he ran for mayor of New York City during World War I.[10] With the end of the war there was no revival of the Socialist Party. Thomas did increase his vote in 1948 to 139,521, but this was by no means a good record.

In 1950 the Socialist Party met in convention at Detroit and debated whether or not to give up the political ghost. Thomas announced he would not run again and urged the convention not to run a national ticket in 1952. After long consideration the party declared it was not yet dead. The decision to continue running a presidential ticket was largely to lend prestige to the municipal tickets in Reading, where the Socialist pacifists had come back into the party just before the war, and in Milwaukee. In 1952 the Socialist candidate for President was Darlington Hoopes, a Reading lawyer. He received only 20,189 votes. Never before had a Socialist presidential candidate done so poorly at the polls. Running ahead of Hoopes were the candidates of the Progressive Party, the Socialist Labor Party, and even the Prohibition Party. In 1954 the once mighty Wisconsin organization voted not to run a slate of candidates.[11] There is not as yet a signed certificate of the Socialist Party's death, but when its presidential candidate is outvoted by the Prohibition Party few will deny that an autopsy is in order. Let us examine the corpse. Why did it die? Why was it never stronger than it was?

Elsewhere in Western civilization Socialists of various kinds have retained their strength or become stronger as American Socialism deteriorated to almost nothing. The British Labor Party at mid-century is at its strongest. There are vigorous social democratic movements in Australia, New Zealand, and western Canada. Socialists are a major political force in western Germany and in the Scandinavian nations. In almost all the democratic nations of the Western world Socialists of some variety are a significant political force, but in the United States, the most powerful of the Western democracies, there is no Socialist political movement.

The decline and death of American Socialism has occurred despite the fact that the course of recent American history has demonstrated the validity of much of the Socialist analysis and criticism of capitalism. As Socialists predicted, economic power has become increasingly concentrated. As Socialists predicted, capitalism has not provided the American nation with a confidently stable economy. What economic stability and health there has been in the nation's economy since 1940 has been largely attributable to past, present, or possible future war. As Socialists predicted, American businessmen have become increasingly interested in and dependent upon foreign markets. There are, of course, very important aspects of the Socialist analysis and prediction that time has shown to be in error. The lot of the worker in the American economy has improved, contrary to Socialist predictions. Real wages have risen. And the Socialist doctrine of the inevitability of socialism, although not susceptible of proof or disproof, certainly does not seem to be validated by recent American history. But if some Socialist predictions have turned out to be mistaken, others were quite acute. Yet in America at mid-century there is no Socialist political movement. It is the purpose of the balance of this book to seek an explanation of why this is true.

At the outset it must be made clear that this discussion is concerned only with Socialism as a political movement. As an intellectual movement an autopsy is not in order, for intellectually Socialism is far from dead. Many historians, economists, and sociologists employ at times what originally were Socialist concepts, and the extent to which Socialism has forced an examination of the assumptions of capitalism is probably great. Undoubtedly there are some major-party voters who adhere to some Socialist principles. But here we are concerned with Socialist politics, not Socialist theory.

There are two categories of factors to be considered in dealing with the question of why the American Socialist Party died. There are, first, weaknesses, inadequacies, failures, errors of commission and omission on the part of the Socialist Party. Besides these internal factors there are external factors, basic conditions in American society that militated against Socialist success and were largely beyond the power of the Socialists to change. This book, concerned primarily as it is with the Socialist Party's internal history, comes nearer offering insights into the internal factors than into the external ones. The external factors of Socialist failure, however, are probably the more important. A full investigation of these external factors requires much more than a history of the Socialist Party; it requires an investigation into all of American history.[12]

One of the most serious errors of the Socialist Party was its failure to behave the way political parties in the United States must in order to be successful. The Socialist Party never fully decided whether it was a political party, a political pressure group, a revolutionary sect, or a political forum. It tried to play all these roles at the same time. One of the first rules of American politics is to build strong local and state organizations. Outside of a few places, notably Milwaukee and Oklahoma, the Socialists failed to establish political machines. Indeed, they usually did not even try to build them. The Socialist Party time and again committed itself to political action, rejecting first the "direct action" of the syndicalists and later the revolution of the Communists, but it usually made little attempt to organize political machines at the local level. And it is at the local level, of course, that voting is done. Only in Milwaukee and Oklahoma and a few small cities did the Socialists have an organization in each precinct to distribute literature, get voters registered, get voters to the polls, watch the count of the vote, and all the other routine tasks of political party workers. Watching the count of the vote is a critical activity, especially critical for minor parties. After the election of 1932 it was estimated that only about half the Socialist vote was counted. Socialists cried fraud when Debs was defeated in his race for Congress in 1916. They claimed that at least 70 per cent of the voters of Terre Haute, Debs's home town, had promised their votes to Debs, but that Debs had been "counted out." If the charge were valid—and considering the aroma of Indiana politics of that era it was not beyond the realm of possibility—the Socialists had no one to blame but themselves. Watchers would have assured Debs a fair count.

But most Socialists never saw the value of political organization. They regarded the building of local machines as "ward heeling," sordid truckling for votes beneath the ideals of Socialism. Debs wrote during his 1916 campaign: "Let it not be supposed for a moment that on the part of the Socialists this is going to be a vote-chasing campaign. . . . We shall explain socialism and make our appeal to the intelligence, the manhood and womanhood of the people, and upon that . . . high plane, whatever the outcome, we are bound to win." [13] With such an approach he had no grounds for optimism.

Nor did Socialists generally concern themselves with local issues. Their interests were nearly altogether in national and international matters. This lack of interest in local matters was a disregard of one of the basic features of American politics. The positions of the major parties on regional and local problems command political loyalties perhaps as much as their positions on national affairs. But usually the Socialists ignored local affairs, and rarely did the Socialists run a full slate of local and state candidates. Evidence of what success the party might have enjoyed from a more intensive concern with local problems can be seen in the experience of those parts of the party that did so concern themselves. The Milwaukee Socialists offered the voters a local program, and they became that city's dominant party. Indeed, Milwaukee voters supported the Socialists because of their local program and record and in spite of their national affiliation. Oklahoma Socialists became strong because of good organization and their concern with local matters. Lacking the money to finance a state Socialist newspaper, Oklahoma Socialists did the next best thing in arranging with the publisher of the *Appeal to Reason*, which circulated very widely in the state, to have inserted a special "Oklahoma page" in each copy mailed to Oklahoma. The "Oklahoma page," edited for many years by J. O. Welday, a high-school principal of Oklahoma City, was concerned almost altogether with state and local matters.[14] The results in the membership rolls and at the polls were gratifying.

When the Socialist Party occasionally strove to become homogeneous, to cast all members in the same mold, it violated one of the basic principles of American political parties. The major American political parties are anything but homogeneous. They are coalitions, and their platforms are compromises, the result of bargaining among the various interests in the parties. In its early days the Socialists were as diverse, regionally and ideologically, as their major-party opponents, and they were a force that caused the major parties some unrest. But over the years the Socialist Party became increasingly homogeneous. By the time the United States entered World War II the Socialist membership was pretty much of the same mold, all social democratic pacifists, and they were very few in number. It is almost a political axiom that any party that is "pure," whose members are unanimous in their opinions, is a weak party. A homogeneous party of Socialists may work in European politics, under a cabinet system with several political parties, where the compromises come *after* the election in the formation of a government, but such a party is not suited to American conditions.

In some of the party's splits, of course, the disagreement among factions was too wide to compromise. In 1912–1913 the differences between the syndicalists and the political actionists were too great to be reconciled. In 1919 the Communist split could not have been avoided. The Left Wing Section had determined that it would either capture the Socialist Party or secede from it. Again in the 1930's there was no hope of party harmony with the Trotskyites. Wide disagreement over basic principles will plague any party of the Left, and splits are likely in parties without the political paste of patronage, or real promise of patronage.

Another of the weaknesses of the Socialist Party was its failure to win organized labor to its cause. This failure was by no means exclusively the fault of the Socialists. There were and are important reasons for labor's shunning the Socialists beyond the power of the Socialists to alter. But, even so, the Socialist wooing of labor's hand was a blundering affair.

The Socialist tactic most regularly used to win the AFL was "boring from within." This device was quite a different thing to the Socialists from what it was to the Communists. Where it seemed to be the aim of the Communist internal borers to get their members into key positions in order to run unions along lines consistent with Communist desires, the Socialists tried actually to convert a majority of the union membership to their point of view. But while such Socialists as Berger, Maurer, and Max S. Hayes of Cleveland bored within organized labor in this fashion they were considerably impeded by the actions of other Socialists. In 1905 Debs helped to organize the Industrial Workers of the World. It is true that the IWW tried to organize workers the AFL had long ignored. But the IWW was a dual union to a degree, and dual unionism is a cardinal sin in the American labor movement. A substantial section of the Socialist Party strongly opposed any yielding to the AFL whatsoever in order to enlist its support. Debs wrote, "Not for all the vote of the American Federation of Labor and its labor-dividing and corruption-breeding craft-unions should we compromise one jot of our revolutionary principles." [15]

But despite Debs and others in the party who seemed to despise the AFL fully as much as the National Association of Manufacturers, the effectiveness of the Socialist kind of boring from within was demonstrated by the progress Socialists made here and there with organized labor. The state federations in Wisconsin, Pennsylvania, and Montana had Socialist officials. Organized labor sometimes gave the Socialists financial help for campaigns in return for the contributions the Socialists gave the unions during strikes. At the AFL's 1912 convention the Socialist Hayes received almost one-third of the convention's vote in his contest with Gompers for the AFL presidency.[16] Whether a consistent Socialist policy of working with the AFL would have won organized labor for Socialism is problematic, but it is certain that Socialist attacks on the AFL neither reformed that body nor attracted it to the Socialist Party.

The Socialist Party made other mistakes. It frequently failed to communicate with the public. A majority of the American people simply does not understand Marxist jargon, and the party could have done well with more of the easily understood language of the *Appeal to Reason*, the *National Rip-Saw*, and the writings of Oscar Ameringer. The Socialist Party also can justly be accused of allowing incompetent persons to rise to party positions of importance and responsibility. Particularly at the state and local level some Socialist officials were too small for their jobs.

But despite all the shortcomings of the Socialist Party, its failure was not primarily its own fault; the failure of the Socialists was due less to their errors than to basic traditions and conditions in American society which the Socialists could do little or nothing to change. Socialist parties in Great Britain, Europe, and elsewhere have also made mistakes, perhaps greater mistakes than their American comrades made. The American Socialists, for example, never suffered a blow like the defection of Ramsay MacDonald. Yet the United States is one of the few important Western democracies not to have at mid-century a significant Socialist movement. One can only conclude that Old World conditions were more conducive to the growth of Socialism than conditions were in the United States. Properly and fully to describe and analyze the American traditions and conditions that impeded and killed American Socialism would be a major task, and it must suffice here only to indicate some of these basic American conditions.

In the first place, there are many features of the American political system that hamper the development of any third party,

whether Socialist or not. The two-party system in the United States
is so strong that no genuine third party has ever succeeded in becoming one of the major parties.[17] The election laws of most of the
states make it difficult for third parties to get on the ballot and stay
on. The large amounts of money necessary to finance an election
campaign handicap third parties. The major parties tend to "steal
the thunder" of minor parties when that thunder seems popular. The
two-party system is very deeply ingrained in American voting habits.
Time and again it has seemed to political observers that a third party
would amass a significant minority of the popular vote, but the
actual returns have seldom borne out the expectation. If all the
people who subscribed to the *Appeal to Reason* to read Debs's editorials, and who paid their money to hear Debs speak, had voted for
Debs as they cheered for Debs, his percentage of the popular vote
would have been considerably higher than it ever was. The same
is true of Norman Thomas, whose measure of respect among the
American people is considerably higher than the vote they gave
him. But many voters are reluctant to vote for a candidate who
does not have a good chance of winning, reluctant to "throw away"
their votes. The emphasis in American politics upon the presidential
campaign is another disadvantage to the development of a national
third party. Citing the difficulties of third parties, however, falls far
short of explaining why American Socialism failed. Socialists never
did as well as many other third parties; Socialism failed to attract
more than a relatively small part of the American people.

The primary reason that American Socialists never developed
the strength of their comrades in other countries was that in America
there is considerably less class consciousness than there is in other
Western nations. The Socialists directed their efforts to "the working class," "the proletariat," "the workers," but generally the members of this class failed to realize their class status. When Debs during his war trial said, "While there is a lower class I am in it; while
there is a criminal element, I am of it; while there is a soul in prison,
I am not free," he expressed a noble sentiment, but relatively few
Americans recognized the statement as an expression of solidarity

with themselves. This is not to say that there are no social classes in America nor that there have been none, nor even that there has been no recognition of social class. It is to say that in the United States class consciousness and solidarity have been considerably weaker than in Great Britain or western Europe.

Late in the Great Depression, when millions were still unemployed, Elmo Roper made a study of public opinion about social class. His conclusions were discouraging for Socialists. When asked, "What word would you use to name the class in America you belong to?" 27.5 per cent of those polled replied they did not know, indicating, if the sample were a fair one, that about one-fourth of the American people were very little if at all aware of social class. The answers to his questions were such that Roper concluded that 79.2 per cent of the population believed itself middle class. Of those whose incomes were so small that Roper considered them "poor," 70.3 per cent thought they were middle class. Only 7.9 per cent of the total considered themselves of the "lower" class. Of the factory workers polled only about one-third thought their interests and those of their employers essentially opposed.[18] Surely in a society with such disregard of social class as this a political movement based primarily upon class appeal will have a difficult time.

But to point out that Americans have relatively little class consciousness or regard themselves as members of a class that has no quarrel with capitalism is not to push back very far the original questions: Why did the Socialist Party die? Why was it never stronger than it was? We must go behind the American attitudes toward social class and seek to explain these attitudes.

The lack of a feudal tradition in America, the result largely of a new civilization on a continent with a vast amount of inexpensive land, is undoubtedly a major factor in the American people's failure to develop a class consciousness comparable to that of European peoples. When a modern capitalistic system of production developed in the United States, it did not displace a large and settled class of craftsmen, as happened in the Old World. From these displaced artisans in Great Britain, for example, came many of the Luddites and Chartists, and these movements tended to create a sense of class solidarity among British workers.[19] The absence of a need for un-propertied Americans to battle for the franchise and political representation in anything like the way the Chartists had to fight for these rights likewise tended to blur class lines. It was difficult for British and European workmen not to conclude that their states were for the advancement and protection of the propertied classes when they had to struggle so long and arduously with these classes for the right to participate in politics. The American workman, on the other hand, received the franchise relatively early and with comparative ease, leaving only social and economic lines between him and men of property, lines less definite than the political line had been.

Similarly, since there has never been a firmly established aristocracy based upon birth in America the middle class has never had a great struggle to assert its superiority. The United States has had nothing comparable to the Puritan Revolution, the agitation for the Reform Bill in 1832, or the French Revolution. This is significant because where there has been sharp conflict between an aristocracy and a middle class, radical and class-conscious ideas have gained circulation among the working class. But in America there has been no middle-class revolt to call forth a Gerrard Winstanley or a Babeuf.

The lack of a feudal heritage, however, has perhaps not been as important a factor in the development of class attitudes in America as has the relative success of American capitalism. The United States' exceptionally rich natural resources, its technical ingenuity, and its tremendous domestic market have combined to produce a huge gross national product. The distribution of the product has been something less than equitable, but the total product has been so great that the United States has enjoyed a better standard of living than have most European nations. The American economy has also, except during a few periods of hard times, been an expanding economy, and this fact has many implications for the question under consideration.

One effect of the tremendous expansion of the American economy has been that as the rich became richer the poor did not, in the long run, become poorer. Industrial capitalism undoubtedly widened the gap between the wealthiest families of the nation and the poorest, but the poor have generally been able, except during economic depressions, to look back upon their fathers' and grand-fathers' status and conclude that their own material comfort is greater. And the widespread assumption that the future holds even greater material comforts reflects an optimism that is not conducive to the development of class solidarity.

The growth of the American economy has also made possible a relatively high degree of class mobility. It has been possible for many able and ambitious young men of working-class origins to escape from their class. Many of their sisters have through marriage similarly risen on the social ladder. Free public schools have played no small part in the process of class circulation. And besides the *actual* degree of class fluidity there is a considerable amount of myth. A firm belief in the story of rags to riches is a part of American folk-lore.[20] Horatio Alger's manly young heroes are a real part of Ameri-can beliefs, whether or not they actually exist. The actuality and the dream have combined to produce an optimism about one's chances to better his position in the social order, an optimism that has militated against the development of class consciousness. Ameri-cans have generally believed it easier and more desirable to rise *from* their class rather than *with* their class. For many the belief proved justified. It is a matter of pure speculation what might have happened had the American class structure been static, but it seems reasonable that there would have been considerably more class consciousness and conflict. It is probable the working class would have had better leadership. It is not inconceivable that the Andrew Carnegies would have been, under different circumstances, leaders of labor.

Still another factor in American history that tended to hamper the development of class consciousness is the ethnic heterogeneity of American workers. The American working class has been com-posed of many races and nations, and there has been a tendency for American workers to identify themselves with their racial or na-tionality group rather than with their class. The steady stream of immigrants to the United States made organization of American workers more than usually difficult. Many American workers were not so aware of class antagonisms as they were of religious, ethnic, and racial tensions. The aspirations of immigrants and Negroes to become assimilated presented a special problem for the Socialist Party. For the Negro it was enough of a burden to be black without also being red. The immigrant who wanted to become an "American" realized that being a Socialist would be a handicap to his assimilation. It was no accident that Debs was the idol of many of the immigrants who did become Socialists; Debs was a living demonstration that it was possible to be both Socialist and American.

Although a major factor, the relative lack of class consciousness of Americans was only one of several basic conditions of American life that hampered Socialists. Perhaps because of the Socialists' inadequate explanation of their philosophy most Americans felt that Socialism would submerge their individualism. Certainly Americans have confused Socialism with communism and have recoiled from the monolithic Soviet state. The Russian Revolution and the subsequent strained relations between the Soviet Union and the United States were undoubtedly a factor in the decline of the Socialist Party even though Socialists were among the earliest of anticommunists.

Another American condition that has militated against Socialist success is the widely held pragmatic view of life that demands visible and practical results, and the quicker the better. Much of Socialism was not attractive to those who held such views. Just as American labor rejected the reformism of the Knights of Labor for the "practical" business unionism of the AFL, it rejected the promises of Socialism for the more immediate results of progressives. Victor Berger was fond of saying: "Socialism is coming all the time. It may be another century or two before it is fully established." In the meantime, one might have concluded, there was little to do but make the best of it and wait for the new day. Surely this vague promise of the millennium was not as attractive as the prospect of achieving less, but achieving it soon, through trade unions and the major parties. To most people half a loaf in the hand, or even a few slices, was preferable to the hope of the whole loaf. The IWW song, "The

Preacher and the Slave," might well have had another verse about this millenarian aspect of Socialism, to be followed by the song's refrain, "You'll get pie in the sky when you die." [21]

These, then, are some of the basic conditions and traditions of American society that prevented the success of the Socialist Party of America. There were undoubtedly other obstacles in the way of Socialist growth, and the author is not prepared to defend these few pages as definitive. In a manner of speaking, it was American history that defeated the Socialists. Thus ends the post mortem examination of the Socialist Party.

Is there a possibility of the Socialist Party's rebirth? Might it revive and embarrass the conductor of the autopsy? In these days of rapid change, when a nation's enemies become its friends and its friends become its enemies within a decade, almost anything seems possible. But today it does not seem at all probable that the Socialist Party shall arise from its grave. Today it seems more likely that the Know Nothing Party might arise from a century's sleep than that the Socialists might revive. The ideals of social democracy will remain part of the American tradition as long as American soil produces rebels, and there may develop some day, under the impact of fundamental social change, another social democratic political movement of significance. But should there again be a vigorous political organization with democratic and socialist principles in the United States, it is most unlikely that the party of Debs, Hillquit, and Thomas will provide its impetus.

BIBLIOGRAPHICAL ESSAY

THERE already exists a published bibliography of American Socialism far more comprehensive than any I could append to this volume, and there is no point in providing the reader with a conventional list of secondary and primary sources. The bibliography I refer to is the second volume of *Socialism and American Life*, edited by Donald Drew Egbert and Stow Persons, and published by the Princeton University Press in 1952. Professor T. D. Seymour Bassett, the chief bibliographer, has performed a great service for students of the subject. His work lists all the major published sources, secondary and primary, and it is well annotated. It is a model of works of its kind.

My purpose here, then, is not to attempt what Bassett has already done so well. I shall instead discuss briefly the manuscript materials I have used and comment upon some publications on the subject that have appeared since Bassett's work. Readers who wish to know specifically what published sources I have used are referred to the footnotes.

Three recent secondary accounts of the Socialist Party deserve special mention. In the first volume of *Socialism and American Life* there is a long chapter by Daniel Bell, labor editor of *Fortune Magazine*, entitled "The Background and Development of Marxian Socialism in the United States." In this admirably written essay the author traces the development, since the late nineteenth century, of all the Marxian political parties and a few other radical political movements as well. The space Bell can devote to the Socialist Party is necessarily limited, but no student of the subject can afford to neglect it. Bell is at his best when he deals with the Socialist Party during the 1930's, a period in which he knew the organization at firsthand. His insights are useful, and his interpretations are stimulating. In my opinion, however, his thesis that American radicals have been "in but not of this world," while a useful concept, fails as an adequate explanation of the failure of American radicalism. For a more detailed statement of my criticisms of Bell's essay, see my review of the two volumes in the October, 1952, issue of *Pennsylvania History*.

Another recent work in this field is Ira Kipnis, *The American Socialist Movement, 1897–1912* (New York: Columbia University Press, 1952). The Kipnis volume is a detailed internal history of the Socialist Party from its origin until the recall of William D. Haywood from the party's National Executive Committee in 1913, with special emphasis on the factional battles within the organization. The appearance of Kipnis's book, with its wealth of detail on the history of the early party, coming as it did after work on the present book was substantially completed, caused me to recast my organization. Seeing no further need for going over the period from 1901 to about 1909 in a detailed, chronological fashion, I abandoned that plan and substituted in the first two chapters of this book a survey of the party during its first years. But because of my disagreement with Kipnis's interpretation of the critical factional fights in the party from about 1909 to 1913, I have in the third chapter of this book gone over the same ground that Kipnis treats. His book, in my opinion, suffers in three respects. First, he is clearly too uncritical of Haywood and his wing of the party and overly critical of the more conservative groups among the Socialists. Second, by his failure to use the official records of the party at Duke University he missed an important dimension of the party's history. And third, his thesis that the failure of the Socialist Party is to be understood in terms of the party's factionalism in general and the defeat of Haywood in particular is far from convincing. For further comments on Kipnis's book see my review in the August, 1953, issue of the *Journal of Southern History*.

Still another recent book in this area is Howard H. Quint, *The Forging of American Socialism: Origins of the Modern Movement* (Columbia: University of South Carolina Press, 1953). Quint has produced an altogether excellent and authoritative account of the various groups and philosophies which evolved into the Socialist Party. The reader who wishes to look back into the origins of the subject of the present book will find *The Forgings of American Socialism* indispensable.

My main sources for this book have been various manuscript collections bearing upon the history of the Socialist Party and Socialist magazines and newspapers. Bassett quite adequately describes the party's publications, and I shall, therefore, confine my comments here to the pertinent manuscript collections. Despite the fact that many Socialists did not foresee that historians would someday be interested in their activities, and consequently destroyed much valuable correspondence and other records, researchers can still turn up a considerable amount of pertinent manuscript material. Some valuable correspondence, of course, is forever lost. Debs's widow, for example, destroyed most of his letters and other papers soon after his death in 1926.

The most important single collection of manuscripts for this book was the Socialist Party Collection at the Duke University Library. This collection of over 95,000 items consists of the official records of the party once kept at the national office. The collection contains official correspondence, membership records, financial records, press releases, photographs, stenographic records of meetings, and many of the mimeographed publications of the party. I have cited materials in this collection so frequently in this book that it seemed proper to abbreviate the full name of the collection to SPC, Duke. Scholars interested in the history of the Socialist Party cannot afford to neglect the Duke collection, and they will be delighted to know that the collection is admirably organized and that its curators are both very gracious and efficient. Scholars doing research in twentieth century American progressivism would be wise to ascertain the possibilities of this collection for their purposes; it contains some materials that extend beyond the history of the Socialist Party itself.

The Duke collection has an interesting history of its own. In the early 1940's the Socialist Party found it necessary to move its national office to smaller quarters. The new offices were too small to hold all the files, and with a disregard for the historian not altogether foreign to the Socialist tradition, the workers in the national office called in a wastepaper dealer to dispose of the records. The wastepaper dealer recognized that the records were worth more than the paper they were written on and sold them to Leon Kramer, a dealer in secondhand books and manuscripts who specializes in the history of radicalism. Kramer then sold the collection to Duke University.

The library of the Wisconsin State Historical Society at Madison is rich for students in this field. The John Rogers Commons collection of labor and radical newspapers and magazines is very useful, and the society also has many pertinent manuscript collections. The file called Labor Collection, Political Parties, is useful. The Henry Demarest Lloyd papers and the Daniel De Leon papers contain correspondence pertinent to the party's early history. I found the Wisconsin Loyalty Legion papers useful in the writing of this book for the activities of A. M. Simons during World War I. Recently the society acquired the Morris Hillquit papers, a collection of paramount importance for a study in this field. I used these papers when they were held by Miss Nina Hillquit of New York

City. Scholars should be gratified that the society has organized them and made them more readily available.

The Socialist Party Collection of the Milwaukee County Historical Society on the seventh floor of the Milwaukee County Courthouse is important for its many letters to Victor Berger. Most of Berger's papers are held by his descendants and are at present unavailable to scholars. The late Frederic Heath of Milwaukee kindly permitted me to use some letters from his personal files.

The nation's capital is rich in manuscript sources for a study of the Socialist Party. Pertinent collections in the Division of Manuscripts of the Library of Congress include the Charles Edward Russell papers, the William James Ghent papers, and the Woodrow Wilson papers. The Russell papers consist for the most part of letters to Russell. Students of English socialism should not overlook the many letters in this collection from H. M. Hyndman. The Ghent papers have relatively little correspondence, but the clippings of Ghent's published writings in obscure periodicals are very convenient. The Wilson papers were very useful to me in tracing the Socialists' relations with the administration during and immediately after World War I. Also in this connection, I used the Josephus Daniels diary in the Daniels papers. The Department of Justice Records in the National Archives abound in pertinent materials for the Socialists during the war years. Particularly useful to me were the Department of Justice Central File and the Records of the Pardon Attorney.

The New York Public Library has the Norman Thomas papers. This large collection is useful not only for its correspondence but also for some minutes of the party's National Executive Committee not in the Duke Collection. This library also has a microfilm copy of the University of Chicago Library's file of the *Socialist Party Official Bulletin*, after 1912 named the *Monthly Bulletin*. No scholar in this field should neglect the Socialist pamphlets in the New York Public Library.

The Louis B. Boudin papers are in the Special Collections Room of Butler Library, Columbia University. This small collection, although not as yet organized, is useful. It contains only letters to Boudin and a box of Boudin's manuscripts.

The Joseph A. Labadie Collection in the library of the University of Michigan, while more fruitful for a study of anarchism than of socialism, nevertheless contains many scattered items impossible to find elsewhere. Scholars of radicalism owe a debt to the late Agnes Inglis, curator of this collection, who gathered the materials. The librarians of the University of Michigan are to be congratulated for their decision to maintain and reorganize the collection.

The Meyer London Memorial Library at the Rand School of Social Science in New York City has the useful Debs Clipping books and many of the records of the New York Socialist organization. J. G. Phelps Stokes allowed me to use some of the materials in his voluminous privately held files, and Mrs. Anna Strunsky Walling graciously put the papers of her late husband, William English Walling, at my disposal. James Oneal, who was very cooperative in many ways, lent me some obscure factional publications of the 1930's. I consulted, but had no occasion to cite, the small collection of Eugene V. Debs papers in the Indiana Room of the Indiana State Library at Indianapolis. The Thomas memoir in the Columbia University Oral History Project, entitled The Reminiscences of Norman Thomas, proved extremely useful. This is a typed transcript, running to three volumes, of some oral reminiscences, and it offers the best biographical information on Thomas now available. It suffers from a lack of editing.

Further detective work undoubtedly would uncover other manuscript sources pertinent to the history of the Socialist Party, and I earnestly urge those who possess or who know of the existence of such sources to communicate with the director of a good library so that the materials may be properly cared for and made available to the community of scholarship.

NOTES

CHAPTER I

The Early Socialist Party: A Regional Survey

¹ For the background of the Socialist Party see Howard H. Quint, *The Forging of American Socialism: Origins of the Modern Movement* (Columbia, South Carolina, 1953), an excellent work, and Ira Kipnis, *The American Socialist Movement, 1897–1912* (New York, 1952), pp. 6–106.

² Quoted in Quint, *op. cit.*, p. 383; *Appeal to Reason* (Girard, Kan.), May 3, 1902.

³ Morris Hillquit, *History of Socialism in the United States* (New York, 1903), p. 338; Carl D. Thompson, Bigger, Better and Stronger Than Ever, MS dated 1913 in Socialist Party Collection, Duke University Library. This important collection will be cited hereafter as SPC, Duke.

⁴ W. J. Ghent, comp., Socialist Officials, typescript dated 1911, SPC, Duke.

⁵ Roosevelt to Charles Ferris Gettemy, Washington, Feb. 1, 1905, and Roosevelt to White, Oyster Bay, July 30, 1907, in Elting E. Morison and others, eds., *The Letters of Theodore Roosevelt* (Cambridge, Mass., 1951–1952), IV, 1113; V, 736–737.

⁶ *Socialism, Promise or Menace?* (New York, 1914).

⁷ Charles Edward Russell, *Bare Hands and Stone Walls: Some Recollections of a Side-Line Reformer* (New York, 1933), pp. 205–209.

⁸ Rand School of Social Science, *Sixth Year Supplementary Bulletin* (New York, 1911); *Worker* (New York), Oct. 27, 1906.

⁹ Russell, *op. cit.*, pp. 196–197; John Spargo, ed., *Proceedings*, National Convention of the Socialist Party . . . 1912 (Chicago, 1912), pp. 137–141.

¹⁰ Quint, *op. cit.*, pp. 150–168, 332–342.

¹¹ *New York Times*, Feb. 13, 1915. The stately *Times* was in this

case as adept at slanting a headline as any of its sensational competitors. One of London's minor points was that if the unemployed had only agitated for their rights and had organized, instead of reading the sport pages and otherwise shirking their class obligations, they would not have been in their present sorry position. The *Times* headlined the story, "Blames the Idle for Lack of Work."

¹² For typical "scientific" writing of the New York party, see Morris Hillquit, *Socialism in Theory and Practice* (New York, 1909). For some ridicule of this language see Oscar Ameringer, *Life and Deeds of Uncle Sam: A Little History for Big Children* (Oklahoma City, 1938, first published, 1909), *passim.* Ameringer defined economic determinism as "the thing that makes people turn their noses in the direction whence they hear the jingle of easy money" (p. 5).

¹³ *Who's Who in America, 1934–1935;* Walter Lippmann to Carl D. Thompson, Schenectady, Oct. 29, 1913, SPC, Duke. Lippmann, then Lunn's executive secretary and a member of the administration caucus, later broke with Lunn and moved further left for a brief period.

¹⁴ F. G. R. Gordon to Victor Berger, Portland, Me., Sept. 8, 1912, Socialist Party Collection, Milwaukee County Historical Society. This collection will be cited hereafter as SPC, Milwaukee. Interview with Louis B. Boudin, Dec. 20, 1949; interview with Algernon Lee, Dec. 21, 1949; interview with James Oneal, Nov. 5, 1951.

¹⁵ Leonard D. Abbott, "The Socialist Movement in Massachusetts," *Outlook,* LXIV (Feb. 17, 1900), 410–412; "The Socialist Defeat at Haverhill," *ibid.,* LXVI (Dec. 22, 1900), 958.

¹⁶ Solon De Leon, ed., with the collaboration of Irma C. Hayssen and Grace Poole, *The American Labor Who's Who* (New York, 1925); James Hudson Maurer, *It Can Be Done* (New York, 1938), pp. 87, 110–118, 139–145, 166, 302–303; Henry Gruber Stetler, *The Socialist Movement in Reading, Pennsylvania: A Study in Social Change* (Storrs, Conn., 1943).

¹⁷ Ralph Korngold to Carl D. Thompson, Spring Lake, Mich., May 10, 1913, SPC, Duke.

¹⁸ Ray Ginger, *The Bending Cross: A Biography of Eugene Victor Debs* (New Brunswick, N.J., 1949), pp. 237–239, 256.

¹⁹ *American Labor Who's Who;* Socialist Party Picture Book, SPC, Duke; Ginger, *op. cit.,* p. 347.

²⁰ *International Socialist Review,* VI (Dec., 1905), 369; VI (Aug., 1905), 77; VII (Oct., 1906), 243; Ginger, *op. cit.,* p. 268; A. M. Simons to the author, New Martinsville, West Va., Jan. 23, 1950; for more on Simons see William A. Glaser, "Algie Martin Simons and Marxism in

America," *Mississippi Valley Historical Review*, XLI (Dec., 1954), 419–434.

[21] *Chicago Socialist*, June 24, 1905; Oct. 13, 1906.

[22] There is no adequate biography of Berger, but see Marvin Wachman, *History of the Social-Democratic Party of Milwaukee* [*University of Illinois Studies in the Social Sciences*] (Champaign, 1945), Victor Berger, *Voice and Pen of Victor Berger: Congressional Speeches and Editorials* (Milwaukee, 1929), and Max Gordon, Victor Berger, Socialist Persuader in Congress, unpublished master's essay, dated 1941, library of the University of Wisconsin.

[23] The *Herald*, a weekly, became the *Milwaukee Leader*, a daily, in 1911.

[24] *Social Democratic Herald*, Dec. 6, May 31, June 7, 1902.

[25] The story is told here as Daniel Bell tells it in "The Background and Development of Marxian Socialism in the United States," Donald Drew Egbert and Stow Persons, eds., *Socialism and American Life* (2 vols., Princeton, N.J., 1952), I, 403n. Bell recounts the 1932 version of the story, but the same joke with different names circulated in the party long before.

[26] *Social Democratic Herald*, July 1, 1905; Frederic Heath to Eugene V. Debs, Milwaukee, July, 1905 (copy), Frederic Heath papers, Milwaukee, possession of Mr. Heath; Debs to Elizabeth H. Thomas, Terre Haute, July 19, 1905, Heath papers; Job Harriman to Victor L. Berger, Los Angeles, July 2, 1912, SPC, Milwaukee.

[27] Oscar Ameringer, *If You Don't Weaken: The Autobiography of Oscar Ameringer* (New York, 1940), p. 295; Berger to Morris Hillquit, Milwaukee, Aug. 20, 1919, Morris Hillquit papers. These papers are now in the Manuscripts Room, Wisconsin State Historical Society, Madison, but the present writer used them when they were privately held by Miss Nina Hillquit, New York City. The "I and my crowd" in this Berger letter is revealing of Berger's personality as well as of his personal strength in the Milwaukee movement.

[28] Summary of Measures Introduced by Victor Berger, SPC, Duke. This document is anonymous, but it may have been prepared by W. J. Ghent, who was Berger's secretary in this Congress.

[29] Berger to Hillquit, Milwaukee, Oct. 23, 1913, Hillquit papers; Frank P. O'Hare to the present writer, St. Louis, Feb. 9, 1949.

[30] Ameringer, *If You Don't Weaken*, pp. 263–269, the quotation from p. 267; *Socialist Songs* (Chicago, n.d.), a pamphlet in SPC, Duke; Ginger, *op. cit.*, pp. 265–268; *American Labor Who's Who*; interview with James Oneal, Nov. 5, 1951. Other Socialist songs were "The Inter-

national," "The Marseillaise" (in a loose translation), "The March of the
Workers" (to the tune of the "Battle Hymn of the Republic"), and
"The Jubilee of Labor" (to the tune of "Marching Through Georgia").

[31] W. J. Ghent, " 'The Appeal' and Its Influence," *Survey*, XXVI
(April 1, 1911), 27; Fred D. Warren to the present writer, Girard, Kan.,
Jan. 20, 1947.

[32] *Appeal to Reason*, May 3, 1902; Oct. 8, Sept. 3, 1904; Aug. 9, 1902;
Aug. 29, 1903; for the *Appeal's* anti-Catholicism see, for example, issues
of March 11, 25, April 1, 1905; for Wayland's early career see Howard
H. Quint, "Julius A. Wayland, Pioneer Socialist Propagandist," *Mississippi Valley Historical Review*, XXXV (March, 1949), 585–606.

[33] George Milburn, "The *Appeal to Reason*," *American Mercury*,
XXIII (July, 1931), 367; *Appeal to Reason*, June 4, 1904.

[34] *Appeal to Reason*, Sept. 23, 1905; March 10, 1906.

[35] Theodore Roosevelt to William Henry Moody, Washington,
March 19, 1906, *Letters*, Morison, ed., V, 186; Irvin G. Wyllie, "The
Socialist Press and the Libel Laws: A Case Study," *Midwest Journal*, IV
(summer, 1952), 72–79.

[36] Ginger, *op. cit.*, pp. 289–290, 303–304; Ghent, " 'The Appeal' and
Its Influence," p. 26.

[37] *Appeal to Reason*, Aug. 5, 1905; July 14, 1906; Oct. 6, 1906; May
13, 1905; Fred D. Warren to Charles Edward Russell, Girard, Kan., April
7, 1905, Charles Edward Russell papers, Manuscripts Division, Library
of Congress.

[38] Some other state membership figures in 1910 were: Texas, 2,079;
Arkansas, 472; Missouri, 1,558; Kansas, 1,300; Massachusetts, 2,856; Pennsylvania, 5,018; Ohio, 3,203; Illinois, 4,173; and Wisconsin, 2,793, Report
of J. Mahlon Barnes, National Executive Secretary, to the National Committee and State Secretaries, Chicago, Jan. 4, 1911, Labor Collection,
Political Parties, Box 3, Wisconsin State Historical Society; Membership
Report, 1916–1917, SPC, Duke.

[39] R. E. Dooley, Oklahoma State Secretary, to John M. Work, National Executive Secretary, Oklahoma City, Nov. 21, 1912, SPC, Duke;
Charles C. Bush, The Green Corn Rebellion, unpublished master's essay,
dated 1932, library of the University of Oklahoma, p. 6n; Socialist Party
of Oklahoma, *Platform and Campaign Book*, 1916 (n.p., but bears Girard,
Kan., ITU label, 1916), back cover; Morris Hillquit, *History of Socialism in the United States* (New York, 5th revised and enlarged ed., 1910),
p. 136.

[40] H. M. Sinclair, Oklahoma State Secretary, to Carl D. Thompson,
Oklahoma City, Aug. 20, 1914, SPC, Duke; Socialist Party of Oklahoma,

Platform and Campaign Book, 1916, the quotation from p. 7; John Riley Thacker to Woodrow Wilson, Altus, Okla., April 6, 1913, File VI, Box 258, Folder 298, Woodrow Wilson papers, Division of Manuscripts, Library of Congress.

[41] Grady McWhiny, "Louisiana Socialists in the Early Twentieth Century: A Study of Rustic Radicalism," *Journal of Southern History*, XX (Aug., 1954), 315–336.

[42] Jack London, "The Dream of Debs," *International Socialist Review*, IX (Jan., Feb., 1909), 481–489, 561–570; William D. Haywood, "Socialism the Hope of the Working Class," *ibid.*, XII (Feb., 1912), 469; for a sample of the open class warfare of the Rockies see Benjamin M. Rastall, *The Labor History of the Cripple Creek District: A Study in Industrial Evolution* [*University of Wisconsin Economics and Political Science Series*, III, No. 1] (Madison, 1905), especially the excellent photographs.

[43] Selig Perlman and Philip Taft, *History of Labor in the United States, 1896–1932: Labor Movements*, in John R. Commons, *et al.*, *History of Labour in the United States* (4 vols., New York, 1921–1935), IV, 285; in Arizona apparently those with a reform Socialist philosophy were Democrats rather than Socialists. A Democratic member of the Arizona Territory's constitutional convention wrote to Charles Edward Russell: "I am going to send to you as soon as printed a copy of the Constitution of the State of Arizona. It was written by men of your ideas tho under the guise of the Democrat party." Thomas Feeney to Russell, Bisbee, Ariz., Dec. 16, 1910, Russell papers; W. H. Kingery, the legislator, to Carl D. Thompson, Shelton, Wash., July 24, 1913; Frans Bostrum, Washington State Secretary, to Thompson, Everett, Wash., Sept. 1, 1913, SPC, Duke. The quotation is from Bostrum to Thompson.

[44] Interview with Jacob Panken, Nov. 5, 1951; Thomas Sladden, "The Revolutionist," *International Socialist Review*, IX (Dec., 1908), 423–430; W. J. Ghent, "The Vagaries of the Reds," clipping from *National Socialist*, Aug. 10, 1912, Box 46, W. J. Ghent papers, Manuscripts Division, Library of Congress.

[45] Ira B. Cross, "Socialism in California Municipalities," *National Municipal Review*, I (Oct., 1912), 611–619.

[46] Kipnis, *op. cit.*, pp. 348–356; Nathan Fine, *Labor and Farmer Parties in the United States, 1828–1928* (New York, 1928), p. 300.

CHAPTER II

IMMIGRANTS, NEGROES, INTELLECTUALS, MILLIONAIRES, AND MINISTERS

[1] Marcus Lee Hansen, *The Immigrant in American History* (Cambridge, Mass., 1942), pp. 85–96; Oscar Handlin, *The Uprooted* (Boston, 1952), pp. 81, 109–110, 133, 196.

[2] John Kolehmainen, "The Inimitable Marxists: The Finnish Immigrant Socialists," *Michigan History*, XXXVI (Dec., 1952), 395–405; James Oneal and G. A. Werner, *American Communism: A Critical Analysis of Its Origins, Development, and Programs* (New York, 1947), p. 43; Socialist Party of America, *Findings* of the Committee appointed by the National Executive Committee to examine into the matters pertaining to the Finnish Controversy (Chicago, 1914), SPC, Duke.

[3] Socialist Party of America, *Proceedings*, National Congress of the Socialist Party, Chicago, May 15 to 21, 1910 (Chicago, 1910), pp. 259–260; Oneal and Werner, *op. cit.*, pp. 43–44; Membership Records, 1916–1917, SPC, Duke; Questionnaires dated April 8, 1913, in papers of the Information Bureau Director, SPC, Duke; *Findings* of the Committee . . . pertaining to the Finnish Controversy.

[4] *Report* of the Executive Secretary of the National Committee in Session, May 10, 1914, in records of the New York State Committee of the Socialist Party, Meyer London Memorial Library, Rand School of Social Science, New York City.

[5] *Findings* of the Committee . . . pertaining to the Finnish Controversy, and appended decision of the National Executive Committee on the matter.

[6] C. E. Ruthenberg to members of the National Executive Committee, Cleveland, Feb. 7, 1915, SPC, Duke.

[7] *International Socialist Review*, XI (July, 1910), 17; *Social Democratic Herald*, July 4, 1902, Oct. 12, 1907; *Appeal to Reason*, Sept. 2, 1905; Aug. 20, 1904; July 8, 1905; for a fuller account of official Socialist policy on immigration see Kipnis, *The American Socialist Movement*, pp. 276–288, which is useful but strongly slanted in favor of those who urged unrestricted immigration.

[8] *International Socialist Review*, X (June, 1910), 1122–1123; Robert William Iversen, Morris Hillquit, American Social Democrat: A Study of the American Left from Haymarket to the New Deal, unpublished doctoral dissertation, dated 1951, library of the State University of Iowa, pp. 60–61.

[9] Socialist Party of America, *Proceedings*, National Convention of

the Socialist Party of America, Chicago, May 10–17, 1908 (Chicago, 1908), pp. 105–122.

[10] *Proceedings*, 1910 Congress, pp. 75–80, 98, 168.

[11] *Social Democratic Herald*, May 31, 1902.

[12] Papers of the Information Bureau Director, SPC, Duke.

[13] *Appeal to Reason*, April 25, 1903; Jan. 21, 1905. The *Appeal* had held this position even before the Socialist Party had been founded. *Ibid.*, Sept. 2, 1899; May 12, 1900.

[14] J. W. Swihart to Carl D. Thompson, Fremont, Neb., April 20, 1913, and attached replies to questionnaires, SPC, Duke.

[15] William English Walling, "Race War in the North," *The Independent*, LXV (Sept. 3, 1908), 529–534; *idem*, "Science and Human Brotherhood," *ibid.*, LXV (June 17, 1909), 1318–1327; *idem*, "The Founding of the N.A.A.C.P.," *Crisis*, July, 1929, p. 226; Charles Edward Russell and Mary White Ovington in *William English Walling: A Symposium* (New York, 1938), pp. 75–81; interviews with Mrs. Anna Strunsky Walling, Feb., 1952; Arthur Link, *Wilson, the Road to the White House* (Princeton, 1947), pp. 501–505.

[16] O. M. Thomason to Carl D. Thompson, Brainerd, Minn., Nov. 12, 1913; Thompson to Thomason, Chicago, Nov. 21, 1913, SPC, Duke.

[17] League for Industrial Democracy, *Twenty Years of Social Pioneering: The League for Industrial Democracy Celebrates Its Twentieth Anniversary* (New York, 1926), p. 7; Frederic Heath of Milwaukee goes so far as to assert that the activity of the ISS was one of the primary reasons for the failure of the Socialist Party. He argues that these intellectuals, although certainly not antilabor, did not truly understand the workingman, and that if they did understand him they did not know how to communicate with him. Heath also argues that the ISS turned the party into a debating society. Interview with Mr. Heath, Aug. 22, 1949. Harry W. Laidler, for many years executive secretary of the ISS and the LID, strongly denies Heath's charges. He points out that the ISS as an organization never participated in the party's internal affairs and that its primary purpose was furthering the study of Socialism among college people. Interview with Mr. Laidler, Dec. 20, 1949. Norman Thomas supports Laidler's position. Interview with Mr. Thomas, Dec. 20, 1949.

[18] *Twenty Years of Social Pioneering*, pp. 6–10; Upton Sinclair, *American Outpost: A Book of Reminiscences* (New York, 1932), p. 159; *Intercollegiate Socialist*, III (April–May, 1915), 3–4; the list of names is compiled from lists in *Twenty Years of Social Pioneering*, pp. 12, 65–67, and *Intercollegiate Socialist*, VI (Oct.–Nov., 1917), 7–19.

19 *Twenty Years of Social Pioneering*, p. 9; Joan London, *Jack London and His Times: An Unconventional Biography* (New York, 1939), pp. 298, 300–301, 325–326; Sinclair, *op. cit.*, pp. 220–222, 233; Mrs. David Graham Phillips to Charles Edward Russell, New York, March 16, 1911, Russell papers.

20 Advertisement for *Masses*, back cover of *Intercollegiate Socialist*, I (Feb.–March, 1913); clipping from Ghent's column, "Here and There," in *California Outlook*, Aug., 1916, p. 107, Box 46, Ghent papers.

21 See, for example, Gustavus Myers, "Our Millionaire Socialists," *Cosmopolitan*, Oct., 1906, pp. 596–605, and Kipnis, *op. cit.*, pp. 173–175.

22 *Proceedings* of the National Convention, 1908, pp. 191–205, quotation from p. 193; "The Church and Socialism," *Arena*, XL (Sept., 1908), 243. These clergymen were all Protestants. There was just one notable case of a Roman Catholic clergyman's supporting the Socialist Party. Father Thomas J. Hagerty of Van Buren, Ark., gave speeches for the party, was one of the founders of the IWW, and wrote for Socialist publications. See *Vanguard* (Green Bay, Wis.), I (Nov., 1902), 13, and *ibid.*, II (Nov., 1903), 6.

23 Eugene V. Debs to Julius Gerber, July 22, 1914, general correspondence of the Socialist Party, Local New York, 1914, Vol. Co–N, Meyer London Memorial Library, Rand School of Social Science; clipping from Ghent's column in *California Outlook*, July, 1916, p. 83, Box 46, Ghent papers; for most of the material on White I am indebted to Professor Irvin G. Wyllie of the University of Missouri, who is writing a biography of White.

24 Hillquit, *History of Socialism*, 1910 ed., pp. 356–357; for accounts of social protest in American Protestantism see Henry F. May, *Protestant Churches and Industrial America* (New York, 1949); Charles H. Hopkins, *The Rise of the Social Gospel in American Protestantism, 1865–1915* (New Haven, 1940); James Dombrowski, *The Early Days of Christian Socialism in America* (New York, 1936); and Aaron Abell, *The Urban Impact upon American Protestantism* (Cambridge, Mass., 1943).

25 For sentimentality, see Eliot White, "A Little World-Waif," *The Christian Socialist*, May 15, 1913; for Christian Socialist intramural struggle, see William S. Prosser, Report of the General Secretary to the 8th Annual Conference of the Christian Socialist Fellowship, 1913, SPC, Duke.

CHAPTER III

PARTY BATTLES, 1909–1913

¹ For details see Kipnis, *The American Socialist Movement,* pp. 183–185.

² Anna Strunsky Walling in *Walling Symposium,* p. 8; Simons to Walling, Chicago, Nov. 19, 1909, quoted in "A Labor Party," *International Socialist Review,* X (Jan., 1910), 596.

³ Anna Strunsky Walling, *op. cit.,* p. 15; William English Walling, "Laborism versus Socialism," *International Socialist Review,* IX (March, 1909), 683–689, quotation from p. 689.

⁴ Alexander Schlesinger to A. M. Simons, New York, Dec. 11, 1909; John Spargo to Simons, Yonkers, Nov. 29, 1909; Walling to Socialist Party membership, New York, Nov. 26, 1909 (mimeographed); Simons to Walling, Chicago, Dec. 1, 1909, SPC, Duke.

⁵ Spargo to Simons, Yonkers, Nov. 29, 1909; Robert Hunter to Simons, Noroton Heights, Conn., Dec. 3, 1909; Berger to Simons, Milwaukee, Dec. 6, 1909, SPC, Duke. The conclusion that Berger was not part of a conspiracy when Walling made his charges is based on the belief that Berger had no reason to feign innocence in a confidential letter.

⁶ *International Socialist Review,* X (Jan., 1910), 609; Walling to Mrs. O. H. P. Belmont, New York, March 10, 1910 (copy), William English Walling papers, possession of Mrs. Anna Strunsky Walling, New York City.

⁷ Charles H. Kerr to Louis B. Boudin, Chicago, March 11, 1910, Louis B. Boudin papers, Special Collections Room, Columbia University Library.

⁸ *International Socialist Review,* X (March, 1910), 855; Report of the National Executive Secretary to the National Executive Committee, Chicago, June 6, 1910, Labor Collection, Political Parties, Box 3, Wisconsin State Historical Society.

⁹ A. M. Simons to G. H. Lockwood, Chicago, July 7, 1910, SPC, Duke, a reply to a friend who had sent Simons an anonymous mimeographed letter he had received which contained extracts from Morgan's *Provoker;* interview with Algernon Lee, Dec. 21, 1949; Reports of the National Executive Secretary to the National Executive Committee, Dec. 16, 1910; Jan. 24, 1911; March 28, 1911, Labor Collection, Political Parties, Box 3, Wisconsin State Historical Society; "Minutes of the National Executive Committee, August 11–15, 1911," *Socialist Party Official*

Bulletin, Aug., 1911. It is difficult for this writer to understand the conclusion of Kipnis, *op. cit.*, p. 380, based upon this last document. The testimony at the "trial" was recorded but not published.

[10] In 1910 the International Union of United Brewery Workmen gave the party $1,000 for the congressional campaigns. Reports of the National Executive Secretary to the National Executive Committee, Oct. 3, 10, 1910, Labor Collection, Political Parties, Box 3, Wisconsin State Historical Society.

[11] Samuel Yellen, *American Labor Struggles* (New York, 1936), pp. 171–204.

[12] William D. Haywood, "Socialism the Hope of the Working Class," *International Socialist Review,* XII (Feb., 1912), 469; Eugene V. Debs, "Sound Socialist Tactics," *ibid.*, pp. 481–486, reprinted also in *Writings and Speeches of Eugene V. Debs* (New York, 1948), pp. 350–357.

[13] Membership Records, 1912–1913, SPC, Duke; Samuel Gompers, *Seventy Years of Life and Labor: An Autobiography* (2 vols., New York, 1943 ed.), II, 35; Socialist Party of America, *Proceedings*, National Convention of the Socialist Party, Indianapolis, Indiana, May 12 to 18, 1912 (Chicago, 1912), p. 60.

[14] Interview with Frederic Heath, Aug. 22, 1949; *Proceedings,* 1912 Convention, pp. 123–137, 199; Debs Clipping Book No. 1, Meyer London Memorial Library, Rand School of Social Science.

[15] Clippings of Ghent's editorials in the *National Socialist,* Jan. 18, Feb. 10, May 25, June 1, 1912, Box 46, Ghent papers. In the Jan. 18, 1912, editorial Ghent had the germ of the argument he was to use a decade later in *The Reds Bring Reaction* (Princeton, 1923). The argument in this case was that Haywood strengthened reaction by sowing dissension in the Socialist Party, thereby helping its enemies, and by arousing major-party conservatives to blind reaction.

[16] *Proceedings,* 1912 Convention, pp. 137–141.

[17] Belle Williams to W. J. Ghent, Texarkana, Tex., June 12, 1913, SPC, Milwaukee; Barnes to Hillquit, Chicago, June 27, 1912, Hillquit papers.

[18] Barnes to Debs, Chicago, June 27, 1912, copy; Debs to Barnes, Terre Haute, July 2, 1912, both enclosed in Barnes to Berger, Chicago, July 3, 1912, SPC, Milwaukee. Berger saw that Debs was trying to "help along the alliance of the Christian Socialists with the Syndicalists." Berger to Barnes, Milwaukee, July 8, 1912, copy, SPC, Milwaukee.

[19] Theodore Debs to W. J. Ghent, Terre Haute, Dec. 18, 1928, Box 26, Ghent papers; Barnes to Hillquit, Chicago, Oct. 13, 1908, telegram,

Hillquit papers. Theodore was Gene's brother and secretary and accompanied him on the Red Special. Theodore, incidentally, looked so much like his brother that when Gene needed sleep on the campaign trains and the scheduled stops did not call for speeches Theodore sometimes impersonated his brother, and the crowds never detected the substitution. Interview with Theodore Debs, Nov. 22, 1941.

[20] H. D. Stettwagen to Victor Berger, Ocean City, N.J., July 3, 1912; Dr. I. A. Wesson to Berger, Wingo, Ky., July 5, 1912; H. B. Kelley to Berger, Mifflintown, Pa., July 1, 1912, SPC, Milwaukee; Ginger, *The Bending Cross*, p. 310.

[21] Clipping from Ghent's editorial in the *National Socialist*, Aug. 31, 1912, Box 46, Ghent papers. Ghent conceded that Debs's opposition to Barnes was genuine and that he probably did not know of the case made against him. If there were such a case worked up against Debs, it probably had to do with his drinking. Debs, while certainly no drunkard, had occasional drinking sprees with his old friends. His enemies made much of his drinking, charging that he was an alcoholic not responsible for his actions. His brother wrote of his drinking: "Gene was in no sense a teetotaler—he took a drink whenever he cared and for this he made neither excuse or apology. It is not apparent to me what this has to do with his public activities any more than if on occasion he drank coffee." Theodore Debs to Ghent, Terre Haute, Dec. 18, 1928, Box 26, Ghent papers.

[22] Berger had written at the bottom of an anti-Barnes letter, "I suppose the best thing poor Barnes can do is to resign his position as campaign manager." H. D. Stettwagen to Berger, Ocean City, N.J., July 12, 1912, SPC, Milwaukee.

[23] Work to Barnes, Chicago, Dec. 30, 1912; Barnes to Carl D. Thompson, Oct. 12, 1913; Thompson to Barnes, Oct. 17, 1913; Report of the Special Committee on Investigation of National Office, 1913, SPC, Duke; Morris Hillquit, *Socialism Summed Up* (New York, 1913), especially pp. 44–75.

[24] Press release, March 1, 1913, SPC, Duke.

[25] William D. Haywood, *Bill Haywood's Book: The Autobiography of William D. Haywood* (New York, 1929), pp. 259–260.

[26] Kipnis, *op. cit.*, p. 418; Bell, "The Background and Development of Marxian Socialism in the United States," in *Socialism and American Life*, I, 289; Membership Records, 1912–1913, SPC, Duke.

[27] A. M. Simons, "The Future of the Socialist Party," *New Republic*, IX (Dec. 2, 1916), 118; Ginger, *op. cit.*, pp. 322–325; Eugene V. Debs, "A Plea for Solidarity," *International Socialist Review*, XIV (March, 1914), 534–538, quotation from p. 538.

CHAPTER IV

Socialists Face the War in Europe, 1914–1917

[1] William English Walling, ed., *The Socialists and the War* (New York, 1915), pp. 212–213.

[2] M. E. M. [Mary E. Marcy], "Socialist Unpreparedness in Germany," *International Socialist Review*, XV (Oct., 1914), 245.

[3] Walling, *op. cit.*, p. 6; Harry W. Laidler, "The Conference Speakers," *Intercollegiate Socialist*, V (Oct.–Nov., 1916), 14, 16; A. M. Simons, "Pacifism vs. Revolution," *New Republic*, X (March 24, 1917), 221.

[4] A. M. Simons, "The Future of the Socialist Party," *New Republic*, IX (Dec. 2, 1916), 118–120; Georges Clemenceau, "Degradation in the Hope of Conquest," *International Socialist Review*, XV (Oct., 1914), 205–209.

[5] *Appeal to Reason*, Aug. 28, 1915; *American Socialist*, Jan. 9, 1915; clipping of a Simons letter that appeared in *London Justice*, July 25, 1918, SPC, Duke; interview with Frederic Heath, Aug. 22, 1949.

[6] Hillquit to Lanferseik, New York, Sept. 21, Nov. 21, 1914, Hillquit papers.

[7] Camille Huysmans to National Executive Committee, Jan. 7, Jan. 28, 1915, SPC, Duke; Report of the National Executive Secretary to the National Executive Committee, Feb. 15, 1915, SPC, Duke.

[8] Iversen, Morris Hillquit, American Social Democrat, pp. 170–173; *American Socialist*, Feb. 19, 1916.

[9] Merle Curti, *Peace or War, The American Struggle, 1636–1936* (New York, 1936), pp. 228–261.

[10] Phillips Russell, "Europe in the Clutch of War," *International Socialist Review*, XV (Sept., 1914), 133; Vincent St. John, "The Working Class and War," *ibid.*, XV (Aug., 1914), 117; W. J. Ghent, "Socialists Should Have Prevented the War," *Intercollegiate Socialist*, IV (Feb.–March, 1916), 8.

[11] Ameringer, *If You Don't Weaken*, p. 305; Curti, *op. cit.*, pp. 232–233; *Socialist Hand Book. Campaign 1916* (Chicago, 1916).

[12] *Appeal to Reason*, Dec. 11, 1915; *American Socialist*, Dec. 9, Jan. 29, 1916; Harry W. Laidler, "The Intercollegiate Socialist Society Convention," *Intercollegiate Socialist*, IV (Feb.–March, 1916), 14. Russell had privately expressed his advocacy of armament almost a year earlier. Russell to Carl D. Thompson, Washington, Jan. 15, 1915, SPC, Duke.

[13] M. E. M., "Socialist Unpreparedness in Germany," p. 245; William

D. Haywood, "Jaurès and the General Strike Against War," *International Socialist Review*, XV (Sept., 1914), 146.

¹⁴ Curti, *op. cit.*, p. 250; Benson to Carl D. Thompson, Yonkers, Jan. 9, 1913; Hillquit to Thompson, New York, Jan. 20, 1915, SPC, Duke; *Socialist Hand Book. Campaign 1916*, p. 7.

¹⁵ *New York Times*, Jan. 4, 1914, March 12, 1916; Ginger, *The Bending Cross*, p. 334; J. Mahlon Barnes to Morris Hillquit, Philadelphia, Aug. 16, 1915, Hillquit papers.

¹⁶ Easley to Joseph Tumulty, Washington, Jan. 24, 1916, Wilson papers, File VI, Box 164, Folder 121; Benson to H. M. Hyndman, reproduced in Rosalind Travers Hyndman, *The Last Years of H. M. Hyndman* (London, 1923), p. 307; Edgar Eugene Robinson, *The Presidential Vote*, 1896–1932 (Stanford, 1947), pp. 379–399; *New York Times*, Nov. 9, 1916.

¹⁷ Membership Records, SPC, Duke; C. Hanford Henderson, "Socialism and the Wilson Regime," *Intercollegiate Socialist*, II (Feb.–March, 1914), 15–16.

¹⁸ John Reed to National Executive Committee, Oct. 13, 1916, SPC, Duke; Gustavus Myers, "Why Idealists Quit the Socialist Party," *Nation*, CIV (Feb. 15, 1917), 118–120; Simons, "The Future of the Socialist Party," pp. 118–120.

¹⁹ Felix Grendon, "In Defense of Socialism," *New Republic*, X (April 7, 1917), 297–298.

²⁰ The call to the convention appeared in *American Socialist*, March 17, 1917.

²¹ Fiorello H. La Guardia, *The Making of an Insurgent: An Autobiography, 1882–1919* (Philadelphia, 1948), p. 138; Delegates to National Emergency Convention Held April 7th to 14th, 1917, at St. Louis, Mo., SPC, Duke. This list is valuable as it includes the country of birth and occupation of each delegate. The lists published in the party press did not present this information.

²² *New York Call*, April 9, 1917; *Milwaukee Leader*, April 10, 1917.

²³ Interview with Louis B. Boudin, a member of the War and Militarism Committee, Dec. 20, 1949.

²⁴ *Appeal to Reason*, April 21, 1917; the most convenient complete report of the committee majority is in Fine, *Labor and Farmer Parties in the United States*, pp. 310–314.

²⁵ *Appeal to Reason*, April 21, 1917; *American Socialist*, April 7, 1917.

²⁶ *New York Call*, April 13, 16, 1917.

²⁷ The exact vote on the two proposals, the majority report and the

Spargo report, is impossible to determine. On the referendum ballot each report was divided into eight sections. The voter could choose to vote Yes or No on the sections of either report. Nearly 23,000 members chose to vote on the sections of the majority report, and every section but one received over 21,000 votes. Less than 8,000 chose to vote on sections of the Spargo report. The majority report of the War and Militarism Committee, therefore, was accepted by the party membership as originally written. Oneal and Werner, p. 35n.

[28] Interview with Frederic Heath, Aug. 22, 1949; *American Socialist*, May 26, 1917.

CHAPTER V

MAKING THE WORLD SAFE FOR DEMOCRACY, 1917–1918

[1] *New York Times*, June 2, 1917.

[2] A. M. Simons, "The Pro-Prussian Socialist Machine," undated MS in Wisconsin Loyalty Legion papers, Wisconsin State Historical Society; Winfield Gaylord to Senator Paul O. Husting, Milwaukee, April 28, 1917; copy enclosed in Husting to Joseph Tumulty, Washington, April 30, 1917, Wilson papers, File VI, Box 258, Folder 298.

[3] Gustavus Myers to W. J. Ghent, March 2, 1921, Box 11, Ghent papers; William English Walling to Theodore Roosevelt, Indianapolis, July 12, 1917, copy, Walling papers; *Our Town* (Greenwich, Conn.), May 5, 1917, Walling papers; Stokes to Champ Clark and Thomas Marshall, New York, Sept. 28, 1917, Wilson papers, File VI, Box 575, Folder 4244.

[4] John Spargo, *The Pro-German Cry of "No Indemnities"* (New York, n.d.), p. 7; Eugene V. Debs, "Mr. Russell and the Socialists," *Social Revolution*, Oct., 1917; Russell, *Bare Hands and Stone Walls*, p. 287; Joseph Tumulty to Wilson, Washington, March 24, 1919, cable, Wilson papers, File VI, Box 611, Folder 4963; Benson to Russell, May 14, 1917, Russell papers; *New York Times*, June 3, 1917; *Revolutionary Radicalism* (4 vols., Albany, 1920), I, 546. This last was the so-called Lusk Committee Report.

[5] Interview with Algernon Lee, Dec. 21, 1949; W. J. Ghent, "Disloyalty, Past and Present," *California Outlook*, July, 1917, pp. 74–75.

[6] Open letter, Upton Sinclair to Woodrow Wilson, Pasadena, Oct. 22, 1917, SPC, Duke. Soon after the war Sinclair regretted his support. See his novel *Jimmie Higgins* (New York, 1919).

[7] Kopelin to Wilson, Chicago, Dec. 4, 1917, telegram copy, Wilson papers, File VI, Box 164, Folder 121; *Appeal to Reason*, Dec. 15, 1917.

[8] *New York Times*, June 3, 1917; Matthew Hale, Chairman of the Progressive Party; Virgil G. Hinshaw, Chairman of the Prohibition Party; and John Spargo of the Social Democratic League, *Confidential Report of Informal Preliminary Conference for the Union of the Forces of Industrial Democracy in a United Political Party* (New York, 1917), p. 3, in J. G. Phelps Stokes papers, possession of Mr. Stokes, New York City; John Spargo to "Dear Friend," Old Bennington, Vt., Sept. 14, 1917, a form letter sent with a draft of a party platform, Stokes papers; National Party press release, Oct. 4, 1917, Stokes papers.

[9] Iversen, Morris Hillquit, American Social Democrat, p. 213.

[10] *New York Times*, Oct. 30, Nov. 2, 1917; Woodrow Wilson to Darrow, Washington, Aug. 10, 1917, in Ray Stannard Baker, *Woodrow Wilson: Life and Letters* (New York, 1939), VII, 210; Iversen, *op. cit.*, pp. 186–187, 202–203.

[11] Henry Best, "The Melting Pot in the United States," *Social Forces*, XIV (May, 1936), 591–596.

[12] Eugene V. Debs, "The November Elections," *Social Revolution*, Dec., 1917, p. 5; Paul H. Douglas, "The Socialist Vote in the Municipal Elections of 1917," *National Municipal Review*, VII (Dec., 1918), 131–139.

[13] John Riley Thacker to Woodrow Wilson, Altus, Okla., April 6, 1913, Wilson papers, File VI, Box 258, Folder 298; Bush, The Green Corn Rebellion, pp. 1–42; Ameringer, *If You Don't Weaken*, pp. 347–355.

[14] *American Civil Liberties Union Press Service Bulletin*, No. 47, Jan. 23, 1922; Ameringer, *op. cit.*, p. 356.

[15] Proceedings, National Joint Conference at Chicago, Aug., 1918, unpublished stenographic report, SPC, Duke.

[16] James R. Mock, *Censorship 1917* (Princeton, 1941), pp. 24, 49–50, 53; Zechariah Chaffee, Jr., "The Milwaukee Leader Case," *Nation*, CXII (March 23, 1921), 428–429.

[17] Mock, *op. cit.*, 149–150; Fine, *Labor and Farmer Parties in the United States*, pp. 317–318; Ameringer, *op. cit.*, pp. 318–320; interview with Freda Hogan Ameringer, April 21, 1950.

[18] Herbert Croly to Woodrow Wilson, New York, Oct. 19, 1917, and Wilson to Croly, Washington, Oct. 22, 1917, Box 575, Folder 4244; Burleson to Wilson and attached note, Sept. 4, 1917, Box 554, Folder 3896; Upton Sinclair to Wilson, Oct. 22, 1917, and Wilson's attached note to Tumulty, Baker, *op. cit.*, VII, 318–319; John Spargo to Wilson, New York, Nov. 1, 1917, and Wilson's attached note to Tumulty, Box 575, Folder 4244; Arthur Brisbane to Wilson, Washington, April 20, 1917, Box 554, Folder 3896; Resolution of Cloverleaf Grange No. 520,

Cloverleaf School House, Okanogan, Washington, Oct. 20, 1917, Box 575, Folder 4244. All in File VI, Wilson papers, unless otherwise indicated.

[19] Walter Nelles, ed., *Espionage Act Cases* (New York, 1918), pp. 45–47.

[20] Kansas City *Star*, March 18, 20, 1918; Nelles, *op. cit.*, pp. 66–74; George Creel to Wilson, Washington, June 8, 1918; Wilson to Thomas W. Gregory, Washington, June 24, 1918; Gregory to Wilson, Washington, June 24, 1918, Wilson papers, File VI, Box 598, Folder 4692.

[21] Fine, *op. cit.*, p. 319. Landis had said he regretted he could sentence Berger to only twenty years in prison "because I believe the laws . . . should have enabled me to have Berger lined up against a wall and shot."

[22] The Canton speech is in David Karsner, *Debs, His Authorized Life and Letters from Woodstock Prison to Atlanta* (New York, 1919), pp. 229–237, and in *Writings and Speeches of Debs*, pp. 417–433.

[23] A. B. Bielaski, Chief, Bureau of Investigation, to Rudolph Forster, Executive Clerk at the White House, Washington, Aug. 13, 1917, Wilson papers, File VI, Box 573, Folder 4202, explains the loose connection of the League to the Department of Justice; *Cleveland Plain Dealer*, June 17, 1918.

[24] E. S. Wertz to Thomas W. Gregory, Cleveland, June 17, 1918; John Lord O'Brian, Special Assistant to the Attorney General for War Work, to Wertz, Washington, June 20, 1918, Record Group 60, Department of Justice Central File, National Archives.

[25] The entire speech to the jury is in Karsner, *op. cit.*, pp. 23–44; *Writings* . . . 48–54.

[26] Joseph Tumulty to Wilson, Washington, March 24, 1919, cable, Wilson papers, File VI, Box 611, Folder 4963. The letter from the three pleaders for respite was incorporated into the text of Tumulty's cable. Tumulty reminded Wilson that Russell "has been your friend and has done much to stem the tide of bolshevism in this country." Wilson to Tumulty, Paris, April 3, 1919, copy of cable, enclosed in Tumulty to Palmer, Washington, April 3, 1919; Palmer to Wilson, Washington, April 3, 1919, copy, Record Group 60, Department of Justice Central File, National Archives.

[27] A. B. Bielaski to John Lord O'Brian, Washington, Sept. 25, 1918, Record Group 60, Department of Justice Central File, National Archives.

[28] Wilson to Gregory, Jan. 18, 1918, Baker, VII, 457.

[29] Maurer, *It Can Be Done*, pp. 223, 227–228; interview with J. G.

Phelps Stokes, Dec. 14, 1951; Morris Hillquit, *Loose Leaves from a Busy Life* (New York, 1934), pp. 170–179; the author interviewed one person, who prefers to remain anonymous, who asserted that he received money from Wilson's "secret fund" in 1917 and 1918 "to promote unity behind the war effort."

[30] Maurer, *op. cit.*, pp. 228–230.

[31] Louis Waldman, *Labor Lawyer* (New York, 1944), pp. 70–71; Eugene V. Debs, "The War and What Might Have Been," *Social Revolution*, Feb., 1918, p. 15.

[32] Fine, *op. cit.*, p. 320; Harry Rogoff, *An East Side Epic: The Life and Work of Meyer London* (New York, 1930), p. 96; Thomas to Wald, New York, March 1, 1918, copy, Norman Thomas papers, New York Public Library.

[33] Germer to Morris Hillquit, Chicago, March 4, 1918, Hillquit papers; copy of resolution adopted by Bohemian Socialist Federation of Chicago, Feb. 25, 1918, enclosed in Adolph J. Sabath to Woodrow Wilson, Washington, March 6, 1918, Wilson papers, File VI, Box 258, Folder 298; Fine, *op. cit.*, p. 321; Thompson to Socialist Party membership, open letter, no place, no date, Wisconsin Loyalty Legion papers; Ginger, *The Bending Cross*, p. 355.

[34] Proceedings, National Joint Conference at Chicago, Aug., 1918, unpublished stenographic report, SPC, Duke.

[35] Membership Records, 1916–1917, 1917–1918, SPC, Duke.

[36] Quoted in Ghent, *The Reds Bring Reaction*, p. 5; Pomerene to Joseph Tumulty, Canton, Ohio, April 6, 1919, Record Group 60, Department of Justice Central File, National Archives; Arch C. Klumph to Warren G. Harding, Cleveland, March 26, 1921, Record Group 204, Records of the Pardon Attorney, National Archives.

[37] See Eldridge Foster Dowell, *A History of Criminal Syndicalism Legislation in the United States* [*The Johns Hopkins University Studies in Historical and Political Science*] (Baltimore, 1939); Maurer, *op. cit.*, p. 203.

[38] *New York Times*, Nov. 24, 26, 1919.

[39] Fine, *op. cit.*, pp. 320–321; *Nation*, CX (Jan. 17, 1920), 66; *ibid.* (March 6, 1920), 110; Lewis S. Gannett, "Socialists' Trial at Albany," *ibid.* (March 20, 1920), 361–363; *ibid.* (April 10, 1920), 450; Carl Becker, "A Little More Grape, Captain Bragg," *ibid.* (Feb. 28, 1920), 260–261; *ibid.*, CXIII (Nov. 9, 1921), 521–522.

CHAPTER VI

SOCIALIST VERSUS COMMUNIST, 1919

[1] Granville Hicks, with the assistance of John Stuart, *John Reed, The Making of a Revolutionary* (New York, 1937), pp. 324, 344.

[2] John Reed, for example, wrote that "Fully a third" of Socialist voters were "middle-class persons who think that Karl Marx wrote a good anti-trust law." *Ibid.*, p. 327.

[3] Fine, *Labor and Farmer Parties in the United States*, p. 329.

[4] *Report of the National Executive Committee to the Members of the Convention*, p. 5, mimeographed document, dated 1919, Meyer London Memorial Library, Rand School; Adolph Germer to Bishop William Montgomery Brown, Chicago, Aug. 14, 1919, SPC, Duke; Hicks, *op. cit.*, p. 345; Benjamin Gitlow, *The Whole of Their Lives* (New York, 1948), pp. 37–39; Jesse D. Clarkson, " 'Big Jim' Larkin: A Footnote to Nationalism," in Edward Mead Earle, ed., *Nationalism and Internationalism: Essays Inscribed to Carlton J. H. Hayes* (New York, 1950), pp. 45–63; Kate Richards O'Hare, "The Story of an Irish Agitator," *National Rip-Saw*, April, 1914, pp. 6–9.

[5] Proceedings, National Joint Conference at Chicago, Aug., 1919, unpublished stenographic report, SPC, Duke.

[6] Louis Fraina, *Revolutionary Socialism: A Study in Socialist Reconstruction* (New York, 1918); Oneal and Werner, *American Communism*, pp. 91n–93n; interviews with Agnes Inglis, Aug. 25, 1949; Theodore Muller, Aug. 22, 1949; and August Claessens, Dec. 19, 1949. Later, after he had changed his name to Lewis Corey, Fraina was a professor of economics in Midwestern colleges and a respected economic historian. His political views later were considerably more conservative than they were when he edited *Revolutionary Age*.

[7] Hicks, *op. cit.*, p. 420; Harry W. Laidler, "Present Status of Socialism in America," *Socialist Review*, VIII (Dec., 1919), p. 35; *Manifesto and Program of the Left Wing Section Socialist Party* (New York, 1919); program quoted in full in Oneal and Werner, *op. cit.*, pp. 375–377. This document appeared between the calling of a meeting to form a new Communist international and the actual formation of the Third International, March 2–6, 1919. Lewis L. Lorwin, *Labor and Internationalism* (New York, 1929), p. 170.

[8] Walter M. Cook, State Secretary of New York, open letter to New York Socialist Party membership, New York, Aug. 1, 1919, Meyer London Memorial Library, Rand School; Hicks, *op. cit.*, pp. 349–350.

⁹ Resolution adopted by the State Committee of the Socialist Party, New York State, at annual meeting held at Albany, April 13, 1919, SPC, Duke; Adolph Germer to Morris Hillquit, Chicago, March 22, 1919, Hillquit papers.

¹⁰ Adolph Germer to Bishop William Montgomery Brown, Chicago, Aug. 14, 1919, SPC, Duke; Laidler, "Present Status of Socialism," p. 35.

¹¹ *Report . . . to the Convention*, p. 4.

¹² For the Berne Conference, Lorwin, *op. cit.*, pp. 166–168, 202, 209–211; *Report . . . to the Convention*, p. 3; Alexander Trachtenberg, ed., *The American Labor Year Book, 1919–1920* (New York, 1920), p. 405.

¹³ Oneal and Werner *op. cit.*, pp. 53–54; Fine, *op. cit.*, pp. 339–340. The problem of help for indicted Socialists and prisoners had long been a source of dissension among the various Socialist factions. Early in 1918 the NEC had refused to cooperate with the Kate O'Hare Defense Committee on the grounds that it must deal with all war cases alike and show no special attention to any. When Frank O'Hare went to New York to enlist support and funds for his wife's defense, he got a cold reception that Hillquit had prepared. Germer to Hillquit, Chicago, Feb. 8, 1918, Hillquit to Germer, New York, Feb. 12, 1918, Hillquit papers. Similarly, Berger complained that the *New York Call* had "deliberately sabotaged" him during his trial and that the Socialist press in general had given more publicity to the O'Hare and Debs cases despite his longer sentence. Berger to Hillquit, Milwaukee, Aug. 20, 1919, Hillquit papers.

¹⁴ "Call for a National Conference of the Left Wing," broadside in SPC, Duke.

¹⁵ Laidler, "Present Status of Socialism," p. 36; Louis A. Arnold, Wisconsin State Secretary, to Germer, Milwaukee, July 3, 1919, SPC, Duke.

¹⁶ Adolph Germer to the Socialists of Michigan, Chicago, June 11, 1919, SPC, Duke; Hicks, *op. cit.*, p. 351; Germer to Glenn H. Pangborn, Chicago, June 12, 1919, SPC, Duke.

¹⁷ Laidler, "Present Status of Socialism," p. 113. The ballots in this election have long since been destroyed, and it is impossible accurately to determine how much irregularity there was or which candidates would have won had the election been completely honest. However, on the basis of the number of Socialists who left the party either to join one of the communist parties or to abandon socialist politics altogether, it appears that the Left Wing candidates won.

¹⁸ L. E. Katterfeld and Alfred Wagenknecht to Massachusetts State Convention of the Socialist Party, telegram copy, Chicago, May 31, 1919, SPC, Duke; Oneal and Werner, *op. cit.*, p. 55; telegrams to Germer from

Dan Hogan, Fred Krafft, Morris Hillquit, F. W. Holt, James Oneal, A. Shiplacoff, Victor Berger, and George Goebel, SPC, Duke.

[19] Alfred Wagenknecht to the Socialist Press and State secretaries, Cleveland, June 10, 1919, SPC, Duke; many of the mimeographed seconds are in the official correspondence for June, 1919, SPC, Duke; Report of the Executive Secretary to the National Executive Committee on Motion No. 55, Chicago, July 11, 1919, SPC, Duke. The vote was seven to three.

[20] Lloyd was generous with his money for radical causes. He donated $1,000 to the Socialists for their 1918 congressional campaigns, and later lost a large sum of money when Bill Haywood jumped bail. Lloyd to Oliver C. Wilson, Chicago, March 1, 1918, SPC, Duke; interview with Theodore Muller, Aug. 22, 1949.

[21] Hicks, *op. cit.*, pp. 355–356; Oneal and Werner, *op. cit.*, p. 56; Laidler, "Present Status of Socialism," p. 37; letterhead of the Left Wing Section of the Socialist Party, SPC, Duke.

[22] Germer to Hillquit, Chicago, July 14, 1919, Hillquit papers; Oneal and Werner, *op. cit.*, p. 59; Hicks, *op. cit.*, p. 357; Laidler, "Present Status of Socialism," p. 37.

[23] Report of the Executive Secretary to the National Executive Committee on Motion No. 56, Chicago, Aug. 20, 1919, SPC, Duke. The motion had been submitted August 1, and the voting ended August 13. Berger, Hogan, Hillquit, Krafft, Oneal, Shiplacoff, Stedman, and Work voted for the expulsion. Holt of Oklahoma City voted against it, although he was not a Left Winger, on the grounds that expulsion proceedings had gone quite far enough. Wagenknecht of the Left Wing refused to vote, arguing that only the "new," or Cleveland, committee was valid. Clark, Goebel, Herman, Katterfeld, and Mills submitted no votes.

[24] Minutes of the Left Wing Caucus, Aug. 29, 1919, mimeographed document, Meyer London Memorial Library, Rand School.

[25] Adolph Germer to the present writer, Portland, Ore., July 14, 1950.

[26] Accounts of the encounter between Reed and Gerber vary considerably. The writer has reconstructed the story as presented here from the accounts of Adolph Germer in his letter to the writer, July 14, 1950, Hicks, *op. cit.*, p. 359, and Laidler, "Present Status of Socialism," p. 106. Gerber, according to Old Guard accounts, is supposed to have said that the battle proved that swinging a sledgehammer with the proletariat—Gerber was a tinsmith, who normally had little occasion to swing sledgehammers—was as good physical training as playing college

football. Reed, of course, had been a cheerleader rather than a football player, which fact would have delighted Gerber. A Left Wing version was that Gerber might have hurt Reed if Reed had not held him so far up in the air Gerber couldn't reach him.

[27] Germer to the writer, July 14, 1950; Laidler, "Present Status of Socialism," p. 106. The Left Wing later made much of the point that the Old Guard had used the capitalist police in its behalf.

[28] Laidler, "Present Status of Socialism," pp. 106–107; Oneal and Werner, *op. cit.*, p. 60.

[29] Hicks, *op. cit.*, p. 361; Laidler, "Present Status of Socialism," p. 107.

[30] Hicks, *op. cit.*, pp. 361–362; Fine, *op. cit.*, p. 352. Hicks's description of the raid agrees with other accounts, but he has the wrong convention being raided.

[31] Laidler, "Present Status of Socialism," pp. 108–111; Oneal and Werner, *op. cit.*, pp. 80–82.

[32] Laidler, "Present Status of Socialism," p. 108. Marguerite Prevy was another who bolted with Boudin. Boudin's whole connection with the party at that time was curious and his presence at the convention illogical. He had not been active in the party since 1917 because he disagreed with the party's antiwar position. Yet he retained his membership because he thought the persecuted party needed his aid. When his local, Kings County (Brooklyn), went Left Wing early in 1919, a delegation of Left Wingers led by Ernest Lindgren called upon him to urge him to join them. Boudin was in basic sympathy with their position, but refused to sign a card endorsing the Left Wing Manifesto because he thought it contained "syndicalist undertones." He was thus a nominal member of the Brooklyn local, which the state organization had expelled, but not a member of the Left Wing, when, to his surprise, the local elected him to be a delegate to the Emergency Convention. The Brooklyn delegation was not seated at the Emergency Convention, and Boudin went downstairs. Interview with Boudin, Dec. 20, 1949.

[33] Hicks, *op. cit.*, p. 363; Oneal and Werner, *op. cit.*, pp. 70, 80–98.

CHAPTER VII

From Left to Right, 1919–1925

[1] Berger to Hillquit, Milwaukee, Aug. 20, 1919, Hillquit papers. Berger's analysis of the party's trouble was typical of Milwaukee Socialism. "We have always played too much with the revolutionary phrase. In this game of would-be radical phrases the one who can play the game the hardest will naturally win. And the emptier the barrel the louder

the sound. . . . that continuous threat of 'revolution' reminds me of a man who is continually brandishing a revolver which is not loaded."

[2] Iversen, Morris Hillquit: American Social Democrat, p. 281; *New York Call*, May 21, 1919; Hillquit did not keep copies of all his outgoing letters in 1919, but it is clear from the letters of Adolph Germer to Hillquit, Chicago, April 9, 17, 1919, Hillquit papers, that Hillquit in his letters to Germer had expressed criticism of the Socialist leadership and urged a more aggressive policy.

[3] Oneal and Werner, *American Communism*, p. 60; *Report . . . to the Convention*, p. 9. The signers of the *Report* were Oneal, Shiplacoff, Hogan, Berger, Stedman, Work, Krafft, and Goebel.

[4] Oneal and Werner, *op. cit.*, pp. 60–61; *American Labor Year Book, 1919–1920*, pp. 408–409; Laidler, "Present Status of Socialism," p. 113. Germer argued that the action of the federal government in holding up the mail of the national office had prevented communication with the membership of the offending organizations. Germer claimed that Washington was trying to divide the American Left by aiding the Left Wing Section to split the party, charging that both publications and first-class mail of the national office was frequently held up while the publications of the Left Wing Section were allowed freely to circulate. Germer to Hillquit, Chicago, April 17, 1919, Hillquit papers; Germer to the present writer, Portland, Ore., July 14, 1950.

[5] *American Labor Year Book, 1919–1920*, pp. 410–411, 414; Oneal and Werner, *op. cit.*, p. 63.

[6] Alexander Trachtenberg and Benjamin Glassberg, eds., *The American Labor Year Book, 1921–1922* (New York, 1922), pp. 393, 400–402, 405–406.

[7] The Twenty-one Points are reproduced in Fine, *Labor and Farmer Parties in the United States*, pp. 332–337; Lorwin, *Labor and Internationalism*, p. 217n.

[8] Labor Research Department of the Rand School of Social Science, ed., *The American Labor Year Book, 1923–1924* (New York, 1924), p. 133.

[9] *Ohio Socialist*, July 30, 1919.

[10] National Executive Committee of the Socialist Party, *The Socialist Party Campaign Book* (Chicago, 1920); *New York Times*, May 14, 1920.

[11] *Campaign Book; New York Times*, May 15, 16, 1920; *Congressional Record*, 66th Congress, 2d session, Vol. 59, pp. 4112, 5815, 6118–6119, 7327.

[12] *New York Times*, June 25, July 22, June 12, 1920; *New Day*, Sept. 25, 1920.

[13] Clipping from Washington *Herald*, Oct. 31, 1920, in Debs Clipping Book No. 2, Meyer London Memorial Library, Rand School.

[14] Summary of Revenue and Expenses, 1920 Campaign, SPC, Duke; *New Day*, Nov. 27, 1920.

[15] *Nation*, CXI (Nov. 17, 1920), 545.

[16] *New Day*, April 13, 1921; the reels of petitions are stored in the Records of the Pardon Attorney, National Archives.

[17] "Minutes of Conference between the Attorney General and Representatives of the American Federation of Labor, September 14, 1920," Wilson papers, File VI, Box 556, Folder 3899; Lucy Robins to Joseph Tumulty, New York, Dec. 11, 1920, and attached copies of telegrams from the labor officials, Wilson papers, File VI, Box 556, Folder 3896; *American Federationist*, XXVII (July, 1920), 640–641; Gompers to Wilson, Washington, Dec. 15, 1920, Wilson papers, File VI, Box 611, Folder 4963; Gompers, *Seventy Years*, II, 416; *New York Times*, Sept. 17, 1921.

[18] Darrow to Wilson, Washington, July 29, 1919, and Hapgood to Wilson, Washington, Nov. 8 and 9, 1920, Wilson papers, File VI, Box 611, Folder 4963; Gavit to Wilson, New York, Feb. 24, 1919, Wilson papers, File VI, Box 556, Folder 3896; Blatch to Wilson, New York, Feb. 28, 1921, Wilson papers, File VI, Box 611, Folder 4963.

[19] John Barton Payne to Joseph Tumulty, Washington, March 22, 1920, Wilson papers, File VI, Box 556, Folder 3896; Josephus Daniels Diary, p. 223, entry for Aug. 10, 1920, Josephus Daniels papers, Division of Manuscripts, Library of Congress.

[20] Westenhaver to Palmer, Cleveland, Oct. 6, 1920, Records of the Pardon Attorney, National Archives; the commutation of sentence document signed by Palmer with Wilson's note of rejection is in Record Group 60, Department of Justice Central File, National Archives; Joseph Tumulty, *Woodrow Wilson as I Know Him* (Garden City, 1921), p. 505.

[21] *New York Times*, Feb. 2, 23, 24, 1921; *New York Call*, Feb. 26, 1921.

[22] *New York Times*, March 18, 25, 1921; Samuel Hopkins Adams, *Incredible Era: The Life and Times of Warren Gamaliel Harding* (Boston, 1939), pp. 254–255; Harry M. Daugherty, with the collaboration of Thomas Dixon, *The Inside Story of the Harding Tragedy* (New York, 1932), pp. 115–121.

[23] Emil Herman, Political Situation in the Northwest, unpublished MS dated 1923, SPC, Duke; letter to the editor from S. A. Swanson, Rosebud Ranch, Wineville, Calif., *Nation*, CXVI (Jan. 17, 1923), 72.

24 *American Labor Year Book, 1921–1922*, pp. 391–392; Fine, *op. cit.*, p. 326; Average Membership and Apportionment of Delegates, 1923, SPC, Duke; Membership and Financial Reports, 1924–1928, SPC, Duke. The 1922 membership document is marked, understandably, "Not for Publication."

25 Interview with August Claessens, Dec. 19, 1949; "Debs Meetings," undated mimeographed report, filed in 1923 material, SPC, Duke; anonymous to Branstetter, no place, no date, filed in 1923 materials, SPC, Duke.

26 Arthur G. McDowell, "The Socialist Youth Movement," *American Socialist Quarterly*, III (Summer, 1934), 44.

27 Undated draft of an article, Ghent papers, Box 45; Joel Seidman, *The Needle Trades* (New York, 1942), pp. 155–168; The Reminiscences of Norman Thomas, Part I, p. 27, Columbia University Oral History Project, Columbia University Library.

28 See, for example, Bell, "The Background and Development of Marxian Socialism in the United States," in *Socialism and American Life*, pp. 337n, 365.

29 James Oneal (affirmative) and Robert Minor (negative), *Resolved: That the Terms of the Third International Are Inacceptable to the Revolutionary Socialists of the World* (New York, 1921), pp. 13, 20, 5–7, 17–18.

30 Bertha Hale White, "The Socialist Party in the Coming Campaign," *Socialist World*, Feb., 1924, p. 4; Thomas Reminiscences, Part II, pp. 157–158; Kenneth Campbell MacKay, *The Progressive Movement of 1924* [*Columbia University Studies in History, Economics, and Public Law*, No. 527] (New York, 1947), pp. 55, 61.

31 White, "Socialist Party in the Coming Campaign," pp. 4–5; MacKay, *op. cit.*, pp. 60–65, 68–72, 80–81, 266–269; Fine, *op. cit.*, pp. 404–405.

32 Fine, *op. cit.*, pp. 406–408; MacKay, *op. cit.*, pp. 72–73; David A. Shannon, "Eugene V. Debs: Conservative Labor Editor," *Indiana Magazine of History*, XLVII (Dec., 1951), 357–364.

33 MacKay, *op. cit.*, pp. 76–78; *Socialist World*, Feb., 1924, pp. 12–15, June, 1924, pp. 10–11.

34 MacKay, *op. cit.*, pp. 110–115, 118–121; Fine, *op. cit.*, p. 411; Jacob Panken, "What We Expected," *Socialist World*, Jan., 1925, pp. 9–11.

35 The entire platform is in *La Follette-Wheeler Campaign Text-Book* (Chicago, 1924); *Socialist World*, July, 1924, pp. 1–2; MacKay, *op. cit.*, pp. 134–135.

36 MacKay, *op. cit.*, pp. 188, 190–191, 199; William English Walling, "Labor's Attitude Toward a Third Party," *Current History*, Oct., 1924,

pp. 32–40; Thomas Reminiscences, Part I, pp. 32–33; Part II, pp. 159–160; "Résumé of Speech Delivered by Andrew J. Biemiller at the New Party Conference in Chicago, July 5th, 1935," attached to National Executive Committee minutes, July 13–15, 1935, Thomas papers.

[37] MacKay, *op. cit.*, pp. 163–166; Thomas Reminiscences, Part I, p. 41.

[38] Foster to Debs, July 15, 1924; Debs to Foster, July 23, 1924, in Debs Clipping Book No. 2, Meyer London Memorial Library, Rand School; David Karsner, "The Passing of the Socialist Party," *Current History*, June, 1924, p. 402; *New York Times*, Sept. 24, 1924.

[39] Robinson, *The Presidential Vote*, pp. 21–24, 380, 390; MacKay, *op. cit.*, pp. 219–221, 277.

[40] Herbert M. Merrill, Secy. of the New York State Committee, to Bertha Hale White, New York, Nov. 21, 1924, SPC, Duke; Fred R. Zimmerman, Wisconsin Secy. of State, "Results of Presidential, State, Congressional, and Referenda Elections, State of Wisconsin, November, 1924," mimeographed document, SPC, Duke.

[41] *American Federationist*, XXXII (Jan., 1925), 55; Eric F. Goldman, *Rendezvous with Destiny: A History of Modern American Reform* (New York, 1952), p. 295.

[42] Eugene V. Debs, "The American Labor Party," *Socialist World*, Jan., 1925, pp. 1–2; Morris Hillquit, *Loose Leaves from a Busy Life* (New York, 1934), p. 321; MacKay, *op. cit.*, pp. 231–238; Bertha Hale White, "The Chicago Convention," *Socialist World*, March, 1925, pp. 3–5. The CPPA, under the name National Progressive Headquarters, with such men in its fold as Oswald Garrison Villard, Arthur Garfield Hays, and Peter Witt, limped on for three more years before it too gave up the progressive ghost.

CHAPTER VIII

Enter Norman Thomas

[1] Iversen, Morris Hillquit: American Social Democrat, pp. 393–396, 406–408.

[2] *Socialist World*, Feb., 1924, p. 12; *American Labor Who's Who*; National Convention Minutes, 1926, typescript in Thomas papers.

[3] Henry to Williams, Chicago, Jan. 11, 1929; Williams to Henry, Dugger, Ind., marked received at national office Feb. 13, 1929, SPC, Duke; interview with James Oneal, Nov. 5, 1951.

[4] Membership Report, 1928, SPC, Duke; National Convention Min-

utes, 1926, Thomas papers; B. Charney Vladeck, manager of the *Forward*, to Henry, New York, Feb. 11, 1929, SPC, Duke.

⁵ New York *Herald Tribune*, Feb. 24, 1926, Sept. 28, 1926; *New York Times*, Sept. 28, 1926; New York *World*, March 25, 1929.

⁶ J. G. Hodges to Joseph W. Sharts, Kansas City, June 27, 1925, SPC, Duke; Thomas Reminiscences, Part I, pp. 79–82.

⁷ Henry Gruber Stetler, *The Socialist Movement in Reading, Pennsylvania, 1896–1936: A Study in Social Change* (Storrs, Conn., 1943), pp. 65–66, 169–170, 177; Henry G. Hodges, "Four Years of Socialism in Reading, Pennsylvania," *National Municipal Review*, XX (May, 1931), 281–289; Harry W. Laidler and Norman Thomas, eds., *New Tactics in Social Conflict* (New York, 1926), p. 22.

⁸ Thomas Reminiscences, Part I, pp. 3–26, 120–121; Teachers College, Columbia University, *School of Education Announcement, 1918–1919* (New York, 1918), p. 45.

⁹ Minutes of the 1928 National Convention of the Socialist Party, pp. 9–11, typescript, Thomas papers.

¹⁰ Interview with Norman Thomas, March 14, 1952; G. August Gerber to National Office of the Socialist Party, New York, Feb. 11, 1929, SPC, Duke; Lilith Wilson to Women's National Committee, Sinking Springs, Pa., Dec. 6, 1928; Annual Report of the National Women's Committee from May, 1928, to Jan., 1929, typescript, SPC, Duke.

¹¹ "From Dogmatism to Pragmatism," *New Republic*, LIV (May 2, 1928), 310–311.

¹² Norman Thomas, "Why Not a New Party?" *North American Review*, CCXXVII (Feb., 1929), 150; Thomas Reminiscences, Part II, p. 162.

¹³ Bell, "The Background and Development of Marxian Socialism in the United States," in *Socialism and American Life*, p. 127.

¹⁴ Norman Thomas, Socialists and the Tariff, typescript dated 1928, SPC, Duke; *Platform of the Socialist Party for the Presidential Election of 1928* (Washington, 1928), pp. 6–8, 16–17, 4; Thomas, "Why Not a New Party?" p. 149.

¹⁵ *New York Times*, Nov. 3, Aug. 11, Sept. 30, Nov. 6, 1928.

¹⁶ *Ibid.*, Sept. 30, 1928; for the Socialist anti-Klan policy, see *Socialist World*, Feb., 1924, p. 3.

¹⁷ Thomas, "Why Not a New Party?" p. 147.

¹⁸ G. W. Beloit to William H. Henry, Boonville, Mo., Jan. 14, 1929; H. A. Hedden to Henry, Los Angeles, Jan. 16, 1929; Henry to Hedden, Chicago, Feb. 5, 1929, SPC, Duke.

¹⁹ *Weekly Press News*, Feb. 23, March 23, Aug. 17, 1929. This was

a mimeographed press release, later renamed *Labor and Socialist Press Service*. A nearly complete file is in SPC, Duke.

[20] G. August Gerber, Report of the National Campaign Manager to the National Executive Committee, Feb. 3-4, 1929, SPC, Duke; J. W. Brown to William H. Henry, Bath, Me., Jan. 10, 1929, SPC, Duke.

[21] *Weekly Press News*, July 27, 1929; Summary of Findings and Decision of the NEC in the Case of David G. George, Thomas papers.

[22] Interview with James Oneal, Nov. 5, 1951; *Labor and Socialist Press News*, Aug. 24, 1929.

[23] Reports of Mabel H. Barnes, Acting Executive Secretary, to the National Executive Committee, June 11, June 19, June 26, 1929, SPC, Duke; *Weekly Press News*, July 5, July 20, 1929; press release, dated 1929, SPC, Duke.

[24] Mabel H. Barnes to the National Executive Committee, Chicago, June 27, 1929, SPC, Duke; J. Van Roosbroeck to William H. Henry, Zurich, Dec., 1928, Friedrich Adler to Henry, Zurich, June 1, 1929, SPC, Duke; press release, May 5, 1929, SPC, Duke; Henry to Herbert Merrill, Chicago, Feb. 4, 1929, SPC, Duke.

CHAPTER IX
The Socialists and the Depression, 1929–1933

[1] Broadus Mitchell, *Depression Decade: From New Era Through New Deal, 1929–1941* [*Economic History of the United States*, Vol. IX] (New York, 1947), pp. 451, 128, 439, 446, 227.

[2] "The Story of a Novel," *Short Stories* (Penguin edition, 1947), p. 135.

[3] *Labor and Socialist Press News*, Sept. 16, Oct. 26, Nov. 9, 1929; *New York Times*, Oct. 2, 3, 18, 23; Nov. 4, 6, 1929.

[4] Clarence Senior to states, locals, branches, and members at large, Chicago, Dec. 31, 1929, SPC, Duke; Senior to National Committee, NEC and state secretaries, Chicago, May 7, 1930, and attached list, SPC, Duke; Ethel Watson to proposed speakers, July 26, 1930, and attached mailing list, SPC, Duke; Clarence Senior to bureau speakers, Oct. 1, 1930, and attached mailing list, SPC, Duke.

[5] *Labor and Socialist Press News*, May 16, Feb. 7, 1931; *American Labor Year Book*, XI (1930), 126–130.

[6] *Labor and Socialist Press Service*, Sept. 1, 1932; July 11, Oct. 24, March 21, May 23, 1931.

[7] *American Labor Year Book*, XII (1931), 141–142; Stetler, *The Socialist Movement in Reading, Pennsylvania*, pp. 66–67. In 1930, be-

sides Mayor Hoan of Milwaukee and Mayor Stump of Reading, there were Socialist mayors at Beaver Dam, Manitowac, and Iola, Wis. In 1931 Socialists of Racine, Wis., elected William J. Swaboda as mayor and the following year expelled him from the party on charges of accepting bribes from gamblers. *Labor and Socialist Press Service*, April 15, 1932.

[8] *American Labor Year Book*, XII (1931), 142–143.

[9] Clarence Senior to Mary Brite, Chicago, Nov. 17, 1932, copy, and Senior to Brite, Chicago, Dec. 1, 1932, copy, SPC, Duke; *Labor and Socialist Press Service*, July 29, 1932.

[10] *American Labor Year Book*, XII (1931), 147–149; Theodore Shapiro, "The 'Militant' Point of View," *American Socialist Quarterly*, I (April 15, 1932), 29–37, a criticism of the Old Guard that equates it with conservative European socialism; Waldman, *Labor Lawyer*, pp. 194–195.

[11] Shapiro, "The 'Militant' Point of View," p. 32.

[12] Quoted in Granville Hicks, *Small Town* (New York, 1946), pp. 221–222.

[13] Morris Hillquit, "Problems Before the National Convention," *American Socialist Quarterly*, I (April 15, 1932), 5; *Labor and Socialist Press News*, Aug. 1, June 20, Sept. 5, Oct. 31, 1931.

[14] *Labor and Socialist Press Service*, May 27, 1932, Dec. 31, 1931; Anna Bercowitz, "The Milwaukee Convention," *American Socialist Quarterly*, I (summer, 1932), 54.

[15] *Labor and Socialist Press Service*, May 27, 1932.

[16] Bercowitz, "The Milwaukee Convention," pp. 51–53; interview with Norman Thomas, March 14, 1952; *New York Times*, May 24, 1932; *Labor and Socialist Press Service*, May 27, 1932. Hillquit's sincerity in taking offense at the remarks of Quick and Broun has been doubted. Norman Thomas believes Hillquit very skillfully exploited what might be called anti-anti-Semitism. Interview with Thomas, March 14, 1952. Hillquit's biographer, Iversen, does not think Hillquit exploited his opposition's blunder, and for his reason cites Hillquit's lack of "Jewishness." Hillquit was not religious, knew little Yiddish, and did not belong to Jewish organizations. Iversen, Morris Hillquit: American Social Democrat, p. 414n. This evidence suggests to the present writer that Hillquit did intentionally exploit Socialist opposition to anti-Semitism.

[17] *Labor and Socialist Press Service*, May 27, 1932; Bercowitz, "The Milwaukee Convention," p. 54.

[18] *Labor and Socialist Press Service*, May 27, June 3, Aug. 19, 1932;

Socialist Party of America, *A Plan for America: Official 1932 Campaign Handbook of the Socialist Party* (Chicago, 1932), p. 14.

[19] Iversen, *op. cit.*, pp. 415–416; John Dos Passos, "Four Nights in a Garden: A Campaign Yarn," in Alfred M. Bingham and Selden Rodman, eds., *Challenge to the New Deal* (New York, 1934), p. 78; *Labor and Socialist Press Service*, June 3, 1932; press release, July 13, 1932, SPC, Duke. Dos Passos thought very little of the Socialists. He conceded Thomas was an effective public speaker but objected to Thomas's "faint reminiscence of the Episcopal pulpit, as if he were always on the edge of dropping into, 'Dearly beloved brethren.'" "Four Nights in a Garden," p. 77.

[20] *A Plan for America*, p. 10; Norman Thomas, *What Socialism Is and Is Not* (Chicago, 1932), a pamphlet.

[21] *A Plan for America*, pp. 10–12; National Executive Committee to Socialist Party Members, Friends, and Sympathizers, Chicago, May 10, 1929, SPC, Duke; Minutes of the National Executive Committee Meeting, Newark, N.J., Nov. 15, 16, 1930, SPC, Duke; *Labor and Socialist Press News*, Aug. 29, 1931.

[22] Thomas Reminiscences, Part I, p. 67; Paul Blanshard, "Tammany and the Roosevelt Myth," *A Plan for America*, pp. 43–48; Henry J. Rosner, "The Myth of a Progressive Governor," *ibid.*, pp. 49–54; Norman Thomas and Paul Blanshard, *What's the Matter with New York: A National Problem* (New York, 1932), pp. 177–195, quotations from p. 177. The Roosevelt fairy tale, wrote the authors, part of the Library of Presidential Fairy Tales, sat on the shelf beside "How Coolidge Crushed the Boston Police Strike" and "How the Great Engineer Brought Efficiency to Washington."

[23] *Labor and Socialist Press Service*, Aug. 12, July 8, July 22, Aug. 19, 1932. Fred Suitor, president of the Quarry Workers, was Socialist candidate for governor of Vermont.

[24] Hillquit, "Problems Before the Convention," pp. 12–13; Clarence Senior to Editors, American Labor Press, Chicago, Oct. 26, 1929, SPC, Duke; *Labor and Socialist Press News*, Nov. 9, 1929; July 3, 1931; *Labor and Socialist Press Service*, April 1, March 11, 1932; Clarence Senior to National Executive Committee, State Secretaries, and State Executive Committees, Chicago, Dec. 4, 1931, SPC, Duke.

[25] Letterhead of the Thomas and Maurer Committee of One Hundred Thousand, Box 53, Ghent papers; press release for afternoon newspapers of Nov. 5, 1932, Thomas papers; press release, no date, Thomas papers; *New Republic*, LXXII (Oct. 26, 1932), 272–274; *Labor and*

Socialist Press Service, Sept. 30, May 19, July 29, Sept. 1, 30, Oct. 14, 28, 1932; press release for newspapers of Oct. 7, 1932, SPC, Duke.

[26] *Labor and Socialist Press Service*, Sept. 1, 30, Oct. 14, 28, 1932; clipping from unidentified newspaper, by-line of William Hard, New York, Oct. 29, 1932, Box 53, Ghent papers; press release for newspapers of Nov. 8, 1932, Thomas papers.

[27] Clarence Senior to editor of *Nation*, Chicago, Nov. 14, 1932, copy, SPC, Duke; *Labor and Socialist Press Service*, Sept. 1, 30, Oct. 7, 14, 21, 28, 1932.

[28] W. H. Miller to Socialist Party of America, Fraziers Bottom, West Va., Nov. 11, 1932, SPC, Duke; League for Industrial Democracy press release for newspapers of Jan. 22, 1931, SPC, Duke.

[29] F. E. McCay to National Campaign Committee, Boyd, Ky., Nov. 2, 1932, SPC, Duke; Helen-Elise Biemiller, organizer of Erie County, Ohio, to Clarence Senior, Sandusky, Nov. 15, 1932, SPC, Duke.

[30] *Labor and Socialist Press News*, June 6, 1931; quoted from *Emergency Plans for Domestic Disturbances* by Norman Thomas and Clarence Senior in an open letter to Congress, Jan. 18, 1932; *ibid.*, Jan. 19, 1932.

CHAPTER X

The Socialists and the New Deal

[1] *Labor and Socialist Press Service*, May 11, 1933.

[2] Statement on the National Industrial Recovery Act Adopted by the National Executive Committee, Reading, Pa., July 4, 1933, *Labor and Socialist Press Service*, July 7, 1933; John Francis Sullivan, Andrew J. Biemiller, and Maynard C. Kreuger, *The National Industrial Recovery Act* [*Issues of the Day* pamphlet series, No. 1] (Chicago, 1933), p. 11.

[3] *A Plan for America*, pp. 11–12; Frank W. Bennett to Clarence Senior, Nashville, Mich., Nov. 15, 1932; Senior to Bennett, Chicago, Nov. 18, 1932, copy; C. W. Crum to Senior, McBrides, Mich., Dec. 1, 1932, SPC, Duke; Socialist Party of America, *Notes for Speakers*, Feb. 20, 1933, SPC, Duke.

[4] Norman Thomas, *The New Deal: A Socialist Analysis* [*Issues of the Day*, No. 3] (Chicago, 1933), pp. 4–5; Maynard Kreuger, *Inflation: Who Wins and Who Loses?* [*Issues of the Day*, No. 4] (Chicago, 1934).

[5] Mitchell, *Depression Decade*, pp. 200–201.

[6] Thomas Reminiscences, Part I, pp. 92–101; Norman Thomas to Henry Wallace, Wichita, Kan., Feb. 22, 1934, copy, Thomas papers;

Norman Thomas, "The Forgotten Man," radio address delivered from Cincinnati over the Columbia Broadcasting System, Feb. 21, 1935, SPC, Duke; Norman Thomas, *The Plight of the Share-Cropper* (New York, 1934), an LID pamphlet. The personal relations between Roosevelt and Thomas were interesting. Thomas liked FDR personally, and apparently Roosevelt held Thomas in some regard. He replied personally to all of Thomas's letters except one in which Thomas objected to the Smith Act. "Sometimes I didn't think his answers were relevant, but at least he answered." At one time, "Roosevelt was willing . . . to line me up on his side, but on terms that were not consistent with the Socialist position which I wished to keep." Thomas Reminiscences, Part I, pp. 103–104.

⁷ Norman Thomas, *Shall Labor Support Roosevelt?* (Chicago, 1936), p. 10; see also Thomas, *Is the New Deal Socialism? An Answer to Al Smith and the American Liberty League* (Chicago, 1936).

⁸ Kreuger, *op. cit.*, p. 16; Thomas, *The New Deal*, pp. 8, 10.

⁹ Thomas, *The New Deal*, pp. 10, 13; National Executive Committee Minutes, New York City, Nov. 20–22, Thomas papers.

¹⁰ *Labor and Socialist Press News*, July 18, 1931; *Labor and Socialist Press Service*, March 23, May 4, 1934; Jerry Voorhis to Norman Thomas, San Dimas, Calif., Sept. 18, 1933, Thomas papers; A Confidential Statement by Paul Blanshard Concerning His Resignation from the Socialist Party, Thomas papers; Norman Thomas to Andrew Biemiller, New York, Sept. 14, 1933; Thomas to John Haynes Holmes, New York, Sept. 14, 1933, copy, Thomas papers; Andrew J. Biemiller, "Socialism and Democracy," *American Socialist Quarterly*, III (spring, 1934), 24.

¹¹ Thomas Reminiscences, Part I, p. 65.

¹² Norman Thomas, Memorandum on the Situation in the Fur Industry, Especially As It Affects the Socialist Party, New York, June 14, 1933, copy, Thomas papers; Thomas to Leo Krzycki, New York, Jan. 16, 1934, copy, Thomas papers.

¹³ James Oneal to Clarence Senior, New York, July 7, 1933, copy; Oneal to Senior, New York, July 12, 1933, copy; Senior to Oneal, Chicago, July 24, 1933, copy; all enclosed in Senior to NEC members, Chicago, July 24, 1933, Thomas papers.

¹⁴ Andrew Biemiller to Norman Thomas, Milwaukee, Sept. 12, 1933; Thomas to Biemiller, New York, Sept. 14, 1933, copy, Thomas papers.

¹⁵ John Murphy Collins of Chicago took Hillquit's seat on the NEC, and Leo Krzycki, an Old Guard opponent, became NEC chairman. *Labor and Socialist Press Service*, Oct. 20, Nov. 3, 1933.

¹⁶ *New York Times,* Jan. 3, 1934; Norman Thomas to Julius Gerber, New York, Jan. 4, 1934, copy; Thomas to Louis Waldman, New York, Jan. 16, 1934, copy; Waldman to Thomas, New York, Jan. 24, 1934; Thomas to Waldman, New York, Jan. 25, 1934, copy, Thomas papers.

¹⁷ Waldman, *Labor Lawyer,* p. 194; Reinhold Niebuhr, "The Revolutionary Moment," *American Socialist Quarterly,* IV (June, 1935), pp. 9–10; for provocation of irritation with the Militants, see Joseph Lash to Norman Thomas, New York, March 1, 1934, and Kenneth Meikeljohn to Thomas, New York, March 1, 1934, Thomas papers; Thomas Reminiscences, Part I, pp. 62–63.

¹⁸ *American Socialist Quarterly,* III, special supplement (July, 1934), pp. 5–6; the Detroit Declaration also appears in a pamphlet, *National Constitution, Declaration of Principles and Congressional Platform As Adopted in Convention at Detroit, 1934* (Chicago, 1934), pp. 28–34.

¹⁹ *American Socialist Quarterly,* III, special supplement (July, 1934), pp. 3, 9. The convention's boldness in adopting the Declaration was mitigated by the NEC's subsequent action of submission of the Declaration to a committee of Socialist lawyers to determine whether it violated any state criminal syndicalist laws. Minutes of the National Executive Committee, Detroit, June 4, 1934, Thomas papers.

²⁰ *Labor and Socialist Press Service,* Oct. 19, June 6, 1934. The two Old Guardsmen elected were James D. Graham of Montana and James Oneal of the *New Leader.* The others elected were Leo Krzycki, chairman; Albert Sprague Coolidge, a Harvard chemist; Franz Daniel, then of Pennsylvania and later of Tennessee; Powers Hapgood of Indianapolis; Daniel Hoan of Milwaukee; Maynard Kreuger of the University of Chicago; Max Shadid, an Oklahoma physician; Darlington Hoopes of Reading; and Norman Thomas.

²¹ For a description of the many leftist organizations, see William Isaacs, Contemporary Marxian Political Movements in the United States, unpublished doctoral dissertation in political science, dated April, 1939, library of New York University.

²² Paul Porter to Norman Thomas, Trudeau, N.Y., Jan. 28, 1934; Thomas to Porter, New York, Jan. 30, 1934, copy, Thomas papers. This Porter, Paul Robert Porter, is not to be confused with Paul Aldermandt Porter, who was in the Office of Price Administration under Roosevelt and Truman; *New York Times,* Oct. 30, 31, Nov. 2, 3, 5, 1934.

²³ Revolutionary Policy Publishing Association, *Evaluation of the Meeting of the National Executive Committee, Buffalo, March 22–24* (New York, 1935), pp. 1, 4; *Build the YPSL into a Revolutionary*

Organization Based on Revolutionary Principles, a four-page mimeographed leaflet, undated, but about June, 1935.

²⁴ *Draft for a Program for the Socialist Party of the United States as Formulated by the Left Wing at the Socialist Call Institutes, Bound Brook, N.J., Sept. 7–8, Chicago, Ill., Oct. 19–20* (New York, 1935), quotation from p. 13; Paul Porter, *America for All: The Commonwealth Plan* (Chicago, 1934); clipping from *New York American*, undated, but internal evidence suggests about Nov., 1935, Thomas papers. The Communists, of course, held that Thomas had sold out to American reactionaries.

²⁵ Herbert Merrill, New York State Secretary, to State and Local Organizations and the Members of the Socialist Party, New York, March 22, 1935, SPC, Duke; Minutes of the National Executive Committee, July 13–15, 1935, and Jan. 4–5, 1936, Thomas papers.

²⁶ *Labor and Socialist Press Service*, April 10, 1936.

²⁷ Proceedings, The Socialist Party of the United States of America, May 22–26, 1936, Public Hall, Cleveland, Ohio, typescript in library of Columbia University, pp. 112–113, ten-page insert following pp. 120, 273, 288–293, 302–308, 315–319, 310–314a, 631–651. Neither New York delegation voted on the report of the credentials committee.

²⁸ Press release from national headquarters, Chicago, July 29, 1936, SPC, Duke.

²⁹ *New York Times*, April 12, 1936; Daniel Bell, "Labor's Coming of Middle Age," *Fortune*, XLIV (Oct., 1951), 137; interview with Norman Thomas, March 14, 1952; Matthew Josephson, *Sidney Hillman: Statesman of American Labor* (Garden City, 1952), pp. 397–401.

³⁰ *Labor and Socialist Press Service*, Oct. 2, 1936. The party's position on the Negro began to change in the early 1920's. At the 1923 convention the Socialists called upon white workers to treat Negroes as equals, to encourage Negro unionism, and to help break down anti-Negro prejudice. *American Labor Year Book*, V (1923–1924), 133; Ernest Doerfler, "Socialism and the Negro Problem," *American Socialist Quarterly*, II (summer, 1933), 23–36. In 1936 there was a special Negro committee of the Labor League for Thomas and Nelson, on which Randolph and Frank Crosswaith, many times a Socialist candidate in Harlem, were the most prominent. Minutes of the National Executive Committee, July 12–13, 1936, Thomas papers.

³¹ *Labor and Socialist Press Service*, Aug. 4, Oct. 2, 16, 1936; "How They Are Voting," *New Republic*, LXXXVIII (Sept. 30–Oct. 28, 1936), 223–224, 249–250, 277–278, 304–305, 347–348, LXXXIX (Nov. 4, 1936), 14–15.

³² Norman Thomas, *To Huey Long and Father Coughlin: An Open Letter* (Chicago, n.d.); Thomas, *Emancipate Youth from Toil, Old Age from Fear* (Chicago, 1936), pp. 9, 10–11.

³³ Edgar Eugene Robinson, *They Voted for Roosevelt: The Presidential Vote, 1932–1944* (Stanford, 1947), pp. 188–189, 191, 192, 199, 201, 207; Stetler, *The Socialist Movement in Reading, Pennsylvania,* p. 43.

³⁴ Thomas Reminiscences, Part I, p. 65.

CHAPTER XI

LAST RITES AND POST MORTEM

¹ Minutes of the National Executive Committee, New York City, Nov. 20–22, 1936, Thomas papers; Clarence Senior to Local and Branch Secretaries, State Secretaries, and State Executive Committee members, Chicago, Dec. 10, 1936, SPC, Duke.

² Proceedings, Special National Convention, the Socialist Party of the United States of America, March 26–29, 1937, La Salle Hotel, Chicago, Illinois, typescript in Columbia University library, pp. 18–19, 1007; "Report to the Special National Convention of the Socialist Party," a long insert following p. 46 of *ibid.*, pp. 2, 6, 9, 18, 43, 45.

³ Proceedings, Special National Convention, 1937, pp. 75–84, 95–97, 124–125, 83, quotations from 82, 96, 97.

⁴ *Ibid.*, pp. 149, 152, 154–158, 166–167, 358–416, 514–521, quotations from 149, 152.

⁵ Minutes of the National Executive Committee, New York City, Sept. 1–4, 1937, Thomas papers.

⁶ Norman Thomas, *Last Night in Jersey City* (New York, 1938); American Civil Liberties Union, *Civil Rights vs. Mayor Hague* (New York, 1938); American Civil Liberties Union, *Eternal Vigilance! The Story of Civil Liberty, 1937–1938* (New York, 1938); *New York Times*, Sept. 27, 1937; Thomas Reminiscences, Part I, pp. 139–140.

⁷ John B. Carter, American Reactions to Italian Fascism, 1919–1933, unpublished doctoral dissertation, dated June, 1953, Columbia University library; Inner-Party Information, No. 2, mimeographed document, SPC, Duke; Minutes of the National Executive Committee, New York City, Nov. 20–22, 1936, Thomas papers; Statement on Neutrality Legislation Recently Passed by Congress, issued by Roy E. Burt, Jan. 8, 1937, SPC, Duke; *Proceedings*, National Convention of the Socialist Party, April 6–8, 1940, Washington, D.C. (Chicago, 1940), pp. 3–6, quotations from 3–4, 6.

[8] Robinson, *They Voted for Roosevelt*, p. 199. States increasing their vote for Thomas were California, Colorado, Illinois, Kentucky, Minnesota, Montana, North Dakota, Washington, and Wisconsin. *Ibid.*, pp. 188, 189, 191, 193, 195, 197, 200, 206, 207.

[9] *New York Times*, Feb. 4, July 29, May 24, 1941.

[10] Thomas Reminiscences, Part II, p. 182; Robinson, *op. cit.*, p. 40.

[11] *New York Times*, June 4, 1950; *Milwaukee Journal*, Aug. 15, 1954.

[12] Many writers have been concerned with the question of why the United States has not developed a strong Socialist movement, and to these authors the present writer is indebted. Perhaps the most important of these works is Selig Perlman, *A Theory of the Labor Movement* (New York, 1928). Among others are Ghent, *The Reds Bring Reaction;* Hiram Elfenbein, *Socialism from Where We Are* (New York, 1945); Werner Sombart, *Warum gibt es in den Vereinigten Staaten keinen Sozialismus?* (Tübingen, 1906); Norman Thomas, *A Socialist's Faith* (New York, 1950); Fred E. Haynes, *Social Politics in the United States* (Boston, 1924); William B. Hesseltine, *The Rise and Fall of Third Parties: From Anti-Masonry to Wallace* (Washington, 1948); Murray S. and Susan W. Stedman, *Discontent at the Polls: A Study of Farmer and Labor Parties, 1827–1948* (New York, 1950); and Daniel Bell, "The Background and Development of Marxian Socialism in the United States," in *Socialism and American Life*. This is only a small sample of the writing on the subject. The present writer is also indebted for the benefits he has received from many conversations with participants in the Socialist movement and from academic colleagues.

[13] Thomas Reminiscences, Part I, pp. 42–43; *Appeal to Reason*, Nov. 25, 1916; *American Socialist*, Aug. 5, 1916.

[14] Interview with Freda Hogan Ameringer, April 21, 1950.

[15] *Writings and Speeches of Debs*, p. 335.

[16] Report of the Executive Secretary to the National Executive Committee, Oct. 3, 1910, SPC, Duke; Carl D. Thompson to Fred Warren, Chicago, March 26, 1913, copy, SPC, Duke; Perlman and Taft, pp. 364–365. The AFL delegates who voted for Hayes by no means endorsed Socialism with their votes, but they did express their dissatisfaction with Gompers's leadership and at least dissented from his strongly anti-Socialist position.

[17] The Republican Party is the only possible exception to this statement, but it was not a typical third party. It was more of a second party, built upon the wreckage of the Whigs. Even so, the Republican victory in 1860 was the result of a split in the Democratic Party, and the Repub-

licans did not have a majority in Congress until the Southern Democrats
seceded.

[18] "The People of the U.S.A.—A Self-Portrait," *Fortune*, XXI (Feb.,
1940), 14, 20, 28, 133–134, 136.

[19] Max Beer, *Fifty Years of International Socialism* (London, 1935),
pp. 111–112, makes much of this difference between British and American
conditions.

[20] Irvin G. Wyllie, *The Self-Made Man in America: The Myth of
Rags to Riches* (New Brunswick, N.J., 1954).

[21] Ameringer, *If You Don't Weaken*, p. 295; Paul Frederick Brissenden, *The I.W.W.: A Study of American Syndicalism* [*Columbia University Studies in History, Economics and Public Law*, LXXXIII] (New
York, 1919), p. 376.

INDEX

Abbott, Leonard D., 55
Adams, Franklin P., 222
Agard, Walter, 56
Agricultural Adjustment Act, 230-232
Allen, Devere, 191, 218
Amalgamated Clothing Workers, 23, 210, 245-246
America First, 256
American Alliance for Labor and Democracy, 117-118
American Civil Liberties Union, 186, 187
American Economic Association, 210
American Federation of Labor, 10-11, 13, 188, 210, 261-262, 267; James Maurer and, 15-16; Milwaukee Socialists and, 21-24; and war, 90, 117-118, 152; and amnesty, 159; election of 1924, 176, 179-180; election of 1932, 221
American Federation of Teachers, 246
American Federationist, 176
American Fund for Public Service, 186-187
American Labor Party, 245-247, 255
American League Against War and Fascism, 252-253
American Legion, 124, 161
American Peace Society, 87
American Protective League, 114
American Railway Union, 3
American Socialist, 110
American Union Against Militarism, 87
Americans for Democratic Action, 250

Ameringer, Oscar, 27-28, 73, 156, 215, 217, 230, 262
Anarchosyndicalism, 38, 106-108
Anthony, Susan B., 157
Appeal group. *See* Trotskyites
Appeal to Reason, 26, 36, 68, 118, 121, 209, 262; on prospects of Socialism, 4; publishes *The Jungle*, 6; character of, 28-34; on immigration, 48-49; on Negroes, 51-52; and war, 90-91, 102-103, 111; "Oklahoma page," 260

Babeuf, Gracchus, 265
Baer, John M., 101
Baker, Newton D., 160
Baldanzi, George, 246
Baldwin, Roger, 56, 127, 186, 208
Ballan, John, 141
Barnes, J. Mahlon, 16, 69, 73-77, 202
Barnes, Mabel H., 202
Batt, Dennis E., 137-138, 146
Beard, Charles A., 9, 103
Bell, Sherman, 39
Bellamy, Edward, 3, 230
Benét, Stephen Vincent, 222
Bennett, William F., 104
Benson, Allan L., 90-92, 99, 102, 116, 155
Berger, Meta, 216, 218, 252-253
Berger, Victor, 42, 79, 85, 129, 149, 155, 158, 181, 192, 209, 261, 267; elected to Congress, 1910, 5; compared with Debs, 17; as Milwaukee "boss," 21-25; on immigration, 48-49; on Negroes, 50-51; opposition to, 62-63;

....t Party of Amer